PIASA Books

are imprints of
The Polish Institute of Arts and Sciences
of America,
New York

His Holiness
Pope John Paul II

A Commemorative Volume of Essays
from the Members
of the Polish Institute of Arts and Sciences of
America

Edited and Introduced by

Charles S. Kraszewski

PIASA Books
NEW YORK
MMVI

Published by PIASA Books, The Polish Institute of Arts and Sciences of America, 208 East 30th St., New York, NY 10016

www.polishbooks.org

Library of Congress
Cataloging-in-Publication Data

His Holiness Pope John Paul II : a commemorative volume of essays from the members of the Polish Institute of Arts and Sciences of America / edited and introduced by Charles S. Kraszewski.
    p. cm.
 ISBN 978-0-940962-67-5
 1. John Paul II, Pope, 1920-2005. I. Kraszewski, Charles S. II. Polish Institute of Arts and Sciences of America.
 BX1378.5.H56 2010
 282.092—dc22

                          2010005347

Cover designed by Mariusz Bargielski.

CONTENTS

INTRODUCTION
Karol Wojtyła — John Paul II: The Man Transcendent
CHARLES S. KRASZEWSKI

When writing of the late Holy Father, it has become commonplace to begin with an enthusiastic litany of his multifarious qualities. The list is familiar: Actor, Bishop, Confessor, Diplomat, Economist, Footballer, "Góral," Hiker, Intellectual, Jurist... one could almost run through an entire alphabet marking down his identities, talents and avocations — perhaps more than one, for what should one choose when one arrives at "p" — Priest, Professor, Poet, or Playwright? Were this introduction biographical — which it is not — we would be discouraged at the outset by the words of Lord Byron from *Don Juan*:

> But words are things, and a small drop of ink,
>   Falling like dew, upon a thought, produces
> That which makes thousands, perhaps millions, think.
>   'Tis strange, the shortest letter which man uses
> Instead of speech, may form a lasting link
>   Of ages; to what straits old Time reduces
> Frail man, when paper — even a rag like this,
> Survives himself, his tomb, and all that's his!
>   (III. lxxxviii)

All biography is doomed to futility. This is as true of the seas of ink spilled in attempts to capture the gigantic personality of a man such as John Paul II as of the dew-drops that seek to refract the lives of less noticed mortals. How little of the living person is contained in the footnotes that remain after his death! How inexact the "immortality," to speak the language of Byron's countryman Thomas Hardy, that we enjoy in the frail memories of loved ones left behind! Far better, it seems, to admit at the very beginning that man is a mystery. Each man, including the Holy Father, is an unplumbable mystery, intimately and fully known to God alone. We can neither comprise nor elucidate anyone fully in speech or print. We can only continue to love and honor him or her. And thus my purpose in beginning this essay in such a fashion. My aim is twofold: to describe at the outset the nature of the book in hand, and to confess to its inadequacy. Incomplete, in many ways unabashedly subjective, but completely sincere, *His Holiness Pope John Paul II* is an offering, by several hands, to the memory of a man loved by so many.

Several of the distinguished members of the Polish Institute of Arts and Sciences of America were fortunate enough to have met the Holy Father, both before and after his election to the Papal See. In his essay, our Executive Director, Tadeusz V. Gromada, recalls the then-Cardinal of Kraków's visits to America in 1969, when he introduced him to the faithful assembled at the "American Częstochowa" in Doylestown, PA, and again in 1976 when, during a trip to the International Eucharistic Congress in Philadelphia, Cardinal Wojtyła was kind enough to visit our headquarters in New York City. Our President, Piotr Wandycz, likewise recalls his three visits with the Holy Father in Rome as member of the Polish Institute of Christian Culture. It was our Vice President, Zbigniew Brzezinski, who, as Jimmy Carter's National Security advisor, telephoned the Holy Father on the eve of the imposition of martial law in December of 1980, informing him of the imminent threat of the Soviet invasion of his homeland. In one of his recent interviews (not reprinted here), Dr Brzezinski recalls once seeing a KGB analysis prepared for the Politburo of the USSR, accusing him of having orchestrated the election of the "Polish Pope!" The Holy Father himself was aware of this absurd suggestion, and once admonished Dr Brzezinski to visit him more often. "After all," he told him, "you're the one who elected me!"[1]

Among the prized possessions of the PIASA archives, none is more valued than the Pope's 1982 letter, written on the occasion of our fortieth anniversary, in which the Holy Father was so kind as to comment:

> Instytut uzyskał stałe prawo obywatelstwa w nauce i kulturze Stanów Zjednoczonych i całego świata, zdobył zasłużony szacunek i wielu przyjaciół. Stał

---

[1] Cf. Marcin Gadziński, "Zbigniew Brzeziński wspomina papieża," [Zbigniew Brzeziński remembers the Pope], *Gazeta Wyborcza* April 5, 2005.

się jednym z ważnych punktów na świecie żywego kontaktu i osmozy owoców polskiego ducha i polskiej myśli z dorobkiem duchowym narodów świata.

[The Polish Institute has achieved the right of permanent citizenship in the academe and culture of both the United States and the entire world. It has won a well-deserved respect, and many friends. It has become one of the important global points of contact and osmosis of the Polish spirit and Polish thought with the spiritual heritage of all the world's nations.]

Likewise, the pride of the present collection is the article entitled "John Paul II's Message of Hope and Meaning in the Context of Postmodern Challenges," written especially for this book by His Excellency Archbishop Józef Życiński of Lublin. Grand Chancellor of the Catholic University of Lublin, organizer and patron of the Congresses of Christian Culture that have drawn so many illustrious minds from all over Poland, and beyond, to discussions on many of the same topics that so moved the late Holy Father, Archbishop Życiński is a respected author and one of the most highly valued intellectuals in Europe. It is fitting that this accomplished Prelate, the author of so many seminal texts on the interplay of Christianity, humanism and science in the modern world, should open the scholarly portion of our book with his reflections on John Paul II as a cultural force and an important bridge in the ongoing dialogue between the Church and the academic world.

The Church is indeed an institution of divine establishment. At the same time, it is of this world, made up of people living in particular parts of the world, at particular moments in history, serving them in very practical ways on their road towards their ultimate fulfillment in Christ. The Church in the world and, in a certain sense not to be misunderstood, *for* the world, is a keynote of many of the documents of the Second Vatican Council, which John Paul II helped to form. He never lost sight of the Church's significance for real human beings, and the symbiotic interplay of the Church and human culture. As he noted in his encyclical *Slavorum apostoli* of June 1985:

> The Brothers from Salonika were not only heirs of the faith but also heirs of the culture of Ancient Greece, continued by Byzantium. Everyone knows how important this heritage is for the whole of European culture and, directly or indirectly, for the culture of the entire world. The work of evangelization which they carried out as pioneers in territory inhabited by Slav peoples contains both a model of what today is called "inculturation," the incarnation of the Gospel in native cultures and also the introduction of these cultures into the life of the Church.
>
> By incarnating the Gospel in the native culture of the peoples which they were evangelizing, Saints Cyril and Methodius were especially meritorious for the formation and development of that same culture, or rather of many cultures. Indeed all the cultures of the Slav nations owe their "beginning" or development to the work of the Brothers from Salonika. For by their original and ingenious creation of an alphabet for the Slavonic language the Brothers made a fundamental contribution to the culture and literature of all the Slav nations.[2]

By accepting human culture, that is, the cultures created by real human beings, the Church both aids in the development of said cultures, and is enriched by them in turn. In this sense, John Paul II is an example of an intellectual, "homocentric" in the best sense of the word. His thought is constantly focused on man, in the concrete, and his epidermal awareness of the consequences ensuing

---

[2] Pope John Paul II, encyclical *Slavorum Apostoli*, 6:21. June 2, 1985. Text from official Vatican website: http://www.vatican.va/edocs/ ENG0220/_P1.htm Here and below, where the texts were promulgated in languages other than Latin, we give only the English text.

there from for *Servus servorum Dei* suffuses both his theology and his social thought. Such is the sense one gets from Héctor Lozada and Richard J. Hunter's essay, "John Paul II and the World's Poor: 'Extreme Poverty is a Violation of Human Rights'," which shows the Pope's ideas in action, and describes his theologically-based pronouncements in the context of their significance for the real, practical problems faced by so many human beings throughout the world.

John Paul II was one of the most popular and approachable pontiffs in the history of the Church. He was no "prisoner of the Vatican." From the very start of his reign, we grew accustomed to seeing him as a human person himself, indulging in very human pursuits and sharing our own interests. We saw him hiking, skiing, joking. Although not many of us have had the opportunity of knowing the Holy Father personally, and growing under his influence (such is the topic of dramatist Kazimierz Braun's contribution, "'You Have Gone, but Through Me You Walk On': A Testimony of a Director and Writer"), his poetic talent has allowed many people to make a personal contact with him. Indeed, his literary *opus*, certainly the most significant by a Pope since Maciej Kazimierz Sarbiewski's patron Urban VIII, has afforded us a greater than usual perspective on the inner person of the Holy Father. It should not be surprising that Karol Wojtyła-writer should attract the vibrant interest of the literary scholars of PIASA. The present book is graced with several eminently interesting works on this topic. Fr. Janusz A. Ihnatowicz, himself a noted contemporary Polish poet and translator, meditates on John Paul II's approach to art and artists in his essay "Serving Beauty, Goodness and Truth: A Hesitant Primer to Karol Wojtyła's Theory of Art." Harold B. Segel, the dean of American Slavists, presents an in-depth discussion of the Pope's major plays in his "Karol Wojtyła, Playwright," while the poet Bolesław Taborski, one of the Pope's major translators and the author of an important study of Karol Wojtyła as an artist of the word, has created a generous introduction to the Pope's poetry in "The Poetry of Karol Wojtyła — Pope John Paul II." Beginning with his juvenilia and concluding with the *Tryptyk rzymski* [Roman Triptych], Taborski leads the reader through the poetic *oeuvre* of Karol Wojtyła with a sensitivity and

xi

acumen that not only elucidates the major themes of the Pope's lyrical works, but definitely excites a desire to reach for the works themselves.

Besides such essays written especially for this book, we have also included some materials that appeared in past issues of our quarterly *The Polish Review*. Continuing with the literary theme is this writer's article on the Pope's most widely-talked about dramatic work, *Brat naszego Boga* [Our God's Brother]. "Our God's Other Brother: Karol Wojtyła, Adam Bunsch, and Saint Brother Albert on Stage" was first published in Vol. XLVII nr. 3 (2002) of *The Polish Review*, as was the text that immediately follows it: "*Our God's Brother*: a Conversation with Krzysztof Zanussi." A great friend of our Institute, Krzysztof Zanussi, one of the leading voices in world authorial cinema and a humanist of the widest horizons, was a personal friend of Pope John Paul II and a member of the Pontifical Council for Culture. The interview is focused on his cinematic version of the Pope's play. This was his second film concerning John Paul II, the first being the biopic *From a Far Country*. With his frequent trips to the Vatican (in 2004, he even arranged a performance of break-dancers and rappers for the Pope, in the context of an ongoing dialogue between "high" and "low" culture), Zanussi was one of John Paul II's most important links to the world of culture and art, and through Zanussi's films, the contact of John Paul II, as an artist, with the world in general, was greatly facilitated.

Some twenty-five years ago, at the accession of Karol Wojtyła to the Throne of Peter, the editors of *The Polish Review* dedicated the second number of the XXIVth volume year (1979) to the Pope. *Gaude Mater Polonia: a Special Issue Dedicated to Karol Cardinal Wojtyła, John Paul II Pontifex Maximus* included essays written especially for the occasion, as well as a selection of texts published elsewhere in Polish, in English translation. A rather large (for the time) Bibliography of selected materials written in English by and about Karol Wojtyła/Pope John Paul II was printed therein, and the Book Reviews section of the number was entirely given over to books in English written by and about the Pope.

From this issue, we have chosen two of the original essays. Rev. George A. Williams' article on the historical context of Poles and the Vatican still stands on its own as a solid work of scholarship elucidating Polish participation in Papal conclaves, which bore fruit in 1978 with the election of John Paul II, the first Slavic Pope in the history of the Church. Joseph L. Lichten's essay is a joyful, and at the same time soberly confident, consideration of the ecumenical *humanitas* of the Pope, the roots of which reach back to his childhood in Wadowice. Because of his own background, Lichten was most interested in the Pope's significance for Jewish-Catholic relations. To re-read this essay, written at the very beginning of John Paul II's pontificate, from a 2005 perspective that remembers not only the Pope's visit to the Roman synagogue and the Holy Land, but the countless gestures of good will and indeed love that the Pope extended toward the Jewish people over the past twenty-six years, is to witness inspiring evidence of Karol Wojtyła's personal integrity and authenticity.

In considering the character and person of the late Holy Father, it is this personal integrity and authenticity that is so very striking. Certainly, given his genius and natural demeanor, John Paul II — John Paul the Great — can certainly be grouped with St. Thomas More as "a man for all seasons." Aware of his temporal as well as his eternal mission, joyfully participating in God's creation, the world about him and the time in which he was given to live and serve, the Pope's arms were ever outstretched to all men and women, who found him patient and attentive to their concerns and worries. Thus did His Excellency Archbishop Stanisław Dziwisz, for many years the Pope's personal secretary, and recently appointed Metropolitan of the Archdiocese of Kraków, describe his master and friend on 4 November 2005, at the inauguration of John Paul II's beatification process in Wawel Cathedral:

Mamy w pamięci Jego ręce wyciągnięte do człowieka, Jego otwarte ramiona przygarniające każdego. Nawet gdy te ręce zranił niegodziwy człowiek, one nie zacisnęły się w pięść w geście nienawiści czy chęci odwetu / . . . / Miałem szczęście być z nim blisko czterdzieści lat i mogę zaświadczyć, że nigdy nie skrzywdził człowieka.

Szanował każde zdanie wypowiedziane przez drugiego, nawet jeśli się z nim nie zgadzał.[3]

[We have in our memory His hands stretched out to man, His open arms drawing each person close to him. Even when those hands were wounded by an ignoble man, they did not clench as fists in a gesture of hatred or the desire for revenge /. . . / I was so fortunate as to be by his side for nearly forty years and I can affirm that he never hurt a single person. He respected every opinion voiced by another, even if he did not agree with it.]

Yet he was just as attuned, if not more so, to the Truth to Whom he was to witness, of Whom he was Vicar on this earth. In him, openness and understanding never devolved into a perilous relativism. While assenting to the salutary dictum *audiatur et altera pars*, his response to all issues and problems was consistently Christ-centered. Sympathy, understanding and good will can never be diluted into an easy willingness to compromise, which would betray the truth, betray the charge he was selected by the Holy Ghost to champion. As he stated in his 1995 encyclical *Ut unum sint*, concerning the formulation of doctrine vis-à-vis ecumenism:

Here it is not a question of altering the deposit of faith, changing the meaning of dogmas, eliminating essential words from them, accommodating truth to the preferences of a particular age, or suppressing certain articles of the *Creed* under the false pretext that they are no longer understood today. The unity willed by God can be attained only by the adherence of all to the content of revealed faith in its entirety. In matters of faith, compromise is in contradiction with God who is Truth. In the Body of Christ, "the way, and the truth, and the life" (Jn 14:6), who could

---

[3] Cf. "Jego życie było modlitwą. . ." [His life was a prayer. . .] *Dziennik Polski* LXI:259, November 5, 2005, p. 1.

consider legitimate a reconciliation brought about at the expense of the truth? The Council's Declaration on Religious Freedom *Dignitatis Humanae* attributes to human dignity the quest for truth, "especially in what concerns God and his Church," and adherence to truth's demands. A "being together" which betrayed the truth would thus be opposed both to the nature of God who offers his communion and to the need for truth found in the depths of every human heart.[4]

Five years earlier, in *Redemptoris missio*, a similar, determined and yet joyful, note is struck:

Christ is the one mediator between God and mankind: "For there is one God, and there is one mediator between God and men, the man Christ Jesus, who gave himself as a ransom for all, the testimony to which was borne at the proper time. For this I was appointed a preacher and apostle (I am telling the truth, I am not lying), a teacher of the Gentiles in faith and truth" (1 Tm 2:5-7; cf. Heb 4:14-16). No one, therefore, can enter into communion with God except through Christ, by the working of the Holy Spirit. Christ's one, universal mediation, far from being an obstacle on the journey toward God, is the way established by God himself, a fact of which Christ is fully aware. Although participated forms of mediation of different kinds and degrees are not excluded, they acquire meaning and value *only* from Christ's own mediation, and they cannot be understood as parallel or complementary to his.[5]

---

[4] Pope John Paul II, encyclical *Ut unum sint*, 1.18. March 25, 1995. Text from official Vatican website: www.vatican.va/ edocs/ENG0221/_INDEX.htm.
[5] Pope John Paul II, encyclical *Redemptoris missio*, 1.6. December 7, 1990. Text from official Vatican website:www.vatican.va/edocs/ENG0219/_INDEX. htm

The theological understanding of the Church has traveled a long way since the days of Cyprian of Carthage, who in the third century is credited with stating *Extra Ecclesiam nulla salus* [there is no salvation outside the Church]. A literal reading of these words is what is behind Dante's description of Limbo in Canto IV of his *Inferno*, that *bella scola* where are gathered the virtuous pagans whose greatest fault was their unwilled exclusion from the Judeo-Christian community during life. As his guide Virgil explains:

> / . . . / s'elli hanno mercedi,
> non basta, perchè non ebber battesmo,
> ch'è porta de la fede che tu credi;
>
> e s'e'furon dinanzi al Cristianesmo,
> non adorar debitamente a Dio:
> e di questi cotai son io medesmo
>
> Por tai difetti, non per altro rio,
> semo perduti, e sol di tanto offesi
> che sanza speme vivemo in disio.[6]

[If they had merit, / it was not enough, because they lacked Baptism, / which is the portal of the faith in which you believe; // and as they did live before Christianity, / they did not adore God as they should / and I myself am of their number. // For such defects, not for any other offense, / we are lost, and are afflicted only in this / that we live in desire, but without hope.]

Were Dante living today, the eternal lot of the Greeks and virtuous pagans described in *La divina commedia* might be very different.[7]

---

[6] Dante Alighieri, *Inferno* IV:34-42.
[7] Referring to the "Harrowing of Hell," Virgil goes on to describe that only the Jews inhabiting Limbo were freed and delivered into Heaven by Christ, who descended into Hell for this very purpose after His Crucifixion.

Today, the Church would consider it presumptuous to exclude *a priori* any person from Heaven. Still, by acknowledging that the manner in which Christ may bring non-Christians and non-Jews to Heaven is unplumbable by human reason, the fact remains that only through Him is all salvation effected — and thus John Paul II makes his courageous and unabashed re-statement of Church doctrine. Similarly, although the Church hierarchy, and John Paul II himself, were variously, and viciously attacked from several quarters for the 2000 declaration of the Congregation for the Doctrine of the Faith *Dominus Iesus*, which states, *inter alia*:

> Unica ergo est Christi Ecclesia, subsistens in Ecclesia Catholica, cuius moderatio spectat ad Petri Successorem et ad Episcopos in communione cum eo. Ecclesiae illae quae, licet in perfecta communione cum Ecclesia Catholica non sint, eidem tamen iunguntur vinculis strictissimis, cuiusmodi sunt successio apostolica et valida Eucharistiae celebratio, verae sunt Ecclesiae particulares. Quapropter in his quoque Ecclesiis praesens est et operatur Christi Ecclesia, quantumvis plena desit communio cum Ecclesia Catholica, eo quod ipsae doctrinam catholicam non acceptant de Primatu, quem, ex Dei consilio, Episcopus Romanus obiective possidet et in Ecclesiam universam exercet.
>
> Illae vero Communitates ecclesiales, quae validum Episcopatum et genuinam ac integram substantiam eucharistici mysterii non servant, sensu proprio Ecclesiae non sunt; attamen qui baptizati sunt iis in Communitatibus Baptismate Christo incorporantur, et ideo in quadam cum Ecclesia communione, licet imperfecta, exstant. Per se enim Baptismus tendit ad perfectionem vitae in Christo per integram fidei professionem, Eucharistiam et plenam communionem in Ecclesia.[8]

---

[8] Congregation for the Doctrine of the Faith, *Declaratio „Dominus Iesus" de Iesu Christi atque Ecclesiae unicitate et universalitate salvifica* [Declaration

[Therefore, there exists a single Church of Christ, which subsists in the Catholic Church, governed by the Successor of Peter and by the Bishops in communion with him. The Churches which, while not existing in perfect communion with the Catholic Church, remain united to her by means of the closest bonds, that is, by apostolic succession and a valid Eucharist, are true particular Churches. Therefore, the Church of Christ is present and operative also in these Churches, even though they lack full communion with the Catholic Church, since they do not accept the Catholic doctrine of the Primacy, which, according to the will of God, the Bishop of Rome objectively has and exercises over the entire Church.

On the other hand, the ecclesial communities which have not preserved the valid Episcopate and the genuine and integral substance of the Eucharistic mystery, are not Churches in the proper sense; however, those who are baptized in these communities are, by Baptism, incorporated in Christ and thus are in a certain communion, albeit imperfect, with the Church. Baptism in fact tends *per se* toward the full development of life in Christ, through the integral profession of faith, the Eucharist, and full communion in the Church.]

what other position could they take? In the above-cited *Ut unum sint*, predating *Dominus Iesus* by five years, the Pope addresses this same issue in exactly the same language:

"Dominus Iesus" for the Unicity and Salvific Universality of Jesus Christ and the Church], 17. August 6, 2000. For Latin text: http://www.vatican.va/roman _curia/congregations/cfaith/documents/rc_con_cfaith_doc_20000806_dominus -iesus_lt.html.For English: http://www.vatican.va/roman_curia/congregations/ cfaith/documents/rc_con_cfaith_doc_20000806_dominus-iesus_en.html

The Catholic Church, both in her *praxis* and in her solemn documents, holds that the communion of the particular Churches with the Church of Rome, and of their Bishops with the Bishop of Rome, is — in God's plan — an essential requisite of full and visible communion. Indeed full communion, of which the Eucharist is the highest sacramental manifestation, needs to be visibly expressed in a ministry in which all the Bishops recognize that they are united in Christ and all the faithful find confirmation for their faith. The first part of the Acts of the Apostles presents Peter as the one who speaks in the name of the apostolic group and who serves the unity of the community — all the while respecting the authority of James, the head of the Church in Jerusalem. This function of Peter must continue in the Church so that under her sole Head, who is Jesus Christ, she may be visibly present in the world as the communion of all his disciples.[9]

Again, dialogue with the world, cooperation with and understanding for the multifarious wonder of mankind, certainly — but some things simply cannot be put on the table as bargaining chips. It is worth noting, and just as reassuring, that Pope Benedict XVI, John Paul's successor, has been treading the exact same path in these first few months of his Papacy — and again, how could he do otherwise, since it is the path first trod by Peter himself? He has met and conversed with both the renegade theologian Hans Küng and Bishop Bernard Fellay, Superior General of the Lefebvrist Priestly Society of St Pius X, yet he has not swayed from his fidelity to the doctrinal and disciplinary charges entrusted him.[10] This is not dyed-in-the-wool conservatism, but simple intellectual honesty. If the Church professes to be founded, not on the shifting sands of human consensus, but on the solid rock of divine

---

[9] Pope John Paul II, *Ut unum sint*, 3.97.
[10] See the November 2005 instruction on homosexuals and the priesthood, issued despite the chorus of protests from the more permissive and relativistic quarters of world opinion.

xix

revelation, delivered to us by the Son of God Himself, then the truths of revelation cannot be tampered with or bent to suit the present tastes of society. If there is a transcendent, absolute truth, and if it has been made known to us by no less an authority (!) than God Himself, we ignore that truth and its teachings at our peril:

> If there is no transcendent truth, in obedience to which man achieves his full identity, then there is no sure principle for guaranteeing just relations between people. Their self-interest as a class, group or nation would inevitably set them in opposition to one another. If one does not acknowledge transcendent truth, then the force of power takes over, and each person tends to make full use of the means at his disposal in order to impose his own interests or his own opinion, with no regard for the rights of others. People are then respected only to the extent that they can be exploited for selfish ends.[11]

For those who see steadfastness to ideals as intolerance, there is no convincing counter-argument. However, a glance through the writings of John Paul II will make it apparent to the fair-minded that the Holy Father's convictions of a single Truth,[12] and his devotion to the consequences that flow therefrom, are motivated by nothing other than a loving concern for the human person, threatened today from so many sides. When he states, as in the 1995 encyclical *Evangelium vitae*, "The basis of these values cannot be provisional and changeable 'majority' opinions, but only the acknowledgment of an objective moral law which, as the 'natural law' written in the human heart, is the obligatory point of reference for civil law itself,"[13] it might be stated that he is

---

[11] Pope John Paul II, encyclical *Centesimus annus*, 5.44. May 1, 1991. Text: http://www.vatican.va/edocs/ENG0214/_INDEX.HTM.

[12] And not the "several truths," "relative truths" or "perspectives-as-individual-truth" of the prophets of Postmodernism, who time and again repeat Pilate's question to Christ: "what is truth?"

[13] Pope John Paul II, encyclical *Evangelium vitae*, 3.70. March 25, 1995. Text: http://www.vatican.va/edocs/ENG0141/_INDEX.HTM.

expressing a truth which, in a sense, transcends even Christianity. These sentiments are the very same as those expressed by Sophocles' heroine Antigone already in 442 BC, when faced with the dilemma of obeying the repulsive civil law enacted by the earthly ruler Creon, or that which she knows to be right, that which is "written in her heart." And, like Antigone, if we are attentive to the voice of our conscience, which is the voice of this absolute, objective moral law, we are bound to take action in defense of it:

> Now the first and most immediate application of this teaching concerns a human law which disregards the fundamental right and source of all other rights which is the right to life, a right belonging to every individual. Consequently, laws which legitimize the direct killing of innocent human beings through abortion or euthanasia are in complete opposition to the inviolable right to life proper to every individual; they thus deny the equality of everyone before the law. It might be objected that such is not the case in euthanasia, when it is requested with full awareness by the person involved. But any State which made such a request legitimate and authorized it to be carried out would be legalizing a case of suicide-murder, contrary to the fundamental principles of absolute respect for life and of the protection of every innocent life. In this way the State contributes to lessening respect for life and opens the door to ways of acting which are destructive of trust in relations between people. Laws which authorize and promote abortion and euthanasia are therefore radically opposed not only to the good of the individual but also to the common good; as such they are completely lacking in authentic juridical validity. Disregard for the right to life, precisely because it leads to the killing of the person whom society exists to serve, is what most directly conflicts with the possibility of achieving the common good. Consequently, a civil law authorizing abortion or

euthanasia ceases by that very fact to be a true, morally binding civil law. / . . . / In the case of an intrinsically unjust law, such as a law permitting abortion or euthanasia, it is therefore never licit to obey it, or to "take part in a propaganda campaign in favor of such a law, or vote for it." [14]

In a very real way, what many people in our world take to be "progressive" attitudes to population control, abortion, euthanasia, "quality of life" questions and the such are actually *regressive*. They hearken back to the theoretical underpinnings of some of the most repugnant civil "codes" enacted in the first half of the twentieth century; actually, they regress even further, past the dawn of civilized human life, to that level of existence where everything is subject to individual will, the law of the jungle, might making "right:"

At another level, the roots of the contradiction between the solemn affirmation of human rights and their tragic denial in practice lies in a notion of freedom which exalts the isolated individual in an absolute way, and gives no place to solidarity, to openness to others and service of them. While it is true that the taking of life not yet born or in its final stages is sometimes marked by a mistaken sense of altruism and human compassion, it cannot be denied that such a culture of death, taken as a whole, betrays a completely individualistic concept of freedom, which ends up by becoming the freedom of "the strong" against the weak who have no choice but to submit.

It is precisely in this sense that Cain's answer to the Lord's question: "Where is Abel your brother?" can be interpreted: "I do not know; am I my brother's keeper?" (Gen 4:9). Yes, every man is his "brother's keeper," because God entrusts us to

---

[14] Pope John Paul II, encyclical *Evangelium vitae*, 3.72-73.

one another. And it is also in view of this entrusting that God gives everyone freedom, a freedom which possesses an inherently relational dimension. This is a great gift of the Creator, placed as it is at the service of the person and of his fulfillment through the gift of self and openness to others; but when freedom is made absolute in an individualistic way, it is emptied of its original content, and its very meaning and dignity are contradicted.[15]

Again, readers of Franz Kafka, that "founder of the twentieth century,"[16] in the words of Catholic poet and philosopher Rio Preisner, will recognize that this truth also "transcends" Catholic dogma. For in *Die Verwandlung* [The Metamorphosis], that shockingly prophetic tale that foresaw so many of these questions as early as 1915, the main hero, Gregor Samsa, suddenly traumatized by a debilitating and disfiguring illness (and even more so by the repulsion and rejection he encounters from his closest family members at the time when he most needs their love and support), dies only when his beloved sister Greta deprives him of all hope by exclaiming in exasperation *Ich will vor diesem Untier nicht den Namen meines Bruders aussprechen, und sage daher bloß: wir müssen versuchen, es loszuwerden!* [I will no longer utter my brother's name in the presence of this monster, and state quite simply that we must try to get rid of it].

It is not feigned compassion and legislation aimed at easing our consciences in regard to the weakest among us, but rather a renewed sensitivity to that law written in our hearts, inscribed there by the Holy Ghost Himself, that excites that "still small voice." As the Pope writes in *Dominum et vivificantem*:

Hence the Church constantly implores from God the grace that integrity of human consciences will not be lost, that their healthy sensitivity with regard to good

---

[15] Pope John Paul II, encyclical *Evangelium vitae*, 1.19.
[16] "Franz Kafka, zakladatel dvacátého století." See Rio Preisner, *Pan Schwitter platí účet v DVSP* [Mr Schwitter pays his bills at the DVSP] in *Kapiláry* [Capillaries] (Brno: Blok, 1968), p. 9.

and evil will not be blunted. This integrity and sensitivity are profoundly linked to the intimate action of the Spirit of truth. In this light the exhortations of St. Paul assume particular eloquence: "Do not quench the Spirit"; "Do not grieve the Holy Spirit" (I Thess 5:19; Eph 4:30). But above all the Church constantly implores with the greatest fervor that there will be no increase in the world of the sin that the Gospel calls "blasphemy against the Holy Spirit." Rather, she prays that it will decrease in human souls — and consequently in the forms and structures of society itself — and that it will make room for that openness of conscience necessary for the saving action of the Holy Spirit.[17]

Thus the Pope taught in writing, and thus did he teach by example. And nowhere did he more eloquently, more effectively, express the dignity of mankind — of all men and all women — a dignity based not on wealth, utility, intelligence, physical capacity or any other quality save the inherent human dignity from which none can ever be separated, than he did during his own personal *via dolorosa* of illness in the final years leading up to his death. Amid so many questions as to his capacity to lead the Church during so physically debilitating an illness such as we all witnessed him struggling against — and overcoming in that daily struggle — amid all those calls for him to abdicate the Throne and entrust Peter's keys into "surer" hands, few there were among us who realized that it is precisely *because* of that illness and weakness that John Paul II soldiered on for us, served us, exposed his declining health to us on all the television screens of the entire world. A lesser man would have rested. A vain man would have spared himself the "indignity" of allowing the eyes of strangers to examine his progressing frailty and speculate on the biological causes of his decline. But Karol Wojtyła, Pope John Paul the Great, was no petty, vain man. He looked not to himself, or the eyes of others, but to Christ, Christ

---

[17] Pope John Paul II, encyclical *Dominum et vivificantem*, 2.48. May 18, 1986. Text: http://www.vatican.va/edocs/ENG0142/_INDEX. HTM.

crucified — not the antiseptic, already-resurrected Christ who seems to leap from the Cross on the stylized, modern crucifixes that spare our eyes and our sensitivities above the altars of so many contemporary churches — but Christ in His death agony, Christ suffering on our behalf, Christ displaying our humanity at its weakest and most abject. And thus did John Paul II transform his latter years into a magnificent *imitatio Christi*. He too showed us a suffering humanity, humanity at its weakest and most abject, so that we should hesitate before lightly rejecting the weakest and most abject among us. Thus, just like Christ Himself, mocked by the crowds who demanded Him to "descend from the Cross," did John Paul II imitate his divine Master, and remain at his post to the very end. Karol Wojtyła, theologian, philosopher, artist and pastor, delivered his most eloquent lesson to us virtually without words.

Words are what the authors of the essays contained in this book have to offer You, reader, in honor of Karol Wojtyła, Pope John Paul the Great, dear to so many, and certainly dear to You, as you have seen fit to take this book in hand. These words, like any which seek to describe John Paul II, are frustratingly insufficient. In requesting that you overlook the obvious inadequacies of our literary offering to the memory of that great Man, perhaps I may be permitted to entertain one small hope. It is my wish that these essays not be an object of contemplation, an end in themselves, but, rather, that they excite Your thoughts past them, to the Object they refer to, our late Holy Father. If, through them, You are prompted to remember his example daily, and thus to emulate him, then this lowly offering of sincere respect on the part of our Institute will have justified its existence one thousandfold.

Three Encounters — Reminiscences

PIOTR WANDYCZ

In the Spring of 1981 I received a letter from Rome dated 10 March and signed Stanisław Grygiel. The name was familiar, because I knew that Grygiel had been the Editor of the Catholic periodical *Znak* [The Sign] and taught philosophy at the Papal Theological Academy in Kraków. The letter carried an invitation to come to Rome to a meeting which would discuss the character and future of the Polish Institute of Christian Culture called into being by the Holy Father John Paul II. Grygiel, who had been appointed director of the Institute, explained the new situation and the new possibilities regarding Polish culture which arose with the election of Cardinal Wojtyła to the Papal See. He recalled the great interest in Polish contributions to European culture which this election awakened. The Institute, as he saw it, would concern itself with all that in Polish and European culture was permeated by Christianity, but he emphasized that the adjective "Christian" should not be perceived too narrowly. Convinced that Polish culture was indivisible, he felt it essential that both Poles from the homeland and those whom "fate made to work for Poland abroad" participate in this first workshop-like meeting.

The meeting which took place in Rome on September 15-16 brought together the following: Fathers Józef Tischner and Janusz Pasierb, Bishop Marian Rechowicz (the rector of the Lublin Catholic University, KUL, from 1956-1965), Prof. Andrzej Święcicki, then chairman of the Warsaw Club of Catholic Intelligentsia (KIK), the writer Jan Józef Szczepański, and from the United States Prof. Feliks Gross, president of PIASA, and myself. The participants were lodged in the building on via Cassia 1200 which housed the John Paul II Foundation and a center designed for Polish pilgrims. We were joined for the different sessions by several Rome-based priests connected with this initiative or with the via Cassia center. There were also Krzysztof Zanussi who showed his film about John Paul II and Mrs. Gawrońska whose Foundation had earned the gratitude of many Poles coming to Rome.

The culminating point came on the second day with the invitation of the participants to Castel Gandolfo to attend the Mass in the Papal Chapel and then to have breakfast with the Holy Father during which the idea of the Polish Institute of Christian Culture would be discussed. In the early morning we were driven to the summer residence of the popes which is beautifully located in hills overlooking a lake. We were immediately admitted and greeted by the Holy Father. After the Mass we moved to the breakfast room and I, as one who had not met the Pope before, was seated on his right hand at the table. Right away I noticed his finger grazed by the assassin's bullet. For someone who for the first time in his life could talk to a pope this was a most intimidating experience. I ventured a sentence about John Paul's health which, in the mountainous area of Castel Gandolfo, should improve quicker than in Rome. John Paul II made it clear that he did not consider this region as real mountains — something I should have guessed. I mentioned my wife's family links to Wadowice which interested the Pope but he remarked that these were already such old times. I felt that he did not feel like engaging in small talk and wished to turn quickly to the business on hand. My first impression of John Paul was the strong will which emanated from him and his great personality .

The Pope explained his ideas about the Polish Institute of Christian Culture. Thus far Paris with *Kultura* and the Bibliothèque Polonaise was the real center of attraction for Poles, but with his election the Pope wished for Rome to become another, if not the, center for Poles from the homeland and abroad. He recalled the old Polish-Roman ties and the Hospicjum in Rome founded by the sixteenth-century Cardinal Stanisław Hozjusz for Poles which still exists today. He hoped that the Institute would be in a sense a continuation of this work taking the form of a bridge between Polish intellectuals and their Western colleagues.

A general conversation ensued in the course of which the participants expressed worry about the safety of the Pope. Only recently a paparazzi had been able to penetrate the Vatican gardens and take a picture of John Paul leaving the swimming pool. Thus the security seemed lax. Someone asked the Pope if he had more definite knowledge of who stood behind the assassin's attempt on his life. He mentioned the prevalent suspicions of the Soviet Union and Bulgaria. To our "please take care of yourself" the Pope replied "what can I do?" At the end of the meeting the papal secretary

Msgr. Stanisław Dziwisz put in front of the Pope copies of the newly published Encyclical *Laborem exercens* which John Paul II autographed and gave to each of us. Taking leave I hugged the Holy Father—the gesture was spontaneous and he reciprocated it.

For various reasons the Institute of Christian Culture did not develop along the lines as envisaged. Martial law in Poland interrupted contacts, and plans for an advisory scholarly council did not materialize. Grygiel resigned his directorship and became professor at Lateran University, all the while maintaining close contact with John Paul II.

Nine years were to pass before I saw the Pope for the second time. The occasion was an international conference which took place in Rome from April 28—May 6, 1990. The initiative came largely from the Lublin circle — in which Prof. Jerzy Kłoczowski played a leading role — and émigré institutions such as the Ukrainian W.K. Lypynsky East European Research Institute in Philadelphia, the Belorussian Institute of Arts and Sciences in New York and the Lithuanian Catholic Academy of Science in Rome. The John Paul II Foundation assumed the main task of organizing and largely financing the meeting. Readers interested in the conference which brought together a large number of scholars and intellectuals will find a list of the papers presented in a volume entitled: *Belarus, Lithuania, Poland, Ukraine. The Foundations of Historical and Cultural Traditions in East Central Europe,* edited by Jerzy Kłoczowski, Jaroslaw Pelenski, Marian Radwan, Jan Skarbek and Stefan Wylężek and published in Lublin in 1994.

We were received by the Pope in the Vatican on May 1, and he exchanged a few words with each one of us. I was amazed when told before the meeting by Father Radwan that the Pope, looking over the list of participants, remembered my name and knew that I was a historian. Perhaps he connected it with my articles in the *Tygodnik Powszechny* [Universal Weekly] which he read carefully.

The first international meeting was a great success and was followed by similar gatherings each year held respectively in Lublin, Kamenetsk Podolskyi, Hrodna (Grodno) and Trakai (Troki). They were referred to as Rome II, III, IV and V. I was not able to

3

take part in them, and came only to attend Rome VI held in Rome in 1995.

For the third time I was able to see and exchange a few words with the Pope who invited us all to Castel Gandolfo. I took this opportunity to present to him a copy of my book *The Price of Freedom,* which, as Prof. Kłoczowski pointed out to the Holy Father, was published by Znak. At the end of the meeting the Pope led us in the Lord's prayer in Polish.

Four years later, in 1999, I was elected President of PIASA and asked through the intermediary of Prof. Grygiel for the Pope's blessing. Toward the end of June I received a letter from Grygiel in which he cited the words which John Paul II had written to him on June 19, 1999: "Write Prof. Piotr Wandycz that I ask God to bless him in the tasks which he undertook." These words of the Holy Father, as well as the three encounters I had with him, will never fade from my memory.

I was never again in the presence of John Paul II, but I followed his journeys on TV and watched his communing with the huge and enthralled crowds from all the continents. More and more I appreciated and admired his wonderful personality, his wit, his human touch and the charisma which emanated from him. His achievements were legion. He was truly one of the greatest popes, and one could not but be moved by the shouts "santo, santo" which recently rang from the mass of people at St. Peter Square.

Reminiscences: Once in a Millennium
THADDEUS V. GROMADA

Late in the summer of 1969 I received a surprising call from the Prior of the Pauline Fathers, Rev. Michael Zembrzuski. He informed me that the 46 year old Polish Cardinal from Kraków, His Eminence Karol Wojtyła, would be making his first visit to the United States and plans were being made to welcome him on September 28, 1969 at the new Shrine of Our Lady of Częstochowa in Doylestown, PA. Governor Raymond P. Schaeffer of Pennsylvania had proclaimed September 28, 1969 "Karol Cardinal Wojtyła Day." A special outdoor program was arranged to honor the young Cardinal and pay tribute to the Polish Church and the Polish nation for their heroic struggle to preserve basic Christian values in a country governed by Communists. Would I be willing to accept the role of Master of Ceremonies and preside over the program? I wondered why the choice should fall on me, a newly minted PhD. from Fordham and a young faculty member at a New Jersey State College. I did, however, accept this task which I regarded as a high honor and privilege.

At the same time, I realized that I must spend some time in preparation for this event. Whom better might I consult than the great Polish Catholic historian, Prof. Oskar Halecki, who was my mentor and advisor at Fordham University? He was now retired from Fordham and had withdrawn from public life after the death of his beloved wife. But I did not lose contact with him; in fact I had often visited him in his White Plains, New York apartment. When Prof. Halecki heard the news of the impending visit of Cardinal Wojtyła and the part I was to play in it, he was very pleased. Our long and animated conversation revealed that Prof. Halecki was a close and keen observer of the Catholic Church in Poland and was very well informed about its hierarchy including Cardinal Wojtyła. He briefed me thoroughly about the young Prince of the Church whom he held in high esteem for both his intellectual and pastoral abilities.

Just before I left, Halecki, asked me one favor. Would I deliver a personal letter to Cardinal Wojtyła together with the first chapter of his forthcoming book on Queen Jadwiga? It was at this time that Halecki told me about his project, a monograph on Jadwiga of Anjou, which he hoped to complete in time for the 600th anniversary of her birth in 1974. It was his last intellectual passion. It was obvious to me that he wanted the Cardinal to be informed about his research and to encourage him to promote more vigorously the beatification of Jadwiga, the first step toward Sainthood.

Bolstered by Halecki's advice and encouragement, I felt confident when I faced the multitude of several thousands at the American Częstochowa on September 28, 1969. On the dais were many distinguished individuals, among them the first Polish American Cardinal, John Cardinal Krol of Philadelphia, the Governor of Pennsylvania, Raymond Schaeffer, Judge Thaddeus Machrowicz and, of course, Karol Cardinal Wojtyła. In my opening remarks, as the Master of Ceremonies, I said,

> This is the very first time that a Polish Cardinal has visited the United States and thus it is a privilege to welcome and honor a Prince of the Catholic Church of Poland, the Archbishop Metropolitan of Kraków, the successor of St. Stanisław Szczepanowski and Prince Adam Sapieha. There is a rich symbolism in the fact a Polish Cardinal is being welcomed and honored in the American Częstochowa, dedicated to the Black Madonna. No one who is of Polish ancestry needs to be reminded that the Shrine of Our Lady at Jasna Góra in Częstochowa played an important role in Poland's history, never ceasing to be a source of inspiration, always helping the Polish nation to survive in times of persecution and tribulation. It is our hope that this Shrine at Beacon Hill in Doylestown will play a similar role for the Polish American community, helping it to preserve its unity and identity but at the same time not preventing it from joining the mainstream of American life.

When it came time to introduce the Polish Cardinal, I decided to do it in English, Polish and in the Góral (Polish Highlander) dialect. The following are excerpts of these introductions:

Karol Cardinal Wojtyła is one of the reasons why the Catholic Church in Poland continues to be a vital and relevant force in the life of Polish citizens /. . . / He is dynamic. He is a humanist with a deep feeling for all his people. A former worker, a poet, a mountain climber and skier. A great scholar and intellectual who has produced several hundred articles and numerous books not only in the field of theology and Church affairs, but also in Philosophy and Sociology. A former Professor of Social Ethics at the Jagiellonian University and the Catholic University in Lublin who still holds the rank of University Professor / . . . / He took an active part at the Second Vatican Council, especially in the discussion of the Constitution of the Church.

Jego Eminencjo, Polonia Amerykańska, dawna i nowa, stoi wiernie przy Episkopacie Polskim, podziwia jego obronę zasad katolickich w kraju pod przewodem obu kardynałów. Czuję wdzięczność za opiekę nad życiem religijnym emigracji za pośrednictwem dwóch biskupów, Biskupa Szczepana Wesołego i Biskupa Władysława Rubina. Witamy, Jego Eminecję, Karola Kardynała Wojtyłę, w Amerykańskiej Częstochowie, i wyrażamy nadzieję, że pomoże nam w utrzymaniu serdecznych więzów, jakie łączą nas z krajem i wiarą naszych przodków /.../ Jako historyk nie mogę pominąć jego zainteresowania badaniami historycznymi, zwłaszcza związanymi z Tysiącleciem Polski i za sprawą beatyfikacji królowej Jadwigi. Jako duszpasterz, ks. Kardynał Wojtyła, dał się poznać szerokim kręgom społeczeństwa katolickiego jako żarliwy i świetny

7

kaznodzieja. Liczne wizytacje duszpasterskie, przeprowadzane na terenie całej Archidiecezji, zjednały mu powszechną miłość i szacunek.

[Your Eminence, American Polonia, old and new, stands loyally with the Polish Episcopate. We greatly admire your defense of Catholic principles under the leadership of two Cardinals. We are grateful for the pastoral care given to the Polish emigration through your representatives Bishop Szczepan Wesoły and Bishop Władysław Rubin. We welcome Your Eminence in American Częstochowa, and express our hope that you will help us maintain warm and cordial ties with the country and faith of our ancestors /. . . / As a historian, I cannot forget to mention your interest in historical research, especially the research connected with Poland's Millennium and the Queen Jadwiga beatification case. As a Pastor, Cardinal Wojtyła is widely known and recognized by Polish society as a passionate and splendid preacher. His many pastoral visits throughout the Kraków Archdiocese have gained for him the love and respect of his flock.]

Finally, the introduction in the "Góral" dialect.

Dla mnie osobiście, jako Amerykanina polskiego, podhalańskiego pochodzenia, jest mi scególnie miło przywitać gościa urodzonego w Wadowicach, w gwarze Góralskiej. Księże Kardynale, calućko Polonia straśnie sie ciesy i raduje, że mo u siebie Kardynała z Krakowa. Jo zaś w imieniu tych, co tu przyśli i tych, co w domach pozostajali, gorąco i całom dusom, witom Wos, Eminencjo.

[For me personally as an American of Polish Podhalan descent, it is a special pleasure to welcome a guest who was born in Wadowice, in the "Góral" dialect. Dear Cardinal, the entire Polonia is wildly happy and delighted, that we have with us a Cardinal from Kraków. So, in the name of all those who came today, and those who have remained in their homes, I warmly and with all my heart, welcome you, Your Eminence.]

Following the introductions, Cardinal Wojtyła walked slowly toward me, smiling broadly and with arms outstretched. Apparently he was touched by my unorthodox introduction in the Góral dialect. He embraced me tightly and then actually picked me up several inches off the ground. Here was a physically strong man, unafraid to display his warm friendly feelings in front of thousands of people. At the podium Cardinal Wojtyła charmed the audience with his natural humanity. His deep, resonant, strong voice carried a message of hope that made a deep impression on me and the assembled. How fortunate, I thought, that Poland now had two outstanding Cardinals (the other being Cardinal Wyszyński) to lead the Church in these difficult times. But I could hardly have dreamed that in less than ten years he would be chosen the successor of St. Peter, and lead the entire Catholic Church.

After the formal program was over, Cardinal Wojtyła could not resist meeting and speaking with the members of the Polish Tatra Highlander Group of Passaic, N.J. led by my father Jan W. Gromada. They were there with other groups to welcome the Polish Cardinal. He was somewhat surprised and delighted to see authentic "Górale" clad in their costumes and accompanied with "muzyka góralska" in American Częstochowa. As promised I personally delivered Prof. Halecki's letter to Cardinal Wojtyła during the closing festivities. A few days later before returning to Poland, the Cardinal and Professor Halecki met in New York City. I will always have the satisfaction to know that in some small way I was instrumental in bringing about this meeting. As a consequence, Professor Halecki had the opportunity to meet the future Polish Pope face to face. Halecki died in September 1973.

My second encounter with Cardinal Wojtyła was in 1976 when he came to America with 16 other members of the Catholic hierarchy of Poland to attend the International Eucharistic Congress

9

in Philadelphia. During his six week stay in the United States, he took the opportunity to make a whirlwind tour from the Atlantic to the Pacific and to visit America's Polish communities during the Bicentennial celebrations. While in New York he made a point of visiting the Polish Institute of Arts and Sciences and the Kościuszko Foundation on September 4, 1976. At the time I was the Secretary General of PIASA and recall that I received short notice of his impending visit, just a few days before the Labor Day weekend. Most people were still vacationing or planning family Labor Day barbecues, so it was not easy to mobilize our members and friends to assure a proper welcome for the Cardinal Archbishop of Kraków. Only two years later many people who, for one reason or another, could not come to welcome Cardinal Wojtyła at the Institute or at the Foundation regretted it very much! After warmly being greeted by a PIASA delegation headed by the Director, Prof. Feliks Gross and myself, the Secretary General, Cardinal Wojtyła spent a few hours touring our 5 story townhouse at 59 East 66th Street and discussing current issues and problems in Poland. Later that same day, I participated in a well attended public meeting that was held at the Kościuszko Foundation organized by its President Dr. Eugene Kusielewicz. The idea behind the meeting was to start a dialogue between the cultural leaders of American Polonia and the Polish Cardinal.

I was among several speakers (all PIASA members, including Dr. Joseph Wieczerzak, Dr. Stanislaus Blejwas, Dr. Daniel S. Buczek and Bolesław Wierzbiański) who were given an opportunity to present what they considered to be the main problems and concerns of the Polish American community. In my opening presentation I pointed out that the main pillars of Polonia located in the urban centers, which include the Polish Roman Catholic parishes, Polish parochial schools, Polish language press, etc. were declining and in some cases had already collapsed. I stated, "Polish Americans are leaving the old Polish neighborhoods and moving into suburban areas. How can Polish ethnicity and Polish cultural life be preserved in the suburbs without the Polish Catholic parish? Can the Polish hierarchy encourage the American Catholic hierarchy to be more sympathetic and more sensitive to the special needs of Polish Americans who do not want to lose their

Polish identity?" At the end, I emphasized Polonia's solidarity with the Polish nation and declared that "we can never be indifferent to the fate of Poland. How best can Polonia advance the cause of justice and greater freedom for Poland?"

All throughout the presentations Cardinal Wojtyła listened attentively and patiently; taking notes once in a while. His response, delivered extemporaneously, was both brilliant and very blunt. "If American Polonia expects cooperation in matters pertaining to the Polish American community, then we expect American Polonia to cooperate with the Polish nation," he declared. He indicated that the concerns and issues expressed will be brought up to the American Episcopate.

> We feel that some decisive steps must be taken with the Polish American Pastorate, to fulfill the needs of all the generations of Polonia; even for those who are unfamiliar with the Polish language. /. . . / But we cannot dismiss the language issue so easily. It is true enough that knowledge of the language of the country in which one resides is fundamental for any sort of advance within the society, but we have to reinforce bilingual education at any cost and be familiar with the language of our forefathers, too. In this respect I am not so sure that Polonia is not guilty of a few sins.

But what kind of cooperation did the Metropolitan Archbishop of Kraków expect from Polonia? He forcefully reminded everyone that

> We are now standing in the face of the greatest historical confrontation humanity has gone through /.../ the final confrontation between the Church and the anti-Church, of the Gospel versus the anti-Gospel. This confrontation lies within the plans of Divine Providence; it is a trial which the whole Church, and the Polish Church in particular, must take up. / . . . / A great deal of it depends upon the

outcome on the banks of the Vistula. /. . . / It is a trial of not only our nation and Church, but in a sense a test of the two thousand years of culture and Christian civilization with all of its consequences for human dignity, individual rights, human rights and the rights of nations.

He praised Polonia for being most aware of this confrontation but pleaded that it enlighten the "other layers of American society who simply eliminate this problem from their sphere of interests. As the number of people who understand the importance of this confrontation increase in Poland and America, we can look with greater trust towards the outcome of this confrontation." In the short run, Cardinal Wojtyła asked for the support of Polish American Catholics to bring back the distinguished Theology Faculty to the Jagiellonian University, which had been removed therefrom in 1954.

The Polish Institute as well as the Kościuszko Foundation received warm accolades that evening from the Polish Cardinal. He declared,

The Kościuszko Foundation and the Polish Institute which I have just visited are particularly important at this time. We realize that culture creates national identity and in the end, creates the nation itself. /. . ./ These matters are profound and affect us very deeply. I pointed these matters out to emphasize the significance of the work of the Polish Institute, as well as of the Kościuszko Foundation, which attempts to diligently serve the interests of the Polish people. We must be grateful to everyone who has contributed to these efforts, and to those who continue to work towards these goals. This work is one of the greatest components of our national identity.

This unprecedented remarkable meeting ended with Cardinal Wojtyła quoting Wyspiański. "Poles could have more, if they would only will, to want it"[1] and then adding "Perhaps, we have changed enough, so that Poles will want more; if only they want more, they will be able to have more."

Less than two years after this New York meeting Karol Cardinal Wojtyła became Pope John Paul II, the successor of St. Peter. It was a shock to many for a non-Italian, and especially a Pole, to be elected Supreme Pontiff. However, we at the Polish Institute deemed him *papabile* back in 1976. Together with millions of Poles and persons of Polish origin I was proud and jubilant over his selection and thanked God that I was privileged to live at this time. I considered his election to the Papacy in October 1978 to be a major event in Poland's history, second only to the Baptism of Mieszko in 966. When Pope John Paul II made his first pilgrimage to the United States and became the first Pope to visit the White House on October 6, 1979, my wife Theresa and I were among the 6,000 or so guests on the South Lawn cheering him and the Baptist President, Jimmy Carter. It was a moving and memorable event when President Carter greeted the Pope and the thousands of guests with a few words in Polish and in the company of his Polish-born National Security Advisor, Zbigniew Brzezinski, a member of the Polish Institute.

It was not until March 1993 that I, together with my wife Theresa, sister Janina Kedron and brother in-law Henry Kedron, was privileged to have an audience with John Paul II in his private Vatican apartment immediately after morning Mass in the Papal chapel. I could not help but notice the statue of Our Lady of Ludźmierz in the Pope's apartment — the Virgin Mary venerated by the Tatra Highlanders (Górale).

The meeting was arranged by his private secretary, Monsignor Stanisław Dziwisz, a Góral from Raba Wyżna who today is Archbishop Metropolitan of Kraków. The main reason for this audience was to present the Pope with a book, *Jadwiga of Anjou and the Rise of East Central Europe* written by Poland's great historian Oskar Halecki and edited and posthumously published by me, his former student. Just before his death Prof. Halecki entrusted his handwritten manuscript to me, but after

---

[1] From *Wesele* [The Wedding], *Oni by to mogli mieć, ino oni nie chcą chcieć.*

discussions with potential publishers it became apparent that the manuscript required extensive editing. So, it was not until 1991 that it was finally published and distributed by Columbia University Press. The Pope (then Cardinal Wojtyła) had, as previously noted, met Prof. Halecki in New York in 1969 and knew that he was working on a definitive study of Queen Jadwiga. They both believed that Jadwiga was a saintly young woman who profoundly influenced not only the course of Poland's history, but the history of East Central Europe. In 1979 John Paul II had actually beatified Jadwiga during a solemn ceremony in the Wawel Cathedral in Kraków.

Clearly on March 24, 1993, he was overjoyed to receive the newly published Jadwiga biography at the time when the Jadwiga canonization process was in progress. Monsignor Dziwisz directed me to contact Archbishop Edward Nowak, Secretary of the Congregation dealing with Canonization, whom I met the next day. The Archbishop accepted the book with enthusiasm and exclaimed that "it will be very helpful."

Oskar Halecki, the first Director of the Polish Institute, could hardly have imagined that before the end of the 20th Century a Polish Pope would canonize Blessed Queen Jadwiga on the Kraków Commons (Błonie Krakowskie) in front of some 1.5 million Poles on a Sunday morning, on June 8, 1997. It would have made him tremendously happy. He would have received even more satisfaction, however, from the words that were uttered during the Pope's Canonization homily, because they confirmed his views about Jadwiga's heritage. On that fateful day his theme was "Fidelity to Roots" which, as he pointed out, does not mean pious nostalgia and a mechanical copying of the past. Instead, it must always be creative, possessing above all the ability to create an organic synthesis between perennial values and the challenge of today's world. "The young 14th century queen," he said "is the model for the Poland of tomorrow."

The new Polish democracy should be based on moral and ethical cultural values which guided the young monarch. It is this tradition, that will enable you to build a genuinely free society worthy of the half-century of sacrifice you made in the name of freedom.

It was my misfortune not to witness these glorious events even though I was in Poland in the summer of 1997. I missed witnessing them by a few weeks.

"You Have Gone, but through Me You Walk On"
A Testimony of a Director and Writer
KAZIMIERZ BRAUN

Odszedłeś, a idziesz przeze mnie wciąż [You have gone, but through me you walk on] — thus in his poem "Odkupienie szuka twego kształtu, by wejść w niepokój wszystkich ludzi" [Redemption Seeks Your Form to Enter Man's Anxiety][1] did Karol Wojtyła record a thought of Veronica, who rendered the merciful service of wiping Christ's face on His way to crucifixion. This thought precisely and perfectly expresses my own thoughts at the passing away John Paul II: he has gone, but he is still walking through me.

Christ left Veronica with the image of His face on the scarf which she used to alleviate his pain and exhaustion. It was Christ's *znak bliskości* [sign of closeness] as he writes in the same poem. He, himself, Karol Wojtyła — John Paul II (nowadays we might safely say John Paul the Great), in passing through this world left his own "signs of closeness" in the form of the immeasurable richness of both his spiritual and intellectual heritage. He left his prayers, thoughts, and teachings; his homilies, encyclicals and apostolic letters; his poems and plays; and his personal example, actions, and even small gestures, such as kissing the ground wherever he stood on his pilgrim's peregrinations. These riches are saved in books, documents, and albums, on photographs and computer disks. They have penetrated human hearts and minds, have become an integral part of the spiritual and cultural treasury of mankind. They are accessible. In ages to come people will be able to draw from them spiritual energy, intellectual food, incentive for meditation, and direction for prayer.

I also have profited from John Paul II's generous giving and I have my own — minute and modest — share in his legacy. For I had the undeserved privilege and providential grace of being a member of a group called *Holy Linden* [Święta Lipka] whose spiritual pastor and scholarly mentor was Bishop Professor Karol

---

[1] Polish citation from Karol Wojtyła, *Poezje i dramaty* [Poetry and Plays] (Kraków: Znak, 1979). English translation: Karol Wojtyła. *Poezje. Poems.* Translated by Jerzy Pietrkiewicz (Kraków: Wydawnictwo Literackie, 2000).

Wojtyła. The students and faculty of the Catholic University of Lublin [KUL] made up the core of the group. I was studying theater directing in Warsaw at the time but I was invited to join *Holy Linden* by my sister, Maria (Dr. Maria Braun-Gałkowska, then a student of KUL, now professor of the same university), and some of my Warsaw friends, who were already members of the group.

Over the course of the years we had sporadic meetings with Bishop Wojtyła — a man of prayer, wisdom, and charisma. We had seminars, retreats, and vacations with him, including volleyball games with the participation of the future Pope. My wife, Zofia, and I had already read and studied his book *Miłość i odpowiedzialność* [Love and Responsibility, 1960]. In fact, we have based our marriage upon it. I, personally, owed to him guidance and inspiration both as a director and a writer.

Early in my life, theater appeared to me both as art and as service. The theater about which I heard and with which I was confronted had definite artistic and ethical dimensions. During World War II, under Nazi and Soviet occupation (1939-1945), theater in Poland was prohibited, since it was considered an expression of the Polish national spirit. Thus, to do theater against the occupiers' will was an act of bravery and patriotism. During the Stalinist era (1945-1956), theater was treated by the Communist régime as a tool in the political and social engineering of the nation. To do a different kind of theater was an act of resistance. During the long years of Communist captivity (1945-1989), a highly artistic and definitively ethical theater was a refuge from the unacceptable and unbearable reality of everyday life; a weapon in the struggle against that devastating culture and mind-corrupting system; it was a strong thread of Ariadne winding its way through a dark and dangerous world "out of joint" (*Hamlet* I. v, 189). This kind of theater stood at the side of human dignity. It gave hope.

The works of Stanisław Wyspiański, father of Polish modern theater, introduced me to the notion of "theater as the temple of art." Adolphe Appia put forth the idea of the "theater-cathedral." Juliusz Osterwa proclaimed that theater is a "sacrificial art." I came to know their thoughts and works early in my theater life. Under their spell and direction, I started to understand and practice theater the same way. Theater was for me a very special and noble form of art,

18

yet, most of all, an art. This art had to be practiced as a profession, as a craft, using certain methods and techniques.

Karol Wojtyła opened for me the ethical aspect of the theater. One of my early professional assignments led me to Kraków in 1961, where, at that time Karol Wojtyła was a newly appointed bishop. As a member of *Holy Linden* I called upon him. A former actor and playwright, he was always interested in theater life and followed its developments. He wanted to hear about new plays and premières, as well as the situation of the theater milieu. Towards the end of our meeting, he asked me to write a paper for him on the ethical problems which a young director encounters in theater. On the one hand, I was not surprised. It was Wojtyła's way of teaching and guiding people: to let them identify their personal, moral, or professional problems and freely search for just, honest, and proper solutions. As a university professor he habitually asked people to express their problems and views in the form of a paper — then, he would offer evaluation, advice, encouragement. Summer vacations with Father Wojtyła always had three components: prayer, tourism, and an academic program of seminars. On the other hand, I remember that I was struck by that assignment: a director asked to reflect not on art or craft of theater, but on his own morality and attitude within the context of theater. I wrote the paper, which cost me more effort then the usual academic homework. I brought it to the professor-bishop. He called me back for discussion. I remember his questions: How do you want to unite faith with art in your theater work? How will you strive for highest values in terms of both aesthetic and ethics? In the time of trial what would you choose — the world or God?

What my mentor and pastor was steering me toward was unlike anything I had studied at drama school or experienced in professional theater. In time I came to realize how radically different his vision of the theater was from the theater I was a part of. I believe this was one of Wojtyła's peculiar gifts: pointing to new possibilities in every domain of human activity and restoring a proper sense of order to life — beginning with the spiritual life and branching out into politics, economics, scholarship, or art. This gift, among the many other charismas he possessed, he shared with individuals and, later on, with humanity at large.

Soon — focused on everyday theater rehearsals, experiments, tensions, stage catastrophes and victories — I forgot that meeting. Later in my work, I know, I answered Father Wojtyła's question in a way of which he would disapprove. Yet, gradually, more and more recurrently, the fundamental questions about theater's spiritual dimension and ethics returned to me. They have stood as a constant point of reference to which I could return and find my bearings.

On the sixteenth of October, 1978, we — my wife Zofia and I, and our children — heard the news on the radio that Cardinal Wojtyła had been elected Pope. This was stunning news that took our breath away. It pierced our hearts with joy, rousing us to expressions of thanksgiving to God.

We had been avidly studying John Paul's II teachings. We tried to join ourselves to his prayers and imitate his witness. I could not help but return to Wojtyła's teachings when I listened to his — now papal — sermons and read his encyclicals, and when I had the joy of seeing him again. All of his counsels and admonitions became somehow more obliging coming, as they now did, from the Pope. I read again his plays, I studied his biography, including those early chapters when theater meant so much to him. As a young amateur actor Wojtyła enthusiastically participated in the artistic life of free pre-war Poland, and loved proclaiming beautiful poetic words. I could imagine his joy and energy while he recited poetry of Adam Mickiewicz, Juliusz Słowacki, or Cyprian Norwid. Thanks to Mieczysław Kotlarczyk, his teacher and director of school productions in which he performed, Wojtyła became a follower of Juliusz Osterwa, a great actor, director, and reformer of the theater, who was both a devout Catholic and a devoted patriot. His hallmark production was *Książę niezłomny* [The Constant Prince] by Słowacki (based on Pedro Calderón) at his Reduta Theater, which he directed, and in which he played the lead role. It was an open air production, attracting huge crowds, a modern morality play celebrating the values of sacrifice and constancy. During the war, under German occupation, when Poland again lost its independence, when Polish theater productions were prohibited along with the whole of public cultural and artistic life, Kotlarczyk created, under the auspices of Osterwa, an underground theater company, the

Rhapsodic Theater [Teatr Rapsodyczny]. Wojtyła became its leading man. Shows were performed secretly in private apartments. The Rhapsodic Theater's productions were a manifestation of an unbroken spirit, love of freedom, and the will to resist oppression. During one of the shows, when Wojtyła was delivering a poetic monologue, from beyond the windows a German public-address system started to roar from loud-speakers set on the streets, jamming the actor. Wojtyła did not interrupt. Not paying any attention to the noise, he continued his monologue. What an example of constancy!

Thanks to John Paul II, with increasing clarity I saw how inseparable the union of the artistic and ethical dimensions of theater is and I understood that only this union can give a theater production meaning and energy, as well as express the abundant and inexplicable richness of the human person. I tried to express this understanding in the productions I directed.

However, I started to think that I also have to give some kind of written testimony to my personal interactions with the Pope and my — clumsy yet earnest — attempts to follow him. I felt that I had to try to repay at least a small part of my debt to him and give him tribute. I wrote a short story about a young priest who is Karol Wojtyła's student and tries to be his disciple. It was the time of martial law in Poland and it was impossible to publish such a text. Yet many people read the manuscript and they liked it. It occurred to me that this short story can be a part of a long story, indeed a whole novel about that priest, Wojtyła's disciple, and — indirectly — abut Wojtyła himself.

Gradually the fragments of *Dzień świadectwa* [Day of Witness, 1999] began to take shape. The novel was constructed on three levels: on three kinds of witness. The first and most important — which also constituted the point of reference of the entire work — was the witness of Pope John Paul II: the witness of his faith, hope and love; his personal daily witness to Jesus Christ through every word, rosary, encyclical, pilgrimage, suffering, and Holy Mass. The second witness was that of the hero of the novel, Father Andrzej. This young priest strove to model himself on John Paul II, by listening to his teachings and following his example. He tried, often ineptly, to witness to the Pope through his own everyday priestly duties. In particular, he gave honor and witness to the Pope on the sixteenth of every month, and especially on the sixteenth of October of every year, thus commemorating the anniversary of Karol Wojtyła's election to the Throne of Peter in 1978. Father Andrzej's narrative was what knotted the novel together. The third witness contained in the novel was that of the author himself.

The novel, as a whole, belongs to the genre of "historical fiction." The story of Father Andrzej was fiction indeed — but it was solidly rooted in history. Thomas Merton aptly characterized this kind of fiction when he observed that the "integrity of an artist lifts a man above the level of the world without delivering him from it."[2] Thus, the fortunes of my fictitious hero, Father Andrzej, were based on real events. The biography of Karol Wojtyła, his deeds and teachings, were true. The background to the narrative was true as well: the history of Poland during twenty four years of John Paul II's pontificate (1978-2002) — the novel ends in the preparations for the twenty-fifth anniversary. In this way the action embraces the period of the decay of the Communist totalitarian order in Poland; *Solidarity's* sixteen-month bid for freedom, the dark years of martial law, the final demise of Communism in 1989, and the restoration of the nation's sovereignty, with all its attendant hardships, frequent bitterness and great hope as well.

Day of Witness also belongs to the category of "religious fiction," that is, novels in which narration, story, action, characters and events belong — in many different ways, directly and indirectly — to the world of religion. The phenomenon and mystery of faith, human belief in the dependence of God, and "life under God," are the fabric of such a literary work. Gilbert K. Chesterton and Graham Greene both wrote "religious novels." With utter humility, yet consciously, *Day of Witness* associates itself with this kind or prose. My main hero is a priest. He prays, meditates, and tries to model his life on Jesus Christ. His vocation and priestly service lead him to different places and milieux in Poland, America, the Holy Land, Germany, and Rome. Everywhere he tries to measure up in his conduct and teaching to the Pope. Generally speaking, *Day of*

---

[2] Thomas Merton, *The Seven Storey Mountain* (New York: Harcourt, Brace & Co., 1948), p.3.

Witness portrays how John Paul II and his pontificate were reflected, understood, and absorbed by many people who loved him, and, conversely, rejected by those who hated him.

My own recollections of my contacts with "Uncle Wojtyła," as we called him, also constituted part of the real-life backdrop to the novel. My hero reflects:

"When Karol Wojtyła was professor, bishop, archbishop, cardinal, we'd call him simply, *Uncle* or *Unc*." And the narration goes on: "Father Andrzej always had doubts as to whether or not this showed a lack of respect. Should they address him in this way? But Wojtyła had accepted it, and even encouraged the usage. It was also a form of camouflage. They would often speak about him, make reference to his words, thoughts, sermons, teachings and books — and *Uncle* served as a handy cryptonym, enabling them to refer to him freely, to speak about him without drawing attention to themselves in the hall, train, hostel, or bus stop. '*Uncle* says... *Uncle* sends you his greetings... *Uncle* thinks... Is *Uncle* coming?' Strangers had no idea who we were talking about, although the professional informers knew. Well, maybe not always. . . There were instances of betrayal and denunciation. But *Uncle* came in handy. So it was always *Uncle* — instead of Reverend Professor, your Excellency, then, your Eminence. Instead of Bishop or Cardinal it was simply, '*Uncle*' or even '*Unc*.' Anyway, how could they call him otherwise, in view of the fact that their ethics seminars were held in the corner of a hostel cafeteria? That methodology paper which Andrzej presented took place on a meadow, while His Eminence, the professor, made his comments, seated on a life-jacket pulled out of a kayak. Then there was that philosophical discussion they'd conducted on the edge of a volley-ball court, on

23

the heels of three hard-fought sets. The cardinal's shirt and sweat suit were as sweaty and dusty as everyone else's. And what about those retreat meditations and question periods held in the calm of night, broken only by the sound of the dry branches crackling in the campfire? It was the same thing in the classrooms, on the pulpit, at the altar. He was never distant. He never set himself apart, put up barriers, flaunted or paraded himself. He was always present.

This was most striking when he prayed. Before a meal. In a snow-swept forest. On skis. Andrzej recalled the *Angelus* they'd said that time, on the road to Turbacz mountain. It was the same thing, the very same thing at the Lord's table raised above the crowds at the Skałka church. Andrzej couldn't express it any better than to think that Wojtyła really prayed. When he prayed one felt God was there. Presence. Communion. The Spirit.

And he was able to preserve this later. When he was dressed in white. In the glare of camera flashes. Amid the bustle of photo-reporters, the dancing of film and TV cameras, the swarms of secret police and body guards. Always — then as now — there was present in him a concentration of mind and a sense of freedom. A sense of rootedness and of flight.

There was something direct and personal about his relations with me — thought Father Andrzej. That's right — personal. With me. Not just with me, of course. With everyone.

I've always known and felt that there's a bond between us. I with him. He with me. When we're together I feel he's talking to me, now, right this minute, and only to me. He hears me. He devotes time to me. Despite that killing schedule of his, he never rushes things. He focuses his whole attention on me. He has ears only for me. I'm chosen. Raised up. Unique. The most important one. And yet, in some strange way, others are included. There are others as well. Just as important and select. Everyone — individually. He's able to talk to me, and only to me, while addressing a crowd three million strong.

He's always been like this. *Uncle. Unc.* Not very respectful really. But this has never taken away from his stature. Not one bit. And in addressing me, all of us, by name, he has never betrayed a trace of either scorn or undue favor. He was simply there.

He was always himself, whether it be with Mother Theresa, President Reagan, the Rabbi of Rome, the Dalai Lama, a national conference of Bishops on an *ad limina* visit, or the *Juventus* soccer team from Turin. With each of us. With me.

So, for me he's never been an abstract authority, an unapproachable cardinal, and then some distant figure in a white cassock. He's always been close. Like a member of the family. Uncle.

Uncle! Uncle! That's what we shouted during the audience, in Paul VI Hall, on the first anniversary of his pontificate. *Uncle! Uncle!* The whole bunch of us, in raptures, tears. *Uncle!*

He heard us. He looked up and recognized us. Then coming up to us, he said: Isia! Jurek! Wanda! Bogdan! Andrzej!

Our names on the lips of the Pope."[3]

I recall my work on *Day of Witness* in May 2005, at this special time, when we already pray to John Paul, as he is on the

---

[3] English translations from *Dzień świadectwa*: Kazimierz Braun. *Day of Witness.* Translated by Christopher A. Zakrzewski (Toronto: Omnibus Printers, 2002).

road to canonization, without ceasing to mourn him. The sense of loss is overwhelming. We feel orphaned. So, it seems fitting to return to the conclusion of my novel. Father Andrzej, whose life was gravely endangered at this moment of the action thought about John Paul II:

> Suddenly, he recalled the words of the Pope. That great and simple catch-phrase of his which he announced at the start of his pontificate:
> *Be not afraid!*
> It was a summons to the old and young, spouses and children, the lost and the doubters, the despairing, the fearful and the dying — indeed, to the whole of humanity. A prophetic call drawn from depths of Isaiah: "Be not afraid, for I am with you." Christ's fortification directed to the Apostles: "Be not afraid little flock." A bold exclamation proclaimed in our time by John Paul:
> *Be not afraid*!
> Do not be afraid for you are redeemed. Do not be afraid since the Blessed Mother is with you, and she did not fear. Do not be afraid since the apostles, martyrs and saints did not fear. Do not be afraid since the light shines in the darkness and no darkness can quench it. Be not afraid since the power of Christ's cross and resurrection is greater than any evil!
> *Be not afraid!*
> The Spirit of God gave these words to the man called to be Pope from "a distant land." They were to serve him as a sword and buckler, as a torch and seed for sowing. He proclaims these words to the multitudes and he himself professes them in his deeds. He has been proclaiming them for years and he is going to proclaim them for ever. And even when he is no longer able to voice them, these words will continue to sound in our hearts.
> *Be not afraid!*"

Such are the last words of my novel. This exclamation — Be not afraid! — had both a religious and moral dimension: Do not be afraid of affirming Christ, living out his teachings, and using them in your life and work. It had a political and social dimension: Do not be afraid of demanding freedom from tyranny; do not be afraid to stand up for human rights and human dignity, and do not be afraid to always defend human life. Do not be afraid of your neighbor of different religion, race, or culture. It also was en encouragement directed to artists and scholars: Do not be afraid to search for beauty. Do not be afraid to search for truth. Do not be afraid to search for excellence. Do not be afraid to stand alone. And to all: Do not be afraid to love.

John Paul the Great has enabled people to put fear behind them. Like the evangelical bruised reed he has raised and made whole our hope. He has fanned the sparks of faith and courage into a flame. Above all, he has embraced all in unconditional love. My own work is a humble witness to the fact that this has really taken place. And continues to do so.

John Paul II's Message of Hope and Meaning in the Context of Postmodern Challenges

ARCHBISHOP JÓZEF M. ŻYCIŃSKI

In one of his poems, Józef Czechowicz, the great Polish poet who died during a Nazi bombardment at the very outset of the Second World War, begs of God:

Od żywota pustego bez muzyki bez pieśni
Chroń nas.

[From an empty life without music and song
Deliver us.]

The whole pontificate of John Paul II was one great effort at counteracting nihilism, which constitutes an important element in postmodern culture. The messages of hope displayed throughout this pontificate bear the evangelical reaction of our communion to the challenges offered by an "empty" world which, after proclaiming the death of God, has been deprived not only of music and song, but also of sense, hope, and beauty.

THE CULTURAL CHALLENGES OF POSTMODERNISM

The pontificate of John Paul II spanned a period of deep and swift cultural change, much of which brought with it the modification of many values and created a field of new challenges requiring pastoral care. Among the essential cultural transformations of this period must be mentioned the information revolution associated with the broad implementation of the Internet, the fall of the totalitarian system in Eastern Europe accompanied by activities pursuant of European integration and globalization processes, the implementation of technologies leading to new threats to human dignity (cloning), and the domination of nihilistic influences in culture, expressed in disappointment with the heritage of the Enlightenment. In many milieux all of these changes gave birth to feelings of confusion and uncertainty, in the face of which the papal appeal "Be not afraid!" constituted an important alternative.

The quick tempo of the above-mentioned transformations may be witnessed to by prognoses concerning the future of Communism, formulated as late as the 1980s. For example, Sir Isaiah Berlin, the prominent social philosopher from Oxford, expressed his conviction that the fall of Communism would be the most beautiful event of his life—however, such was not to be expected for another one hundred years.[1] Similar prognoses testify to just how far the transformations of the last few decades surpassed the expectations and imagination of competent experts. The cultural and spiritual consequences of these changes exceeded just as dramatically the schemata and prognoses that had up until then functioned quite well. The person educated in the mentality of the deep cultural changes of postmodernity does not simply reject religion, science or philosophy. Much more often, he reacts to them with indifference, which in the long run ends in despair.

Whereas earlier generations referred to Nietzsche's declaration that "God is dead" in our culture, today one speaks ever more often about the death of man and also about the ideas of enlightened Humanism constituting a grand illusion which was consumed in the crematories of Auschwitz or buried in the mass graves of Kołyma. The *Homo postmodernus* appears in such a perspective as a tragic figure sentenced to avoid all great questions and doomed to a surface-oriented pilgrimage through a world empty of vitality. People who were once united in a reflective community, are now to be brought together by the carefree "happening." *Spiel macht frei.* In place of the *animal rationale* there appears the carefree *homo ludens*. Entangled in challenges unknown to previous generations, he appears as a tragic figure similar to the protagonist of Camus' *Myth of Sisyphus*.

The contemporary cultural exhaustion is often compared to the dominant moods of late antiquity, in which Stoicism offered an alternative to Christianity.[2] Today's alternatives are to be offered

---

[1] Beata Sygulska, "Nil desperandum" in *Oblicza liberalizmu* [The Face of Liberalism] (Kraków: Księgarnia Akademicka, 2003), p. 17.
[2] See Chantal Delsol, *Esej o człowieku późnej nowoczesności* [Essay on Late Modern Man] (Kraków: Znak, 2003), p. 12.

by the varied versions of nihilism. As a Christian answer to such propositions there appears the Pope's message of hope and blessings, which points to the dignity of the human person redeemed by Christ as the central value in a culture of deep transformations. Suffering remains an unavoidable element of every person's world. The way in which we accept it testifies to the depth of our faith, as well as to the maturity of the person accepting his life's cross as a sign of love. I love, therefore I suffer. Loving is painful.

JOHN PAUL II'S GOSPEL OF SUFFERING

The beginning years of the Pontificate were dominated by the joyful atmosphere of the Wedding in Cana—expressed in part by journalistic fascination with the new Pope's athletic, poetic, and philosophical interests. Then the path of the Pope's service led through the modern Areopagus, where his evangelical message of humanism, hope, and dialogue was sounded with great clarity. Information concerning his encyclicals began to appear on the first pages of newspapers, where the public was not accustomed to finding either papal pronouncements or the somewhat mysterious Latinate word.

Several years ago, following some lectures at Notre Dame, I asked some of my non-Catholic friends what it was that encouraged them to read these—difficult, after all—papal texts. One of them answered, "I reached for them out of a common feeling of obligation to familiarize myself with new publications. I assumed that they would be stiff and boring. And lo and behold, I became fascinated reading the first encyclical. It hit home— connecting with my personal feelings, causing the most sensitive strings of my soul to tremble." These same strings were touched in a somewhat different way by John Paul II during the last weeks of his life, speaking the language of suffering, which even in complete silence proves itself more eloquent than the earlier papal documents.

Years ago, I asked Professor Alvin Planting, a respected philosopher and Calvinist, which of the papal texts he values most highly. Without a moment of hesitation he replied, "the letter on suffering—*Salvifici doloris*." He explained that in reading the letter one sees quite clearly that John Paul II does not take up the problem of suffering from the perspective of a theorist, who wishes to transmit abstract, general truths. Rather, the formulations of this document clearly show forth the personal experiences and life wisdom of a man who, on the day of his ordination, stood beneath the Cross of Christ.

Preparing us for his departure, John Paul II directed to us his longest apostolic letter written in the language of love expressed in the mystery of the Cross. In this letter, every gesture and every word grows to the dimensions of an exceptional testimony of his faith and union with God. Perhaps it is this very message, touching upon the unavoidable presence of suffering in man's life, that is most necessary to us now, as our civilization seeks to avoid, programmatically, all difficult questions concerning suffering and fidelity, directing instead its chief attention toward success, accomplishment, and pleasure.

I once asked Krzysztof Zanussi if he would be able to identify a contemporary film in which the question of suffering would be taken up in a sensible and critical matter. The famous director thought long and hard before finally offering the title of an Iranian film, completely unknown in the countries of the West. The culture of the West avoids such themes; thus it is that the Pope's witness in suffering carries so much more weight. In our solitary union with the suffering Holy Father it is very important to look upon his suffering with the eyes of faith, not the glance of aesthetes. From the point of view of aesthetics, the entire drama of Golgotha would seem repulsive. For some contemporary observers, the ideal hero would be rather a Jesus signing autographs along the Way of the Cross. The Pope's suffering was a challenge. At the same time it created a deep unity of faith with such as each day must struggle beneath the weight of their cross. It demonstrated the solidarity of the Cross, which unites us all in the experience of pain directed toward the glory of Easter morning.

In the wealth of the varied traditions that came together in the person of John Paul II, we find the prayerful depths of the mystics, the language of poets, philosophical truth and an artistic sensitivity to beauty. In the strophes of his poetry, as in the unprecedentedly poetic language of many of his documents, we find allusions to that grand tradition recognized by a civilization valuing what remains of rationalism and pragmatism. Simultaneously, however, we also meet in the papal documents with an openness to the new discoveries of natural science and the cultural transformations that the exploitation of the new technologies brings in its train. Instead of fear before the new challenges, we find a dialogue full of concern inspired by a striving toward the defense of humanistic values.

In the Pope's teaching we come across a broad current touching upon the ethical aspects of the implementation of new technologies, as well as the broadly conceived ethos of those milieux obligated to the service of reflection. This solidarity of the Church with Academe is of especial importance in an age where success in the field of business is often valued more highly than the new discoveries of science, and where an esoteric and pseudo-intellectual escape from thinking is not infrequently displayed as the result of liberation from the canons of Enlightenment rationalism. John Paul II introduces subtle distinctions, accepting what is positive in the rationalist heritage of the Enlightenment while at the same time pointing out the illusions of an uncritical rhetoric glorifying progress as the unavoidable consequence of scientific development.

The unprecedented opening of his pontificate toward the world of science is no surprise at all. Both as professor of the Catholic University of Lublin and as Archbishop of Kraków, Cardinal Wojtyła developed and inspired this type of dialogue, the substantial consequences of which remain essential to his later thought. As the symbol of this one might take the rehabilitation of Galileo, whose condemnation in 1633 was earlier represented as a symbol of the inevitable conflict of the Church with the world of science. On the very threshold of his pontificate, on November 10,

1979, John Paul II took up this theme during a session of the Papal Academy of Science, on the occasion of the one hundredth anniversary of the birth of Albert Einstein. At that time, he expressed the wish that theologians, scientists, and historians, invigorated by the spirit of sincere cooperation in research, should deepen our knowledge of the matter of Galileo, loyally confessing to the mistakes and overcoming the distrust that this *casus* gave birth to in the minds of many. In answer to his appeal a team of researchers was called into being, who published valuable essays speaking to new aspects of Galileo's drama. These works uncover to us the particular circumstances of the painful condemnation and offer valuable materials for future studies, allowing us at least in part to overcome the distrust that for many years dominated the contacts between religion and science.

Another area of conflict between the representatives of Christian thought and those who support natural theories is constituted by the theory of evolution. Both Darwin's theory of natural selection, as well as the development of the universe displayed in contemporary cosmology as occurring over a period of billions of years, came in for criticism from those communities who strive to explain the Biblical account of the creation of the world, and man, in a literal manner. The document of the Papal Biblical Commission entitled "The Interpretation of Sacred Scripture in the Church," published in 1993, unequivocally stresses that the Biblical accounts cannot be understood in a literal sense, since the Bible's purpose is not to answer questions of physics or biology. As a result, explanations proposed by Biblical fundamentalists in so-called "creation science" cannot be reconciled with the Christian vision of the world, as such attempts to literally explain the texts of the Bible create artificial conflicts between science and religious faith.

The position of the Church in regards to the theory of evolution found its fullest expression in the October 1996 message of John Paul II to the Papal Academy of Science. Referring to Pius XII's statement touching upon these same problems, John Paul II stresses that the newest scientific discoveries support the evolutionary picture of the universe, which can no longer be treated as a mere hypothesis. In Pius XII's 1950 encyclical there is found

34

the statement that the doctrine of evolutionism must be treated as a serious hypothesis, which needs to be considered with the same keenness that one brings to non-evolutionary explanations. In John Paul II's message, the symmetry between the evolutionary explanation and alternative ideas that question the reality of evolution disappears definitively. The papal affirmation of the evolutionary script of the development of nature constitutes an event which cannot be overestimated in the dialogue of Christianity and science.

John Paul II's letter to Fr. George Coyne, published for the three hundredth anniversary of the publication of Newton's *Principia*, is an important document, which emphasizes the complementarity of theological reflection and scientific undertakings toward the discovering of the truth of the world. In 1987, when the world of science was celebrating the first edition of this work, which is symbolically recognized as the first step in modern physics, John Paul II directed his letter to the American Jesuit, the director of the Vatican Astronomical Observatory in Castel Gandolfo. In the message, which historians of ideas quickly acknowledged to be one of the most momentous documents of the pontificate, the Pope underscores his great desire that:

> the dialogue should continue and grow in depth and scope. In the process we must overcome every regressive tendency to a unilateral reductionism, to fear, and to self-imposed isolation. What is critically important is that each discipline should continue to enrich, nourish and challenge the other to be more fully what it can be and to contribute to our vision of who we are and who we are becoming.[3]

John Paul II's message reveals the concrete possibility of overcoming earlier conflicts. It also carries with it the chance of a

---

[3] "Message of His Holiness Pope John Paul II to the Reverend George V. Coyne, S.J., Director of the Vatican Observatory," in: Robert J. Russell, William R. Stoeger, S. J., and George V. Coyne, S.J.,eds., *Physics, Philosophy, and Theology : A Common Quest for Understanding* (Vatican City State: Vatican Observatory, 1988), p. M7.

united integration of our scientific reason and our philosophical and theological convictions.

In answer to the Pope's encouragement to scholarly cooperation, the Vatican Observatory, in union with other prestigious academic institutions, took up interdisciplinary research in connection with the question: how can the presence of God in the process of the world's creation, and the rise of man, the development of the human psyche, be understood?[4] The cooperation of theologians and natural scientists in the search for answers to such questions creates a qualitatively new climate, in which the place of simplified conceptions, so popular in the past, is taken over by cooperative harmony in the discovery of common truth.

THE CULTURE OF EVANGELICAL HOPE

A counterproposition to the vision of culture dominated by pessimism and disillusionment is designated by the Pope's words to UNESCO on June 2, 1980: "Man, who in the visible world is the only ontological subject of culture, is also the only proper object and goal of culture as well. Culture is that through which the human person, as a human person, becomes even more human."[5] John Paul II revealed his vision of dialogue carried out on the field of culture and in service to the full development of mankind in his *motu proprio* of 1982 entitled *Inde a Pontificatus* with which he called into being the Pontifical Council for Culture. He wrote at the time that from the beginning of his pontificate he has been especially interested in the development of a dialogue between the Church and the contemporary world. In his search for new forms, he attempted above all to facilitate encounters with unbelievers on the privileged terrain of culture, that basic dimension of the spirit

---

[4] A bibliographical record of these studies may be found in, for example, Robert J. Russell, William R. Stoeger, S. J., and F.J. Ayala, eds., *Evolutionary and Molecular Biology. Scientific Perspectives on Divine Action* (Vatican City State: Vatican Observatory, 1998).
[5] Jan Paweł II, „Przemówienie w siedzibie UNESCO, Paryż, 2 VI 1980," w: *Przemówienia i homilie Jana Pawła II* [Speeches and Homilies of John Paul II] (Kraków: Znak, 1997), s. 271.

that defines the common bonds between people and unites them in their common humanity. The consequence of embracing this very perspective is the vital presence of the Church in dialogue with the creators of culture. It allows for a common understanding between people of the Church and those milieus which have traditionally demonstrated a reticent distance in regards to religious faith.

The Holy Father frequently reminded the creators of a culture threatened by nonsense, ugliness and emptiness of the words of the Second Vatican Council, which stated that the world in which we live needs beauty in order for it not to sink into despair. In his letter to the artists, composed for Easter Sunday 1999, he restated that the vocation of the artist is the development of a sensitivity to beauty in society, which is in as much need of artists as it is of scholars and technicians, witnesses to the faith, teachers and mothers. The unique spirituality of artistic service determines the wealth of our culture, in which as witnesses to beauty have survived artistic masterpieces of great talents from Händel to Bach, from Mozart to Schubert, from Beethoven to Berlioz.

The paths of art and faith cannot be allowed to diverge, as in the face of the experienced miracles of the world delight constitutes the single proper attitude. Alluding to Norwid, John Paul II reminds us that it is delight that can actually become the wellsprings of enthusiasm for labor. This enthusiasm brings with it a new hope since, thanks to it, we can "resurrect," despite all earlier failures. In this sense one might say that "beauty will save the world." In a very special way this message moved the hearts of young people searching for ideals which should allow us to preserve our faith in sense. The World Youth Days provided ever more performances of the Pope's symphony of hearts, which constituted a common answer to the propositions of the "empty" world, devoid of sense and beauty. In the global village, in which we are so plagued by exhaustion, the lack of spirituality, and anonymity, we were made to feel the invigorating breath of a new hope thanks to the execution of this symphony of the young by the Pope.

In the difficult beauty displayed by the Polish Pope, one might see the special role of the logic of wounds. It was the possibility of touching the Wounds of Christ that allowed the skeptical Thomas the Apostle to whisper "My Lord and my God."

The Pope's prayer of the wounds of life constitutes the crowning of his teachings, which he conveyed to us with his life's blood. His slogan *Totus tuus* took on a visible sense when his unbreakable spirit was made to struggle with the physical rebellions of a weary body, which through the later years of his life accepted without protest an exhaustive dose of labor in the harvest fields of the Lord. Beholding the struggles between a powerful soul and the inexorable laws of biology, we may learn an evangelical radicalism in which only the perspective of the Cross reveals to us the deepest sense of the words *Totus tuus*; words that teach us what exactly an entire surrender to God means.

The empty place that remains after His departure from us will unavoidably bear painful associations, calling to mind those sunny moments, when we could enjoy His nearness. In order to overcome this pain, we must look at human life from the perspective of the Pope's anthropology, in which man cannot be fully understood without reference to Christ. In order to realize the spiritual testament which has been left to our generation, we must ask ourselves every day what we can still do in order to ever more fully adapt His slogan *Totus tuus* to our life, our personal execution of the Pope's symphony of life.

Twenty years ago, Adam Zagajewski posed the question— would Poles in a free Poland continue to be interested in poetry and continue to go to church?[6] The unequivocal answer to that question may be found by looking at the Poles today, who can be found both in church and in bookstores in great numbers. Among the reasons they frequent the latter is in search of the latest books by the Pope, from his poetical musings *Tryptyk rzymski* [Roman Triptych] to *Pamięć i tożsamość* [Memory and Identity]. What causes the poetic message of John Paul II to evoke such a strong resonance in the souls of His countrymen? How might one explain the fact that sections of the public so different and distant from each other are united in this same search for hope and sense in the words of the Polish Pope? Someone writing in the Warsaw newspaper *Rzeczpospolita* [The Republic] strove to rationalize this Polish

---

[6] Adam Zagajewski, *Solidarność i samotność* [Solidarity and Solitude] (Warszawa, 2002).

behavior with the words, "One has to love something, after all, and it's a good thing that the Poles can find this something to love in the Pope's writings."

I am inclined to add that this papal "something" receives a very concrete character in the evangelical message of hope. It remains spiritually close to the tradition represented by Fr. Józef Tischner and Zbigniew Herbert. The world of values accepted and consistently revealed by them allows us to uncover the reality of beauty and sense even in a landscape touched by absurdity and emptiness. Tischner's value-centered thought and the spiritual aristocracy of Pan Cogito find their natural complement in the Pope's discovery of beauty, peace and harmony, which designate an axiological horizon constituted by the elementary spiritual needs of our civilization.

Throughout his entire pontificate, in his witness to Christian Humanism, John Paul II displayed the gravity of a Christian sensitivity to, and responsibility for revealing, the beauty and harmony of the world. The addressees of his messages, open to the truth of God, ought to unite with the figures of the "guards of the morn" looking in the darkness of night for the first optimistic signs of the dawn. Should the witness of an attendance at the springs of God's beauty be lacking, should Christianity be reduced to the mere level of moralism and complaints about a rotten world, our existence would lose the essence of its sense and emptiness and nullity would appear to be the natural environment of man. The poetical sensitivity of the Polish Pope allows us to positively value aesthetical categories in religion, as well as to direct our attention to that beauty, upon which we are to lay our hopes for the salvation of the world.[7]

THE PONTIFICAL SHAPE OF POLISH HOPE

The generation of thirty-odd-year-old Poles might be called the Generation of John Paul II, as practically speaking they have

---

[7] See Bruno Forte, "Bellezza splendore del vero: la rivelazione della bellezza che salva" [Beauty the splendor of truth: the revelation of beauty that saves] in N. Valentini, ed., *Cristanesimo e bellezza* [Christianity and Beauty] (Milano: Paoline, 2002), pp. 72-95.

had no experience of a Church governed by other principles than those revealed during the last pontificate. It was in His teachings that we found the strength to endure, when the prognoses of politicians were singlemindedly gloomy. Much self-abnegation was necessary to break facile pessimism. Jan Nowak-Jeziorański recalls with what skepticism many Western experts in the 1950s considered the possibility of the survival of the Polish national tradition in an ideological system imposed by the USSR. At that time he heard from them, "Considering the matter from the example of the Ukraine, in twenty-five years Poland will be nothing more than a name and a place on the map. The young generations, educated by propaganda and the Communist educational system, will speak Polish and think in Russian."[8] On the day of the Pope's death one might unequivocally state that these prognoses have been proven wrong, in the case of the Ukraine as well as that of Poland.

Pessimism might have a *chic* sound to it, but it departs far from the truth when it is met with the strength of spirit and the message of hope contained in the Gospels. During his first pilgrimage to Poland, John Paul II was able to combine references to the grand national tradition of Poland with a sense of responsibility for Poland's presence in European culture. Invoking the Holy Spirit and believing in His action, not far from the grave of the Unknown Soldier, the Pope recalled the spiritual heritage of those who, by their sacrifice and courage, composed the most beautiful pages in the book of Polish history. At the time he recalled those soldiers who shed their blood dreaming of a free Poland, the workers from the factories and mines, the scholars and the farmers, the artists and people of profound prayer. He spoke with the deepest respect about their sacrificial dedication to the Fatherland, a dedication that also designated a model of action for the believers hanging on his every word. One year after those memorable words we experienced the great solidarity of hearts, which began the process of radical change on the European continent. Summing up the spiritual influence of the Pope on his countrymen during the 1979 pilgrimage, Timothy Garten Ash noted that the spiritual

---

[8] *Będzie mówiło po polsku, a myślało po sowiecku.* Vide Wojciech Karpiński, *Herb wygnania* [Exile's Coat of Arms] (Warszawa: Iskry,1998), p. 252 n.

consequence of this first pilgrimage to the Homeland turned out to be "a nation of an awakened pride and a society with a new feeling of elementary dignity."

In his last book, *Pamięć i tożsamość*, where he strives to uncover to his countrymen the most beautiful models from Polish history, he recalls the "Jagiellonian" model of Polishness, stressing that "Polishness is. . . variety and pluralism, and not narrowness and enclosure."[9] Teaching consistently the posture of openness toward the new problems experienced in the new European fatherland, he writes with the love of a father concerned with the new family of Europe entrusted to his care:

> O Church in Europe! Let the joys and hopes, the sadnesses and anxieties of today's Europeans, above all of the poor and suffering, be your joys and hopes, your sadnessess and anxieties as well, and may nothing which is authentically human remain without an echo in your heart / . . . / And be a Church of blessings, constantly assimilating yourself to Christ.[10]

We must return to these words when discouragement and anxiety are heard in Polish discussions, and when "that which is authentically human" is shouted down by political slogans. It is then that we must invariably pass the threshold of discouragement, displaying that "memory and identity" with which He consistently formed the hope and sense of His message.

---

[9] *Polskość to . . . wielość i pluralizm, a nie ciasnota i zamknięcie.* Jan Paweł II, *Pamięć i tożsamość* (Kraków: Znak, 2005), p. 92.

[10] *Ecclesia in Europa*, p. 104n.

"PIASA Executive Director Prof. Thaddeus V. Gromada presents Pope John Paul II with Oskar Halecki's book on Jadwiga of Anjou."

John Paul II and the World's Poor
"Extreme Poverty is a Violation of Human Rights"

RICHARD J. HUNTER, JR.
HÉCTOR R. LOZADA

It is a noticeably disturbing fact of the 21st century that twenty percent of the world's population holds 83 percent of the world's wealth while the poorest 20 percent receive only 1.4 percent of total income. This not a new phenomenon, however, as such a disparity between rich and poor has persisted since the Industrial Revolution. The Catholic Church's concern for this unfortunate reality is likewise not a new phenomenon. In 1891, Pope Leo XIII issued what has been termed a "revolutionary encyclical," *Rerum Novarum,* in which the Holy Father had noted: "That the spirit of revolutionary change which has long been disturbing nations of the world, should have passed beyond the sphere of politics and made its influence felt in the related sphere of practical economics is not surprising... in the enormous fortunes of some few individuals and the utter poverty of the masses" (Pope Leo XIII 1891). Pope Paul VI, in many ways an important mentor to John Paul II, provided a proper context both to these troubling statistics and to the impending commitment of his successor to the plight of the world's poorest citizens by noting in *Populorum Progressio* (1967) that "No one may appropriate surplus goods solely for their private use when others lack the bare necessities of life."

So, it was no surprise that John Paul II willingly and enthusiastically took up the inspirational mantle of his predecessor as champion of universal economic justice upon assuming the papacy in October of 1978. Writing especially for *The New York Post* on December 2, 1985, the Holy Father commented: "Freedom in justice will bring a new dawn of hope for the present generation as it has done before: for the homeless, for the unemployed, for the aging, for the sick and the handicapped, for the migrants and undocumented workers, for all who hunger for human dignity in this land and the world."

Commenting on John Paul II's immutable and visible commitment to the ideals of social justice, *The Center for American Progress* noted: "His devotion to the Christian message of 'Be Not

Afraid' led him to a lifelong commitment to fierce battles for the rights of the downtrodden, impoverished and oppressed around the globe, including the rights of workers, political freedom and religious tolerance." The Holy Father would repeatedly and without reservation urge the international community to "denounce the existence of economic, financial and social mechanisms that accentuate the situation of uncertainty for many and poverty for the rest" (Trócaire 2005).

The extraordinary work of John Paul II can be seen in the light of three important initiatives that consumed much of the social agenda of his papacy. All are based on a unique insight into the very core of Catholic social teaching which grew out of his unique experiences growing to adulthood and to his vocation as priest, pastor, and teacher in both Nazi-occupied Poland and postwar Communist-dominated society. Based on the Holy Father's reflections on the creation of man, so beautifully portrayed in Genesis, John Paul reminded the world that all human life has value and that all human life is sacred. In traveling throughout the world in 104 foreign pilgrimages, visiting 129 countries, John Paul II personally encountered extreme, raw, and brutish poverty in lands where people barely lived above the mere subsistence level. The Holy Father never ceased to remind the First World of its responsibility of providing for the needs of its brothers and sisters of the Third World. The Pope's apostolic mission to uphold life in all of its stages and to speak in the defense of the poor and those who were tragically marginalized in modern society and to reaffirm his commitment to human rights, democracy, and fair trade can be seen within the prism of efforts to eradicate world hunger and eliminate world poverty, to reduce significantly the staggering burden of world debt, and in the creation and implementation of recognizable and realizable millennial development goals.

This essay is dedicated to an exploration of these three important aspects of Pope John Paul II as social reformer and social conscience to the world in the third millennium. His unified message and clarion call to arms can be summarized succinctly: "Extreme poverty is perhaps the most pervasive and paralyzing form of violation of human rights in our world" (Pope John Paul II 2000).

John Paul II opened an important front in his assault on world poverty by dealing squarely and forthrightly with the issue of world hunger. Ever the optimist about an uncertain future in a new world of globalization, the Holy Father summoned the words of his predecessor that "God intended the earth and everything in it for the use of all human beings and peoples. Thus, under the leadership of justice and in the company of charity, created goods should flow fairly to all" (Pope Paul VI 1967: 22). Paul VI had added: "Goodwill and generous policies must encourage human ingenuity, so that the vital needs of all can be met, also by virtue of the universal purpose of the earth's resources" and praised the work of the many sons and daughters of the Catholic Church who were working to help the poorer nations of the world improve their productive capacity and discover "in full fidelity to their own proper genius, the means for their social and human progress" (Pope Paul VI 1967: 64).

John Paul II was no latecomer to this critical issue. In his stirring address to the United Nations Economic Commission for Latin America and the Caribbean (*Origins* 1987), the Pope had noted: "The moral causes of prosperity... reside in a constellation of virtues: industriousness, competence, order, honesty, initiative, frugality, thrift, spirit of service, keeping one's word, daring—in short, love for work well done. No system or social structure can resolve, as if by magic, the problems outside these virtues." Yet, later in that same year, proving that he was no myopic cheerleader for unbridled capitalism, John Paul wrote in *Sollicitudo rei socialis* (1987b: 16): "It should be noted that in spite of the praiseworthy efforts made in the last two decades by the more developed or developing nations and the international organizations to find a way out of the situation, or at least to remedy some of its symptoms, the conditions have become notably worse."

John Paul II chose the occasion of the World Food Summit in Rome, Italy, in November of 1996 in order to focus attention on the issue of the world's food supply. The Holy Father noted that 800 million people still suffered from chronic malnutrition and that it was the direct moral responsibility of the delegations of the 194 countries in attendance to study the "technical problems" associated with "food insecurity" and to propose reasonable solutions to them (Pope John Paul II 1996).

The spirit of solidarity which the Holy Father first evoked in connection with the birth of Eastern Europe's first democratic movement in his native Poland in 1980 was significantly broadened. John Paul II called forth a "change of attitude and habits with regard to life-styles and the relationship between resources and goods, as well as for an increased awareness of one's neighbor and his legitimate needs." The Holy Father also confronted head-on rather controversial issues relating to endemic overpopulation as the source of world hunger. Steadfast in his views, the Pope stated that "demographic considerations alone cannot explain the poor distribution of food resources. . . A numerous population can become a source of development, for it involves the exchange of and a demand for goods..." John Paul specifically condemned the notion that an "arbitrary stabilization of world population or even its reduction could directly solve the problem of hunger; [such] would ... be an illusion." The Pope boldly made a comparison between normally minimal investments in the agricultural and food sector with those sums allocated for national defense or the "superfluous spending" which is customary in the most developed countries and urged that nations take immediate suitable measures to encourage local agricultural production and the protection of farmland outlined in the *World Food Summit Plan of Action* (No. 14). Included in this *Plan* were concrete suggestions for international aid to the poorest countries and for a "fair determination of trade terms and access to credit." Never again would the relationship of food supply and poverty be viewed in purely sterile economic terms.

POVERTY AND DEBT

Catholic social teaching also offers a unique and compelling insight into the complexities of the international debt crisis and its impact on the whole human community—both debtor and creditor nations—drawing on the *moral dimensions* of economic activities. The foundation of Catholic social teaching is deeply rooted in Scripture and is based on a seminal viewpoint that each individual is sacred. It is against this paradigm of individual dignity that economic activity, and, more broadly, all economic, political, and social systems must be evaluated and measured.

What was the context of the Holy Father's interests and activities? The international debt crisis began in the mid-1970s when many of the nations that comprised the Organizations of Petroleum Exporting Countries (OPEC) amassed enormous amounts of wealth. Banks were more than eager to lend billions of dollars to OPEC nations, as well as to other "developing countries" around the globe. Nations borrowed huge sums of money—some suggest that the amount of developing countries' debt may have exceeded $2 trillion—at low, but *floating*, interest rates. Many underdeveloped and developing nations failed to invest these sums wisely, instead funding projects involving immediate consumption, heavily influenced by corruption and unsound policy perspectives, with private projects benefiting only the national elites. The poor of these nations, of course, had virtually no voice in incurring these debts, nor did they benefit from them in any tangible manner. But unlike the world of globalized corporations, there was no option for impoverished nations to declare bankruptcy, transfer responsibility to third parties, or declare themselves in default, in order to manage repayment and to eventually emerge from the mountain of debt that had been accumulating.

Adjustable loan rates skyrocketed in the early 1980s when the United States attempted to reduce inflation by enforcing stringent monetary policies and at the same time, cutting its income tax rates. Globally, the prices for raw materials fell precipitously, meaning that poor countries had even less money to repay their debts. For example, both Brazil and Mexico nearly were in default on their loan agreements and required even more international aid, more foreign assistance, and more loan guarantees to stave off financial disaster. When private commercial banks became unable to handle the mass of debt and potential defaults, poorer nations turned to both the World Bank and the International Monetary Fund for assistance.

Prior to the *Heavily Indebted Poor Countries (HIPC) Initiative*, the IMF had created a program of "structural adjustment" in many of these nations. In return, debtor nations had to agree to impose stringent economic austerity programs on their nations in order to reschedule or refinance their current debt and to qualify to borrow more money. The cycle of poverty and debt had emerged.

Governments were thus required to drastically limit their domestic social spending by literally slashing social programs for education, health and social services, devaluing their national currencies, creating strict limitations on food subsidies, cutting government sector jobs and wages, converting small "subsistence farms" into large, export-oriented agribusiness operations, and promoting the privatization of state-owned-enterprises (SOEs), often further reducing domestic employment.

How did the Holy Father react to the debt crisis? On his first overseas papal trip in 1979, Pope John Paul II provided a unique insight into the reaches of his papacy and said "I am the voice for the voiceless." During the next two decades, he became a tireless champion of closing the gap between rich and poor, demanding social justice, jobs, and decent health care for the impoverished around the world. John Paul II commented in *Sollicitudo rei socialis* (1987b: 19.4-19.6): "... Debtor nations, in order to service their debt, find themselves obliged to export the capital needed for improving, or at least maintaining their standard of living. It is also because, for the same reason, they are unable to attain new and equally essential financing. Through this mechanism, the means intended for the development of peoples has turned into a brake upon development instead. . . " The Holy Father again framed the issue in terms of an oft-repeated concept of solidarity as a "... firm and persevering determination to commit oneself to the common good; that is to say, to the good of all and of each individual because we are all really responsible for all" (Pope John Paul II 1987b).

Cardinal Roger Etchegaray joined in the discussion in his insightful introduction to the Vatican document, *At the Service of the Human Community*, and stated: "Debt servicing cannot be met at the price of the asphyxiation of a country's economy, and no government can morally demand of its people privations incompatible with human dignity."

48

Later, in *Centesimus annus* (1991), John Paul II returned to this topic and commented: "The principle that debts must be paid is certainly just. However, it is not right to demand or expect payment when the effect would be the imposition of political choices leading to hunger and despair for entire peoples. It should not be expected that the debts which have been contracted should be paid at the price of unbearable sacrifices. In such ways it is necessary to find—as in fact is partly happening—ways to lighten, defer, or even cancel the debt compatible with the fundamental rights of peoples to subsistence and progress." What were the tangible results of the Holy Father's efforts and exhortations?

THE HIPC INITIATIVE

In response to the assertion that the responsibility to promote an "international common good" in which all people would have a real opportunity to achieve their full human development falls upon states, international institutions, and a host of private actors to accept their responsibility, the HIPC Initiative was proposed by the World Bank and the International Monetary Fund in the fall of 1996. The HIPC Initiative was significantly revised in 1999 so that a new initiative resulted in a significant enhancement of the original framework, producing a HIPC Initiative that would be "deeper, broader and faster" and which would strengthen the links between debt relief, poverty reduction, and social policies within a comprehensive development framework. The HIPC Initiative was the first comprehensive approach to reduce the staggering external debt of the world's poorest, yet most heavily indebted countries. The HIPC Initiative was also perhaps the most important step ever taken by the richest nations of the world in attempting to place debt relief in an overall framework of world poverty reduction.

The Holy Father had, in real effect, set the stage for this massive international effort. Linking the biblical concept of the Millennium Jubilee to the imperative of "righting injustice," the Holy Father stated: "Christians will have to raise their voice on behalf of the poor of the world, proposing the Jubilee as an appropriate time to give thought… to reducing substantially, if not canceling outright, the international debt which seriously threatens the future of many nations" (John Paul II 1994: 51). Archbishop Renato R. Martino, Apostolic Nuncio and Permanent Representative of the Holy See to the United Nations, in speaking before the Second Committee of the United Nations General Assembly on October 26, 2000, reiterated the papal viewpoint that "The growing awareness of our interdependence must lead us to great solidarity. Scientific progress must be accompanied by an *ethic of sharing*. The world community cannot miss the opportunity to make even minimal progress toward the eradication of poverty." Stressing that a truly interdependent world cannot be sustained "only on the basis of the defense of narrow private or national interest," Archbishop Martino noted that while developed countries had pledged 0.7 percent of the GNP to official development assistance, the reality was that the amount was more nearly a paltry 0.25 percent, resulting in a gap between commitment and performance of about $100 billion annually.

As a result of the concrete actions undertaken under the aegis of the HIPC Initiative, the thirty-three poorest countries (later increased to thirty-eight) around the world that faced an "unsustainable debt situation" of approximately $90 billion would be eligible to qualify for the HIPC Initiative and for additional debt reduction from so-called Paris Club creditors (amounting to a 67 percent reduction on eligible debt), as well as from other bilateral and commercial creditors (members of the so-called London Club) on terms at least comparable to those agreed with the Paris Club. Under this "enhanced framework," eligible nations would be able to apply revenues generated from exports from traditional government sources to real investment in poverty reduction strategies. Creditors who participated in the HIPC Initiative would share in HIPC debt reduction on the basis of "broad and equitable burden sharing" that was proportional to their share of the debt of eligible countries after the full application of traditional forms of debt relief. The cost of the new framework was estimated to be in the range of $12.5 billion to potentially more than $29.3 billion, with $6.3 billion to be provided by the World Bank's International Development Association (IDA), accomplished mainly through a 50 percent reduction of the annual debt service due on existing IDA debt. The

IMF's share of the cost of the HIPC Initiative would be financed on the net proceeds from "off-market" gold sales in 1999 that were deposited to the IMF's PRGF (Poverty Reduction and Growth Facility)-HIPC Trust. It was expected that the net-present value of public debt would be reduced by about one half after HIPC and traditional debt relief.

HIPC assistance would be provided through special Poverty Reduction and Growth Facility (PRGF) grants. Prior to the HIPC Initiative, eligible countries—especially those in sub-Saharan Africa—were spending slightly more on debt service than on health and education combined. By 2005, HIPC packages had been approved for 27 countries and between 1998 and 2004, debt service fell on average by more than half in relation to both exports and government revenue.

Under the terms of the HIPC Initiative, poor, developing countries have significantly increased their expenditures on health, education, and other critical social services. On the average, such spending is now almost four times the amount of debt service payments—once again, the powerful intervention of the Holy Father, as represented by the comments of Archbishop Martino, proved the litmus challenge for international action: "The failure of the wealthier nations to fulfill their solemnly proclaimed commitment undermines the trust and confidence which must be at the heart of any plan for peaceful world cooperation and of the new international culture of solidarity."

MILLENNIUM DEVELOPMENT GOALS

In a very similar fashion to the manner in which the Holy Father influenced the debate on worldwide debt reduction, so too did John Paul II confront the conventional wisdom surrounding globalization by demonstrating a "weighted concern to the needs of the poor in all economic, political, and social decisions because it is the most impoverished people whose rights and dignity are most often violated" (Caritas 2005). Thus, the Holy Father challenged world leaders to establish what is now known as "the preferential option for the poor," conveying in no uncertain terms Jesus' words that whatever we do unto the least of our brothers and sisters we do unto Him. The organization *Caritas* noted in reflection that "Those members of society with the greatest needs require the greatest attention and response. By assisting those who are most vulnerable, an option for the poor strengthens the entire community, for the deprivation and powerlessness of the poor wounds the whole human community. Such wounds are healed only by a greater solidarity with the poor and the marginalized." Archbishop Renato R. Martino provided the impetus for a major worldwide effort in response to the prodding of the Holy Father. Said the Archbishop, "If the process of globalization which is taking place in our world is to be truly human, it requires the construction of a truly global community. In such a community, there must be concern for all and especially for the weakest."

In September 2000, the member states of the United Nations unanimously adopted the *Millennium Declaration*, and after exhaustive consultations among a host of international agencies of the United Nations—the World Bank, the IMF, the OECD, the General Assembly—recognized the *Millennium Development Goals* as the road map for implementing the Millennium Declaration. Through the process, the Holy Father insisted that the Church's viewpoint be represented at the negotiating table. The Millennium Development Goals committed the international community to a real vision of development, "one that vigorously promotes human development as the measure of sustaining social and economic progress in all countries, and recognizes the importance of creating a global partnership for development." The first seven goals are "mutually reinforcing" and are directed at reducing poverty in all of its insidious forms. The last goal—creating a global partnership for development—concerns the ability to achieve the first seven. It has been recognized that many of the poorest countries around the world will require additional assistance and will look to the world's rich countries to provide it. From the outset, it was known that countries that were both poor and heavily indebted will require further assistance in reducing their debt burdens beyond those found in the HIPC Initiative. Among the Millennium Development Goals may be found the following imperatives:

- Eradicate extreme poverty and hunger... Halve, between 1990 and 2015, the proportion of people whose income is less than $1 a day; halve, between 1990 and 2015, the proportion of people who suffer from hunger;
- Achieve universal primary education... Ensure that, by 2015, children everywhere, boys and girls alike, will be able to complete a full course of primary schooling;
- Promote gender equality and empower women... Eliminate gender disparity in primary and secondary education, preferably by 2005, and in all levels of education no later than 2015;
- Reduce child mortality... Reduce by two-thirds, between 1990 and 2015, the under-five mortality rate;
- Improve maternal health... Reduce by three-quarters, between 1990 and 2015, the maternal mortality rate;
- Combat HIV/AIDS, malaria, and other diseases... Have halted by 2015 and begun to reverse the spread of HIV/AIDS; have halted by 2015 and begun to reverse the incidence of malaria and other major diseases;
- Ensure environmental sustainability... Integrate the principles of sustainable development into country policies and programs and reverse the loss of environmental resources; halve, by 2015, the proportion of people without sustainable access to safe drinking water and basic sanitation; have achieved, by 2020, a significant improvement in the lives of at least 100 million slum dwellers; and
- Develop a global partnership for development... Develop an open, rule-based, predictable, non-discriminatory trading and financial system, including a commitment to good governance, development, and poverty reduction—both nationally and internationally; address the special needs of the least-developed countries, including tariff-and quota-free access for export enhanced program of debt relief for HIPC and cancellation of official bilateral debt; address the special needs of landlocked countries and small island developing states; deal comprehensively with the debt problems of developing countries through national and international measures in order to make debt sustainable in the long term;

53

in cooperation with developing countries, develop and implement strategies for decent and productive work for youth; in cooperation with pharmaceutical companies, provide access to affordable, essential drugs in developing countries; in cooperation with the private sector, make available the benefits of new technologies, especially information and communications.

In the later years of his remarkable papacy, the Holy Father would return to these main themes on a recurring and reinforcing basis. Of special note to Americans were the remarks of John Paul II upon his meeting with President George Bush at Castel Gondolfo (July 23, 2001): "The revolution of freedom of which I spoke at the United Nations in 1995 must now be completed by a revolution of opportunity, in which all the world's people actively contribute to the economic prosperity and share in its fruits. This requires leadership by those nations whose religious and cultural traditions should make them most attentive to the moral dimension of the issues involved."

Noting that "a global world is essentially a world of solidarity," the Holy Father stated that "Respect for nature by everyone, a policy of openness to immigrants, the cancellation or significant reduction of the debt of poorer nations, … these are the priorities which the leaders of the developed countries cannot disregard."

President Bush responded: "Where there's oppression, you speak of human rights. Where there's poverty, you speak of justice and hope. . . Where there's great abundance, you remind us that wealth must be matched with compassion and moral purpose."

CONCLUSIONS

To the very end of his papacy, transformed by time into one of suffering and personal witness, John Paul II would remain faithful to his oft-repeated admonition that Jesus Christ had come into the world to "proclaim good news to the poor." John Paul II would also continue to prod world leaders to reaffirm and the keep their commitments to the poor and destitute. In fact, in July of

2004, an increasingly frail Holy Father announced the establishment of a "Coalition of Support and Promotion for the Financing of Development," and the organization of a conference to be attended by officials from the United Nations, the World Bank, the IMF, as well as representatives from the hierarchy of the Catholic Church, interested national governments, and important nongovernmental organizations. The topic of the Conference would be "Poverty and Globalization: Financing for Development, including the Millennium Development Goals." The Pontifical Council for Justice and Peace may have best summed up the Pope's message by commenting: "Special attention will be given to the present situation of the international debt and innovative financing proposals. . . The objective of the project is to collect funds that will make it possible to obtain the $50 billion needed annually to achieve the millennium's objectives before 2015." The Pope's message on this occasion underscored his earlier comments in which he had exhorted this same group with the words: "It is important, therefore, that the debt relief initiatives launched by the wealthier nations and the international institutions should come rapidly to full fruition, in a manner which will enable the poorest countries to become themselves the driving force of efforts to fight poverty and bring the benefits of economic and social progress to their people." Evoking the blessings of the Blessed Mother, *Mater pauperum*, the Holy Father forcibly reminded world leaders of their "special commitment to all those who are poor and outcast."

Sadly, not all of the Holy Father's efforts were met without criticism nor were all aspects of his message universally approved. The critics almost in unison point to what they identify as a glaring weak spot: AIDS, poverty and the pandemic in Africa. In the latter part of the 1990s, the late Jonathan Mann, founding director of the WHO's Global Program on AIDS, promoted a link between deprived social and economic conditions and vulnerability to AIDS in his pioneering work on the AIDS epidemic in Africa. In 2000, South African President Thabo Mbeki's address to the Thirteenth International AIDS Conference in Durban stirred up a controversy when he suggested that the health crisis facing Africa is due to extreme poverty (Mbeki 2000). Despite his encouraging people to fight against AIDS and other sexually transmitted diseases through his visits to Africa, John Paul II was unyielding regarding the Catholic Church's stance on contraceptive use, and this created a dilemma between the moral guidance that the pontiff was offering and the practical realities of fighting a disease and its potential linkages to poverty. By his detractors, the Pope's opposition to condom use was signaled as significantly contributing to the spread of HIV/AIDS, but they also disparaged John Paul's resolute opposition to contraception as having had a major impact on developing and less-developed nations, in relation to high birth rates, maternal mortality, infant mortality, resource over-exploitation, the crisis in global sustainability, and poverty and mass mortality due to deprivation or malnourishment-exacerbated avoidable and treatable disease. In the particular case of Africa, nearly half of the continent's people live below the poverty line, less than one in five Africans have access to electricity and two-thirds of rural people lack adequate water supplies, while three quarters live without proper sanitation. Bill Fletcher Jr., president of TransAfrica Forum, submits a dichotomy: "The Pope was very outspoken on human rights abuses and war. He was deeply concerned about the AIDS pandemic, but theologically he could not find it in himself to advance a solution necessary for the 20th and 21st century" (Dawkins 2005). Despite the earnestness of the critics and the fact that some issues remain unresolved, John Paul II's appeal for global humanity and the plight of the poor situates him as one of the most important World influencers, and perhaps the most significant moral authority in the World at the end of the second millennium and the beginning of the third. John Paul II championed human rights and better treatment of the poor while condemning war, and many world leaders listened.

What will be the legacy of the Holy Father as champion of God's least fortunate and least disposed? When considering the genuine outpouring of respect and love exhibited during his last illness, as well as at the Holy Father's funeral on April 5, 2005, U2 lead singer Bono, who met with the Pope during the Jubilee 2000 Campaign for African Debt Relief, may have offered the most poignant epitaph. Meant as an obvious compliment, Bono stated that the Pope was a "street fighter and a wily campaigner on behalf of the world's poor." Bono added, "We would never have gotten the debts of 23 countries completely canceled without him" and "Without John Paul II it's hard to imagine the Drop The Debt campaign succeeding as it did."

References

Caritas (2005), "The Debt Crisis Must be Understood in Moral Terms," available at www:worldhunger.org/articles/global/debt/caritas.htm.

Dawkins, Wayne (2005), "Commentary: 'Trapped' Pope John Paul II Blew the Opportunity to Contain AIDS in Africa," available at www.blackamericaweb.com /site.aspx/bawnews/baw commentary/dawkins408

Mbeki, Thabo (2000), "Speech of the President of South Africa at the Opening Session of the 13th International AIDS Conference," July 9, available at www.virusmyth.net/aids/news/durbspmbeki. htm.

Pope John Paul II (2000), *Homily at the Jubilee of Workers*, May 1, available at www.vatican.va/holy_father/john_paul_ii/homilies /2000/documents/hf_jp-ii_hom_20000501_jub-workers_en.htm.

Pope John Paul II (1996), "Food Security Results From Ethic Of Solidarity: Address to World Food Summit," November 13, available at www.ewtn.com/library/PAPALDOC /JPSUMMIT.htm.

Pope John Paul II (1994), *Tertio Millennio Adveniente, Apostolic Letter on Preparation For The Jubilee Of The Year 2000*, November 10, available atwww.vatican.va/holy_father/john_ paul_ii/apost_letters/documents/hf_jp-ii_apl_10111994_tertio-millennio-adveniente_en.html.

Pope John Paul II (1991), *Centesimus annus, Encyclical on the Hundredth Anniversary of Rerum Novarum*, May 1, available at www.vatican.va/holy_father/john_paul_ii/encyclicals/do cuments/hf_jp-ii_enc_01051991_centesimus-annus_en.html.

Pope John Paul II (1987a), "Address to the U.N. Economic Commission for Latin America and the Caribbean," *Origins* 16 (April 16): 775.

Pope John Paul II (1987b), *Sollicitudo Rei Socialis, Encyclical on the Twentieth Anniversary of Populorum Progressio,* (December 15), available at www.vatican.va/holy_father/john_paul_ii/ encyclicals/documents/hf_jp-ii_enc_30121987_sollicitudo-rei-socialis_en.html.

Pope Leo XIII (1891), *Rerum Novarum, Encyclical on Capital and Labor,* May 15, available atwww.vatican.va/holy_father/leo_xiii/encyclicals/documents/hf_l-xiii_enc_15051891_rerum-novarum_en.html.

Pope Paul VI (1967), *Populorum Progressio, Encyclical on the Development of Peoples,* March 26, available at www.vatican.va/holy_father/paul_vi/encyclicals/ documents/hf_p-vi_enc_26031967_populorum_en.html.

Trócaire (2005), "John Paul's Solidarity with the Poor," April 5, available at www.trocaire.org/newsandinformation/ makepovertyhistory/solidarity.htm

United Nations (2000), *United Nations Millennium Declaration,* available at www.un.org/millennium/declaration/ares552e.htm.

World Food Summit (1996), *Rome Declaration on World Food Security,* available at www.fao.org/documents/show_cdr.asp? url_file=/DOCREP/003/W3613E/W3613E00.HTM.

Serving Beauty, Goodness and Truth:
A Hesitant Primer to Karol Wojtyła's Theory of Art

JANUSZ A. IHNATOWICZ

Throughout his papacy John Paul II reached out to artists. He wished to change the tone of the dialogue between the Church and the world of art for so long "marked by opposition and contestation,"[1] and "to consolidate a more constructive partnership between art and the Church."[2] He was convinced that both parties would profit from this partnership.

Surely he had a personal, not to say professional, reason to seek such reconciliation, for he was an artist, a poet. As he confessed in his *Letter to Artists*: "I feel closely linked [to you artists] by experiences reaching far back in time and which have indelibly marked my life."[3] Even though he appears to have given up writing poetry for many years during his pontificate, he did not abandon it. We know that he read poetry regularly, and towards the end of his life he gave us *The Roman Triptych*.

But there was, I think, a more objective and universal motive for his support of the arts. He was convinced that art had an important role to play in the cultural and religious life of all human beings. He brought to his papacy a definite theory of art. He did not leave us a comprehensive statement of this theory, but it is suggested in many of his texts, especially those addressed to artists. In this essay I shall try to glean the basic outlines and elements of this theory by looking at several passages from his various addresses, most notably his *Letter to Artists* from 1999.

Wojtyła's vision of art, as well as his own poetic work, were inspired by Polish Romanticism, refined and universalized by Cyprian Kamil Norwid, as it was interpreted and practiced by Mieczysław Kotlarczyk and the Rhapsodic Theater of Kraków.[4]

---

[1] John Paul II, *Address to Artists and Journalists*, Munich, November 19, 1980, intro. Translation mine.

[2] John Paul II, *Letter to Artists*, April 4, 1999, n.14. Unless otherwise noted all Papal texts are quoted in the official Vatican English version.

[3] John Paul II, *Letter to Artists*, April 4, 1999, n.1.

[4] On the relationship of Wojtyła and the Rhapsodic Theater see, Bolesław Taborski, *"Wprost w moje serce uderza droga wszystkich": O Karolu Wojtyle*

This is universally admitted. What is less noted, as far as I know, is the theological inspiration of his ideas. His esthetic system was dependent on ethics, but ultimately on theology.

ART IS A VOCATION

For Karol Wojtyła art is a vocation. And this, it seems, created tension in his own life. In the preface to an anthology of poems by priests he wrote:

Kapłaństwo jest sakramentem i powołaniem. Twórczość poetycka jest funkcją talentu – ale talenty również stanowią o powołaniu, przynajmniej w sensie podmiotowym. Można więc stawiać sobie pytanie: w jaki sposób te dwa powołania, kapłańskie i poetyckie, współistnieją ze sobą, w jakiś sposób wzajemnie się przenikają w tym samym człowieku. [5]

[Priesthood is a sacrament and a vocation. Poetry is a question of talent — but talents also determine vocations, at least in a subjective sense. Therefore we may ask: how do these two vocations, priestly and poetic, coexist, how do they interpenetrate in one and the same man?]

Karol Wojtyła and his friends thought that art, the theater was his vocation, but then he discovered that God saw it differently. This is how he described it much later: "Mieczysław Kotlarczyk thought that my vocation was the living word and the theater, but Jesus thought that it was priesthood, and somehow we

---

— *Janie Pawle II, Szkice, Wspomnienia, wiersze,* [Straight into my Heart Lead the Roads of All: On Karol Wojtyła — John Paul II. Sketches and Memories, Poems] Toruń 2005, pp. 215-234.

[5] Kard. Karol Wojtyła, „Wstęp," *Słowa na Pustyni: Poezja kapłańska* [The Word in the Desert: Poems by Priests] red. Ks. Bonifacy Miązek, Londyn 1971, p. 5. *Translation mine.*

came to an agreement about it."[6] The priesthood demands everything from the man who is called to it. Wojtyła had no doubt about that. His problem was that in his view, poetry has a similar claim on the talented. Yet finally he came to the conclusion that direct service to the Word in the priesthood had the superior claim to his loyalty. Here, as he confessed, the person of Adam Chmielowski, a painter who gave up art to become Brother Albert, was an example and encouragement.[7] Yet, he was not prepared to give it up altogether—and it is perhaps of some importance that the majority of his published work was written after his ordination. Hence he faced something of a dilemma. At least twice he told Marek Skwarnicki: *Poezja to wielka pani, której trzeba się całkowicie poświęcić; obawiam się, że nie byłem wobec niej zupełnie w porządku* [Poetry is a great lady. One must dedicate oneself to her totally; I fear that I have not been quite in order with her).[8]

Of course most artists are not priests, so this dilemma is not theirs. But the call to total dedication is. Poetry is a matter of talent. Talent always obliges, carries with itself a duty to be used and developed. But when talent is seen as a gift of God, a grace, as John Paul II saw it, the obligation becomes even more pressing and absolute.[9] In a relatively early address the Pope declared that the supernatural action of grace is reflected in the creative work of artists.[10] Sixteen years later he wrote: "Dialogue with grace ... is particularly expressed in the exercise of artistic talents."[11] In both cases his primary concern was with Christian artists, but, as grace

---

[6] John Paul II, Address to Representatives of Science and Culture, Kraków 2 June 1979. *Translation mine.*

[7] He said that both in *Dar i tajemnica* [Gift and Mystery] (p. 34) and in *Wstańcie, chodźmy!* [Arise, Let us Go!], (p. 150).

[8] See *Karol Wojtyła — Poezje Dramaty Szkice: Tryptyk Rzymski Jan Paweł II* [Karol Wojtyła — Poetry Plays and Sketches: Roman Triptych] (Kraków: Znak, 2004), p. 8.

[9] Address to a Polish Group from the Cultural and Artistic Foundation Center, January 25, 2004.

[10] See Homily preached at the Mass for artists, Rome February 18, 1984, n. 5. *Translation mine.*

[11] Address for the Jubilee Celebration for Artists, February 18, 2000, n.4.

works in mysterious ways in all men and women of good will, it applies to all artists, regardless of their confession.

POET PRIEST AND PROPHET

Karol Wojtyła embraced the vision of Polish Romanticism that poetry is a form of service to the people of Poland and through them to all humanity. An artist has "the responsibility to form the spirit of society and of the people."[12] For Wojtyła, as it was for Norwid, this was fundamentally the service of truth.[13] A poet's duty is to speak the truth; he must not be ashamed of the truth or try to hide it to gain acceptance.[14] By being faithful to the truth he gains the right to be the nation's conscience.[15] But this service is more than that of an honest political leader or philosopher. From an early time Wojtyła tended to see it in religious terms. In a youthful poem, written while he was still in high school, he ascribed to the poet the role and functions of a priest.[16] Years later he referred with apparent approval to Beethoven's idea that the artist is in a sense called to priestly service.[17] A priest is one who has the knowledge of mysteries; he is a *mystagogos*; his role is to communicate and interpret mysteries to the people.

But an artist's knowledge of mysteries is not a matter of tradition, as it is for priests, but of inner illumination. Hence another

---

[12] Address to a Polish Group from the Cultural and Artistic Formation Center, January 25, 2004.

[13] Norwid's influence on the thought of Wojtyła is well known. (I have a feeling that this influence extends to his poetic diction; it must have been instrumental in his abandoning epigonic attempts to imitate the poetics of Wyspiański in his early verse.) The Pope admits to his enthusiasm for Norwid in the address to a group of Polish intellectuals on July 1, 2001. In his *Letter to Artists* he quotes him (Nor, in my opinion, is this the only time he does so.)

[14] See C . K. Norwid, *Promethidion: Bogumił*, v. 14: „czy się nie wstydził prawdy i nie stłumił."

[15] See *Promethidion: Bogumił*, v. 11: „naród spowiadał" [The nation confessed].

[16] "Psalterz Renesansowy: 3. Słowo – Logos, Rapsod" [Renaissance Psalter: 3. Word — Logos, Rhapsode] *Karol Wojtyla Poezje Dramaty Szkice: Tryptyk Rzymski Jan Paweł II*, Kraków ZNAK 2004, pp. 55-63. See p. 14.

[17] Address to representatives of the world of science and art, n. 11. Vienna, September 12, 1983.

Romantic comparison: the poet as a prophet or seer of mysteries (*wieszcz*) also found in that youthful poem. Later he will rather speak of "artistic intuition," but the sense remains the same.[18]

There are two elements of this intuition, which together make it the source of art. "[Artistic] intuition—says the Pope—springs from the depths of the human soul, where the desire to give meaning to one's own life is joined by the fleeting vision of beauty and of the mysterious unity of things."[19] Art is a response to human desire to understand, to make our life meaningful, but this response is rooted in an experience of beauty. As it flows from an experience of beauty, it must have beauty as its ultimate object. "In so far as it seeks the beautiful, fruit of an imagination which rises above the everyday, art is by its nature a kind of appeal to the mystery."[20]

ART AND MYSTERY

The Pope says this of artists: "You do not stop at mere representation or the description of the surface of things. . .you seek through word, sound, image and representation, to make comprehensible the truth and the profundity of the world and of man."[21] And again: "Every genuine artistic intuition goes beyond what the senses perceive and, reaching beneath reality's surface, strives to interpret its hidden mystery."[22] Art might be a mirror held up to nature, but it is a mirror of a special kind. "Every piece of art, be it religious or secular, be it painting, a sculpture, a poem or any kind of handicraft made by loving skill, is a sign and a symbol of the inscrutable secret of human existence, of man's origin and destiny, of the meaning of his life and work."[23] For this reason "Every genuine art form in its own way is a path to the inmost reality of man and of the world."[24]

---

[18] *Letter to Artists*, n. 6
[19] *Letter to Artists*, n. 6.
[20] *Letter to Artists*, n. 10.
[21] Address to Artists and Journalists, Munich, November 19, 1980, n. 3. *Translation mine*
[22] *Letter to Artists*, n. 6
[23] Address at Clonmacnois in Ireland, September 30, 1979.
[24] *Letter to Artists*, n. 6

To speak of "inmost reality of man" is to speak of mystery. Therefore "art is by its nature a kind of appeal to the mystery."[25] But the Pope's vision does not stop on the "inscrutable secret of human existence." I think that we may understand that this appeal is to *the* Mystery, the Mystery of God. Every work of art is a symbolic acknowledgment of this Mystery. But by the same token, as the Polish version of the *Letter* understands it, art invites us to open ourselves to this Mystery. In this way "art remains a kind of bridge to religious experience." And not only art more or lest explicitly inspired by religion. The Pope writes, "Even when they explore the darkest depths of the soul or the most unsettling aspects of evil, artists give voice in a way to the universal desire for redemption."[26]

Art goes and makes it possible for others to go beyond "the surface of things," and it does this by creating beauty.

ART AND THE BEAUTIFUL

For Wojtyła there is no doubt that art is about beauty. As he said late in his pontificate in a speech that in a way summarized his thought on the subject of art, "When we speak of creativity, spontaneously we think of the beautiful."[27] For this reason, "the theme of beauty is decisive for a discourse on art." [28] "The artist has a special relationship to beauty. In a very true sense it can be said that beauty is the vocation bestowed on him by the Creator in the gift of 'artistic talent'."[29] Artists are "creators of beauty."[30] Only "in so far as it seeks the beautiful" art is true to itself.[31]

Perhaps the dedication of his *Letter to Artists* expresses it best. It is addressed "to all who are passionately dedicated to the

---

[25] *Letter to Artists*, n. 10. Italian and Polish versions capitalize M; Vatican English version does not.

[26] *Letter to Artists*, n. 10.

[27] Address to a Polish Group from the Cultural and Artistic Foundation Center, January 25, 2004.

[28] *Letter to Artists*, n. 3.

[29] *Letter to Artists*, n. 3.

[30] *Letter to Artists*, n. 1; cf. Address to Members of the Pontifical Council for Culture, January 13, 1983.

[31] *Letter to Artists*, n. 10. The Polish version here has not "the beautiful" but "truth" (*prawda*).

search for new "epiphanies" of beauty so that through their creative work as artists they may offer these as gifts to the world." And this is the great gift that artists can give to humanity. John Paul II made his own the words of the Second Vatican Council in its Message to Artists: "this world in which we live needs beauty in order not to sink into despair."[32] For "beauty is a key to the mystery and a call to transcendence."[33]

As far as I know, John Paul II did not give us a definition of beauty. But I see no reason to doubt that he accepted the classical understanding of it in terms of inner harmony and luminosity.[34] Perception of beauty may not be reduced to pure sensory perception; it is a form of intellectual knowledge: perception of a pattern in what is seen that leads beyond what is seen. This is what, I presume, the Pope means when he writes that beauty sought by the artist is the "fruit of an imagination which rises above the everyday."[35] The search of beauty is, in a real sense, the search of the truth. As Karol Wojtyła said it in his play *The Jeweler's Shop* [Przed sklepem jubilera], truth is the beauty accessible to the mind.[36] A tasty meal cannot be a symbol of anything, but something beautiful gives us a foretaste of "the mysterious unity of things," and it is from a vision of this unity that an artist works.[37] It is the beauty of a work of art that enables it to be an epiphany of "the divine beauty reflected in creation."[38] For all that is harmonious in the world has a luminosity reflecting that unity of unities, that perfect harmony, the Triune God.

I am convinced that John Paul II would sympathize with Hans Urs von Balthasar's belief that beauty is a fitting starting point in our attempts to penetrate the mystery of God, seen as the Supreme Beauty.

---

[32] *Letter to Artists*, n. 6.
[33] *Letter to Artists*, n. 16.
[34] For this concept of beauty see Armand A. Maurer, *About Beauty: a Thomistic Interpretation*, Houston 1982.
[35] *Letter to Artists*, n. 10.
[36] *Przed sklepem jubilera*, I Sygnały [I Signals]. In this sense Polish version's of the *Letter* "poszukiwanie prawdy" [seeking the truth], mentioned earlier, may be justified.
[37] See *Letter to Artists*, n. 6.
[38] Address for the Jubilee Celebration for Artists, February 18, 2000, n.2.

But to Wojtyła's mind there is another consequence of this understanding of beauty. Beauty and the good are intimately and inseparably linked. "In perceiving that all He had created was good, God saw that it was beautiful as well."[39] It was not without reason, the Pope observed, that the Greek version of the book of Genesis translates the Hebrew term for "good" by the Greek word beautiful. Note however, that creation is beautiful because it is good and not vice versa. Therefore the Pope says: "In a certain sense, beauty is the visible form of the good, just as the good is the metaphysical condition of beauty."[40] Indeed, "the beautiful can begin to exist only when the power of good resides in her (*sic*) nature."[41]

This connection is in the work of art itself. Every beautiful thing intimates the goodness of creation. And giving hope inspires to action. The Pope quotes a passage from Norwid's great poem about the nature of art, *Promethidion*: *Bo piękno na to jest by zachwycało / Do pracy – praca by się zmartwychwstało* [beauty is to enthuse us for work, and work is to raise us up].[42] He could quote another line from the poem: *Kształtem miłości piękno jest* [beauty is the shape of love].[43] Beauty, revealing love, charms us and thus impels us to action, which is the condition of achieving our goal, the good. And ultimately this love is Love, God who creates. For John Paul II "Christian artists will ... offer the world new "epiphanies" of the divine beauty reflected in creation."[44] Christian artists certainly do; but all artists may if they "perceive a ray of the supreme beauty among many manifestations of the beautiful."[45]

---

[39] *Letter to Artists*, n. 3.
[40] *Letter to Artists*, n. 3.
[41] Address to a Polish Group from the Cultural and Artistic Foundation Center, January 25, 2004.
[42] *Promethidion: Bogumił*, vv. 185-186, quoted in *Letter* n. 3. Vatican translation of the *Letter* does not really do justice to Norwid. Especially "by się zmartwychwstało" [lit: so that one might rise again] which has, I believe, also an allusion to the resurrection of Poland.
[43] *Promethidion: Bogumił*, v. 115; cf vv. 108-109.
[44] Address for the Jubilee Celebration for Artists, February 18, 2000, n.2.
[45] Address for the Jubilee Celebration for Artists, February 18, 2000, n. 4.

There is another aspect of this connection of beauty and goodness, a personal one. Pope John Paul II does not identify the moral order with the esthetic one, the creation of beautiful works with religious faith or personal holiness, but he is convinced that "each conditions the other in a profound way. In creating their works, artists express themselves to the point where their work becomes a unique disclosure of their own being, of what they are and of how they are what they are."[46] Through artistic creativity an artist, writes the Pope, "accomplishes this task above all in shaping the wondrous 'material' of his own humanity," and this finds its consummation and reflection in his "exercising creative dominion over the universe which surrounds him," by forming material into a thing of beauty.[47] Therefore, even if he would not insist on personal holiness as a condition of being called a genuine artist, the Pope sees a connection: "If creativity is not guided by good, or worse still if it is directed towards evil, it is not worthy of the title 'artist'." Moreover, he is convinced that "for beauty to shine in its full splendor ... it must be united to goodness and the sanctity of life."[48] Creating art is a form of dialogue with others, hence a way of influencing them.[49] "The artist, therefore, is responsible not only for the aesthetic dimension of the world and of life, but also for its moral dimension."[50]

In this perspective, Pope John Paul II was seriously troubled by the fact that beauty seems a category largely eliminated from contemporary art in favor of showing man in his negativity, his contradictions, his loss of meaning.[51] He does not reject the presentation of what is evil and ugly in itself. It probably had a cleansing effect on art, freeing it from falsifying "romantic superstructures." At the same token, he wonders whether "the

---

[46] *Letter to Artists*, n. 2.
[47] *Letter to Artists*, n. 1.
[48] Address to the Participants of the ninth Public Session of the Pontifical Academies, November 9, 2004, n. 3.
[49] *Letter to Artists*, n. 2.
[50] Address to a Polish Group from the Cultural and Artistic Foundation Center, January 25, 2004.
[51] Address to Artists and Journalists, Munich, November 19, 1980, n. 5. *Translation mine.*

mirror of negativity, employed by contemporary art does not become an end in itself? Whether it does not lead to a taste for evil, to pleasure in destruction and collapse, whether it does not lead to cynicism and contempt for man?"[52] This is possible because ultimately elimination of the beautiful flows from a deeper source: despair flowing from a denial that good is a reality.

ARTIST AS CREATOR

There is an analogy between Creator and the craftsman.[53] There are obvious differences: God creates *ex nihilo*; an artist works by molding matter already in existence. But there is also a similarity. All human activity manifests man's status as created in the image and likeness of God. This image is particularly clear in an artist.[54] For John Paul II the artist is given a "creative vocation" in special sense. "God, the sole creator of all things, has wished in some way to associate" artists in the mystery of creation.[55] An artist fulfills his mission by giving "form and substance to reality and the material that the world offers to him."[56] His work somehow resembles the creative work of God: "the human craftsman mirrors the image of God as Creator."[57] The Pope quotes Nicolas of Cusa's words that creative art is a communication of and a share in that creative art which is God himself.[58] "Through his 'artistic creativity' man appears more than ever 'in the image of God', and he accomplishes this task above all in shaping the wondrous 'material' of his own humanity and then exercising creative dominion over the universe which surrounds him."[59] His work

---

[52] Address to Artists and Journalists, Munich, November 19, 1980, n. 5

[53] *Letter to Artists*, n. 1. For the Pope two Polish terms *Stwórca* and *twórca* neatly denote both the similarity and the difference between the two kinds of "creating."

[54] Address to Artists and Journalists, Munich, November 19, 1980, n. 3. *Translation mine.*

[55] *Letter to Artists*, n. 1.

[56] Address to Artists and Journalists, Munich, November 19, 1980, n. 3.

[57] *Letter to Artists*, n. 1.

[58] *Letter to Artists*, n. 1.

[59] *Letter to Artists*, n. 1.

becomes an epiphany of beauty, hence also a signal that the world is good.

CONCLUSION

The Pope's esthetic framework has an ethical foundation not merely, not even primarily, in the sense of the artist's personal life but because of the relationship between beauty and the good. Ultimately his vision of art is theological. The artist through his work re-creates in a symbolic manner the world as God made it and saw it "in the beginning." "Through the language of beauty," says the Pope, we can "see the profound syntony between ... human creativity and the work of God, the author of every authentic beauty."[60] Ultimately art gives us a "reflection of the divine beauty." And here lies its great dignity and its importance for humanity and the Church. But also the artist's responsibility. For the same reason, the Pope insists, religion, that homeland of the soul, where the most important questions of human existence are asked and answers sought, has much to offer to art. It was so in the past, where religious faith became inspiration to great artistic creativity, and there is no reason why it should not happen today.

---

[60] Address to the Participants of the ninth Public Session of the Pontifical Academies, November 9, 2004, n 2.

"PIASA President Prof. Piotr Wandycz and Pope John Paul II."

The Poetry of Karol Wojtyła — Pope John Paul II
BOLESŁAW TABORSKI

Karol Wojtyła's interest in poetry has been as keen and consistent as his involvement with drama and theatre. Both stemmed from similar roots: the love of literature. Both went also through a similar development and transition: from an understandable need for self-expression to becoming a means to an end which ultimately was his pastoral mission. To trace this parallel development is a fascinating though by no means easy task. Fascinating, because the poetry developed with the man: from somewhat modest and conventional beginnings he went to achieve the stature of a major religious poet for our time when his own deep spirituality crystallized itself. Difficult, because the substance of the poetry became complex, characteristic of the formidable religious and moral thinker its author was.

The love of literature I mentioned was imbued in young Karol at the Marcin Wadowita High School in Wadowice where he engaged also in theatre activities. The two were interconnected. After all, the plays he appeared in were written by poets and were for the most part poetic dramas. In 1934 the fourteen-year old Karol was awarded second prize in a poetry reading contest for his rendering of the difficult philosophical poem *Promethidion* by Cyprian Norwid. The love of literature resulted in Karol Wojtyła choosing Polish Philology as his main course of study at the Jagiellonian University in Kraków in the autumn of 1938. Already on October 15, with three other young writers he took part in a poetry reading, reciting his own poems. This was only the first of a number of such readings. As witnesses recollect, those early poems were in the nature of stylized highland folk ballads, with some religious themes included. But in the spring and summer of 1939 the next book of poems was written, known under two titles which well describe the poet's fascinations at that time: *Renaissance Psalter, Slavonic Book.* It contains a cycle of 17 sonnets, a couple of poems called "psalms," with David as their theme, some longer poems, among them the "rhapsodic" *Word-Logos,* written in octaves, and *Poetry — the Czarnolas Feast,* written in quatrains. Czarnolas was the estate of the first great poet of Poland, Jan

Kochanowski (1530-1584). It is to the period of national greatness and prosperity, as well as to Poland's Christian heritage, that the youthful Karol Wojtyła looks back, but for his stylistic inspiration and form he is indebted mainly to the early 20th Century Young Poland movement. Though for this reason his poetry of that period has to be classed as *juvenilia,* not fully original, his thoughts are already maturing in a remarkable way. Even as far as the form is concerned, one can see a considerable development from the first version of the long poem *Mousike*, written on December 31, 1938, and the second version, completed in the following year.

As one could have supposed, the outbreak of World War II, the Nazi occupation of Poland, Karol Wojtyła's attendance as student at the now clandestine University, physical work in a quarry, but also involvement with underground theatre activities, the loss of his father, and his gradual orientation towards spiritual life and priesthood all contributed to the further development of his poetry in all its aspects. Gone is the carefree, joyous self-expression of his pre-war student days; serious thought tending more and more to his single-minded choice is prevalent, while the form becomes subservient to it, though now definitely his own, rid of the ornaments and external influences he had modeled himself on. The poems written during the war show this development clearly. Probably the earliest of them, "The Harpist," still belongs to the theme of "David" and is the most conventional "The Breakthrough" seems to reflect the impending change in his life. "The Avengers" is connected with the patriotic strain in his writing, while "Proletariat" — with his social awareness. Both these strains will find a fuller expression in his later poetry. The war-time poems form, in fact, a transition to Karol Wojtyła's fully fledged poetry which emerged by 1944, at the time when he had begun a new phase of his life that was to take him to priesthood and eventually to the Vatican.

* * *

Poetry, one has the feeling, was to Karol Wojtyła something very intimate, personal. Except for those youthful pre-war readings, he never again brought it into the open, published infrequently, with reluctance it seems, and never under his own name (until October 1978 that is, when the 'secret" was out).

It is symptomatic in this respect that when part of his first mature poetic work, *Pieśń o Bogu ukrytym* [Song of the Hidden God], written over a long period and completed at Christmas 1944 appeared in four issues of the Carmelite monthly *Głos Karmelu* [Voice of Mt. Carmel] in the years 1946-47, it was published anonymously. His next poem was published in the Kraków weekly *Tygodnik Powszechny* in 1950 under the *nom de plume* Andrzej Jawień which he would from then on use for his literary publications (i.e. poems, the only published play and his reviews of the Rhapsodic Theatre's productions until 1975, when he changed it to Stanisław Andrzej Gruda and occasionally others). But he did not publish much, while three late poems remained unpublished until 1979, after his election to the Papacy.[1] And, as. far as one can tell, he never attempted to have them published in a book. A very private poet then. Whereas his reviews and articles on drama tell us a great deal about his conception of the theatre, on poetry (apart from frequent quotations from classics) he has said little. A rare insight into Karol Wojtyła's thoughts on the connection between poetry and religious vocation can be found in an anthology of poems written by priests, brought out by a London-based Polish publisher in 1971. No poems of his are included, but Cardinal Wojtyła supplied the preface where he has this to say:

> Poetry has its own significance, its own aesthetic value and criteria of appreciation which belong to its proper order. And this is what the authors included here are concerned about. But doubtless they are also concerned with making a point about their religious vocation... Priesthood is a sacrament and vocation, while writing poetry is the function of talent; but it is talent too that determines the vocation.[2]

---

[1] All were published either in *Tygodnik Powszechny* [The Universal Weekly] or in the Catholic monthly *Znak* [The Sign], both printed in Kraków.

[2] Karol Cardinal Wojtyła, Preface to *Słowa na pustyni* [Words in the Wilderness], ed. Rev. Bonifacy Miązek (London: Poets' and Painter's Press. 1971), p. 5.

These words may be thought to provide the clue to their author's own poetry. One may call it religious in its deepest, innermost sense and message. But the diction and imagery used is by no means "devotional" or superficially "religious." One should keep in mind that Wojtyła's poetry spans four decades. As time went by it reflected more and more his main task of a concerned and committed pastor. His poetry has always been one of ideas rather than images, notwithstanding the striking and beautiful imagery, which is also to be found in that seemingly cerebral poetry. It could be said that, in time he transcended poetry, as it were, in the sense that while formal aspects, like rhythm or line pattern, and imagery, remained, he later produced philosophical and religious reflections in the form — or even guise — of poetry. But this would not be altogether true.

The fourteen great poetic structures I have in mind are written mainly in blank, free verse. They are open ended, with changeable, often long lines of verse which — sometimes, particularly in later poems — pass into poetic prose. As a rule they are long poems, divided into parts and sections; some give one the impression of being cycles of shorter poems. But it would be wrong to treat those parts as independent entities, because they form elements of a complex, multi-layered structure, like the naves and chapels of a cathedral, and only the whole poem makes the full, intended impact. Complex also is the way in which the author treats his material. The subject described is seen directly, and at the same time becomes the centerpiece of a grand metaphor spreading through the entire fabric of the work, while the detailed images form part of a large canvas. There is in this poetry a flow from the particular to the universal.

Karol Wojtyła's poetry gives one the impression of a monolith by its form and by its content directed to universal values. Unlike most poetry written today, it is not self-centered, or even in a wider sense anthropocentric, but theocentric, directed to God (though the actual word "God" is not often mentioned; the poet is very sparing in employing religious terms). This theocentricity does not mean that his poetry neglects man. On the contrary, it is hard to find a poetry more caring for man. But man is considered not just in relation to his earthly matters, or to history, but also to his ultimate destiny which, as far as this poet is concerned, lies in God. It is also, as has been mentioned, an intensely personal poetry. It deals with inner life and experience; expresses his deeply felt emotions and thoughts about his and other people's place in the world. It is definitely relevant to the problems of modern man. One has the impression that on becoming a priest, Karol Wojtyła continued writing poetry because it was still a natural means of expression for an important aspect of his personality; for the poet who was still in him. But of course it had to be connected with his religious vocation and pastoral work. For such a totally committed person, it would be strange if it were not so. On the other hand, Karol Wojtyła's poems never become philosophical or theological dissertations clothed in the form of poetry. On the contrary, while some early poems are complex, resounding with echoes of his reading of mystics and theologians, late poems contain striking images, lyrical passages of great beauty and direct, simple statements. His is a poetry written truly of the inner necessity of both mind and heart. It also provides proof, if one were needed, that he himself is one of those writers whom John Paul II had in mind when on his first pilgrimage to Poland he said:

> Christian inspiration continues to be the main creative source for Polish artists. Polish culture still flows with a broad stream of inspirations which have their source in the Gospel.[3]

In very broad outline the poems encompass four major themes: the sacraments, aspects of Vatican Council II, the Bible, and poems dealing with Polish history, in particular with the development of Christianity in Poland.

* * *

---

[3] John Paul II, Speech to youth, Gniezno. 3 June 1979. From *Jan Paweł II w Polsce* [John Paul II in Poland] (London: P.K.F., 1979) pp. 13-14.

Song of the Hidden God, his published debut and also his longest poem, is divided into two distinct parts. The first, "Wybrzeża pełne ciszy" [Shores of Silence], is in the nature of religious reflection; the second, "Pieśń o słońcu niewyczerpanym" [Song of the inexhaustible Sun], has the form of a prayer, addressed to God directly. It is a deeply contemplative poem, closely connected with his desire at the time to join the Carmelite novitiate. "Dalekie wybrzeża ciszy" [The distant shores of silence] which "zaczynają się tuż za progiem" [begin just over the threshold, I.1] in all probability refer to monastic life, so close to and yet so far from a seminarian, who was not in fact permitted to execute his plan. There are in the poem echoes of his seminary readings of the Spanish mystics, particularly St. John of the Cross, who a year later became the subject of his dissertation in dogmatic theology: *The Analysis of Faith According to St. John of the Cross. Faith as a Means of Uniting the Soul with God.* In the poem, however, the author contemplates God and his own relation to Him not only on the basis of faith, but above all — love:

> Miłość mi wszystko wyjaśniła,
> miłość wszystko rozwiązała —
> dlatego uwielbiam tę Miłość,
> gdziekolwiek by przebywała.
>
> (I.5:1-4)

> [Love has explained all to me,
> love has solved all
> that is why I adore that Love,
> wherever it might reside.]

Love, personified in God, is the dominant theme, leading to adoration: the adoration of God in His greatness and in the mystery of the Eucharist, as well as in the beauty of Nature. The title of part two, "Song of the Inexhaustible Sun," refers to both. In its deepest essence, *Song of the Hidden God*, as the very title suggests, is a poem about the Eucharist. The poet speaks of his meeting with the Heavenly Father "in the gentle Host" and says that he dwells in God's Thought,

. . . gdy w blasku ukrytym
skupiam siebie całego,
i staję się znów Twoją Myślą,
miłowany białym żarem Chleba.
                                    (II.9:17-20)

[. . . when in the hidden brightness
I focus myself whole,
and again become Thy Thought,
loved with the white heat of Bread.]

There are moving references to the Gospels, as when he
asks the Master to take him to Ephraim, recalls the evening with
Nicodemus, or when he recreates within himself the Biblical events:

jest we mnie kraina przeźroczysta
w blasku jeziora Genezaret —
i łódź. . . i rybacza przystań,
oparta o ciche fale. . .

i tłumy, tłumy serc,
zagarnięte przez Jedno Serce,
przez Jedno Serce najprostsze,
przez najłagodniejsze —
                                    (II.12:1-8)

[There is in me the translucent country
in the brightness of Lake Genezareth —

and the boat. . . and the fishermen's haven,
backed by the still waves. . .

and crowds, crowds of hearts,
captured by One Heart,
by the One simplest Heart,
by the gentlest one —]

As always with this poet, the external landscapes are closely bound with the landscape of the inner soul and one passes into the other. We have the impression throughout that the young poet simply communicates with God (even though with his usual reluctance he does not mention the word). This work, without ceasing to be poetry is a conversation, a prayer. As in the well known medieval legend, an acrobat prayed to Our Lady with his dancing, here, the poet adores God with his poetry. As far as its form is concerned, the poem is characterized by a simplicity almost unparalleled in his work. Later there will be simple fragments but for the most part the contents will be condensed and expressed through long lines of blank verse. In *Song of the Hidden God* short, almost musical phrase dominates, and the poet's ideas and emotions are expressed so directly and spontaneously that comments seem superfluous. The poem is, indeed, a song: a song of the soul.

* * *

If at the core of *Song of the Hidden God* is the Eucharist as approached by the devout young seminarian, some sixteen years later another sacrament, that of Confirmation, is made the subject of a poem written by the bishop, and consequently treated in a somewhat different way. *Birth of the Confessors* is closely connected with its author's mission and is, as it were a spiritual account of one of his pastoral journeys in the diocese. Much later he thus told André Frossard about the importance he attributed to the visits in parishes and how deeply they were connected for him with the meaning of the sacraments:

> As the next crucial moment — which for its inner intensity I could compare to my early youthful experiences, let us accept the moment when as a young bishop I began to visit the parishes. The visits were conducted according to a traditionally accepted liturgical ritual, but also a certain religious and social custom. They were an important event in the life of every visited parish. I soon realized that the aim one had to aspire to is manifold, but fundamentally one

must assume and make real the *common experience of the sacramental dimension of the Church.* What mattered in that new perspective was not just the awareness that the Church is a place where one administers the sacraments and where one receives them — an awareness deeply connected already within the period of the first Confession and Holy Communion — but something else: *the Church lives through sacraments a life which is to the utmost its own* and which at the same time is the life of the community and the life of everyone in that community.[4]

The poem was written in 1961. What importance he attached to that particular sacrament we know from a sermon delivered by Cardinal Wojtyła in June 1969 in the town of Nowy Targ in the Podhale mountain region, on a canonical visit, when he also administered that sacrament:

A person who has been confirmed, in the depths of his soul retains the character and attitude of a child: the child of God. For a man never ceases to be God's child: the more mature in his faith, the more a child of God he is. "I mark you with the sign of the Cross." A novelty? You were marked with that sign at Baptism, then your parents taught you this sign of the cross. But today, the bishop, as it were, draws this sign of the cross to the surface, onto your forehead. Here on your forehead it is written that you are a Christian. You must not erase it, you must not hide it: you are to give testimony — you are to be a confessor.[5]

---

[4] From André Frossard, *"Nie lękajcie się!" Rozmowy z Janem Pawłem II* ["Be not afraid!" Conversations with John Paul II] (Kraków: Znak, 1983), p. 187.
[5] Rev. Adam Boniecki, ed. *Kalendarium życia Karola Wojtyły* [A Calendarium of the life of Karol Wojtyła] (Kraków: Znak, 1983), p. 187.

It is exactly this thought that was expressed in the poem written eight years earlier: that through the sacrament of Confirmation a confessor is born; the conscious confessor of Christ. The poem *Narodziny wyznawców* [Birth of the Confessors] consists of two symmetrical parts, reflecting a simple, yet very original idea: the sacrament of Confirmation is successively reflected upon by the bishop who administers it in a mountain village (Part I) and by a man who receives it, in the same place (Part II). The bishop thinks about the hidden sources of energy with which the world is charged — from the mountain stream to the stream of thought, and he realizes that he himself is the giver, who touches forces in man which ought to rise; the electricity which is a fact in nature but also a symbol. The bishop notices first the rows of human figures, then the eyes of people. We encounter here the image so frequent in his poetry: of eyes being the mirror of the soul. Man comes forward to meet "Tego, który go stale wyprzedza" [Him who always walks ahead, I.8:3], and having met him with spiritual courage becomes a bastion of faith.

In Part II of the poem the man who is being confirmed wonders how he is to be born anew, since he is like a wanderer walking along the mountain stream, with all the hazards of that journey. The image of the source, in its literal and metaphorical sense, which the author will soon develop in detail in his play *Promieniowanie ojcostwa* [Radiation of Fatherhood], is already present here. Man asks questions, resists the demand that he should strive so hard and merely "for himself," but recognizes that:

> Jeśli jednak prawda jest we mnie, musi wybuchnąć.
> Nie mogę jej odepchnąć, bo bym odepchnął sam siebie.
>   (II.2:1-2)

> [If truth is in me, it must break out.
> I cannot reject it, or I would reject myself.]

And so he sets foot on a footbridge which may be his heart, or thought; he thus achieves his purpose through emotion or through perception. With the passing of time man must preserve truth with his life, seeing "Thou" (God) everywhere and by taking into himself "dwa ciężary: ciężar nadziei i grozy" [the dual weight of hope and terror, II.6:4) he will reach the translucent depths. Thus it may be affirmed that the sacrament of Confirmation establishes a harmony between God, nature and man.

Birth of the Confessors, contrary to what one might think, is not limited to narrow "theological" deliberations, but is in fact curiously open to man and the world, with the utmost discretion and subtlety directing the reader's attention to problems of faith. A remarkable achievement is also the author's use of two narrators and the presentation of the theme from both angles: of him who administers and him who receives the sacrament.

* * *

Rozważanie o śmierci [Meditation on Death], Cardinal Wojtyła's last published poem before his election to the Papacy, does not directly focus on the sacrament called in the past Extreme Unction and now the Sacrament of the Infirm, but is none the less decidedly religious in character: it has as its theme the Christian attitude to death. These eschatological reflections on life and death are the work of a poet, thinker and pastor, conscious of the responsibility for human souls. But there is no trace here of moralizing or "pontificating." The poem is in fact a very personal statement on the drama of human existence with its inevitable implications. To overcome the fear of death is possible, but not at all easy: it requires an effort, a conscious act and cooperation with the mystery of grace.

The poem is divided into four, clearly separated yet logically connected parts. In the first, entitled "Myśli o dojrzewaniu" [Thoughts about Maturing], the author considers the dilemma facing man: exactly at a point when he reaches full maturity based on life experience, he nears death, and "dojrzałość jest także bojaźnią" [maturity is also fear, I.2:1] — the fear of death. But maturity means also love; means "pragnienie odejścia ku Temu, w Kim istnienie znajduje całą swą przyszłość" [desire to depart to Him in whom existence finds all its future, I.3:5]. Part Two, "Mysterium Paschale," states even more clearly that though passing of life on earth cannot be halted, the way out of the dilemma can be

81

seen in the view of life as the mystery of passing from death to a new life, in spite of man's material experience. The example of reversal of direction of passing has been given by HIM (i.e. by Christ) through His "Przejście [które] nazywa się PASCHA" [Passing called Pascha, II.4:6]. In Part Three, "Bojaźń, która leży u początku" [Fear which is at the Beginning], the author considers further the drama of passing, witnessed every day in the history of our planet, "miejsce śmierci pokoleń" [the place of death of generations, III.2:8], and states that God alone "może ciała nasze odebrać ziemi z powrotem!" [can retrieve our bodies from earth, III.1:15]. The poet's reflections culminate in Part Four, "Nadzieja, która sięga poza kres" [Hope which Reaches Beyond the End]. Hope counterbalances death. That "nadzieja dźwiga się w porę ze wszystkich miejsc / jakie poddane są śmierci" [hope rises timely from all places / subject to death IV.l:1-2]. Wherever people walk on the streets of cities, they cut across

> przestrzeń wielkiej tajemnicy,
> jaka rozciąga sią w każdym z nich między śmiercią własną
> i nadzieją
>
> (IV.1:7-8)

> [the space of great mystery,
> which stretches in everyone between their own death
> and hope.]

In that space there is HE, Christ, who alone gives sense to man's passing and is able to reclaim our bodies from the grave. Admittedly, "Śmierć jest jednak doświadczeniem kresu / i ma w sobie coś z unicestwienia —" [death is an experience of the end / and has something of annihilation in it, IV.4:1-2] but the hard struggle with oneself and with other people can be won, for hope placed in HIM will give a new life. One must entrust oneself to the mystery of God's Pascha leading to Resurrection. This the poet does in the form of prayer which the poem becomes when in Part III he begins to address God directly.

The thoughts expressed in the poem echo in poetic form those that had been uttered by Cardinal Wojtyła, for instance, in the homily at Rakowice Cemetery in Kraków on All Saints' day, 1967:

The reality of death speaks to us as the truth of eternal life. The reality of death, suffering and the cross speaks to us as the truth of Christ's Resurrection. On the foundations of that truth speaks the faith in body's resurrection and in eternal life. That faith fills our awareness and our hearts which sometimes react very forcefully with pain. Hand in hand with that pain goes faith and the hope of resurrection, that is to say, eternal union.[6]

The poet, however, found it necessary to add an imaginative dimension to the truths spoken in the sermon. The poem abounds in striking juxtapositions and reveals contradictions in that man's strivings and achievements (cosmic rockets are mentioned) do not allow him to surpass his limitations, unless he does it on a non-material level. The poet invokes Festus' admonition to St. Paul as an example of the earthly world's inability to comprehend metaphysical perspectives. His observation stretches from long-haired passers-by in short jackets to an interpolated magnificent definition of "człowiek. . . fragment świata urochomiony inaczej. . ."[man. . . a fragment of the world set in motion in a way that is different, IV.3:4] and there is even an amazingly concise, short-cut yet evocative description of Our Lord's life and Passion in the last section of Part Two. If *Meditation on Death* is a treatise it can also be regarded as a most impressive poetic statement.

* * *

For Catholics religious life is, of course, centered in the Church. The most significant and seminal event in the life of the

---

[6] Karol Wojtyła, *Kazania 1962-1978* [Sermons 1962-1978] (Kraków: Znak, 1979), p. 137.

Church in the 20th century was the Second Vatican Council. The newly elected capitular vicar of the metropolitan see of Kraków, Bishop Karol Wojtyła, took a very active part in the first session of the Council, from October 11 to December 8, 1962. On his return to Poland he recounted his Council experiences and stressed its great importance for the Church, as in this speech on December 20 at the Church of St. Anne in Kraków:

> The Council brought the Church much closer to us... From the very first day the Council was conscious of the fact that it was taking place in the view of all mankind, and from the very first day established contact with all mankind.[7]

Six days later in his homily on the Council at the church of St. Stephen he stated:

> This Council wants to be, in the intention of the Holy Father and in the work of all the bishops, an act of love. . . an act which will make its imprint on the history of modern man, somehow tear man away from hate and push him in the direction of love.[8]

It was not only the pastor, however, who went to the Council but also the poet. Can one wonder that the exhilarating Council experiences and observations touched also that aspect of his personality? Less than a year later the Kraków monthly *Znak* published a poem signed with the cryptonym A.J. entitled *Kościół — Pasterze i źródła* [The Church — Pastors and Sources]. The subtitle defined the place and the time when the poem was written: "St. Peter's Basilica, Autumn 1962: 11.X - 8.XII." Perhaps more than in the case of Karol Wojtyła's other works, *The Church* could be regarded as a cycle of poems rather than a long poem, but for its unifying theme — the church, in a dual sense: material, as a place of worship, in this instance the principal church of Christianity, whose

---

[7] Karol Wojtyła, quoted in Boniecki, p. 197.
[8] Karol Wojtyła, quoted in Boniecki, p. 197.

various parts the poem evokes; and in a spiritual sense, as the congregation of the faithful constituting the mystical body of Christ. This latter sense has been underlined by the participation of the successors of the Apostles — the bishops who have come here, to the grave of the first Apostle and the first bishop of Rome, St. Peter.

The poem consists of nine short parts, or poems, of six to twelve lines each. The subtitle speaks of "fragments." So we may assume that there would be more parts to the poem, but for the fact that duties of a father of the Council, more absorbing and responsible with the progress of the proceedings, made the poet give way to the bishop. But even what he had time to write down is a significant poetic evocation and record of his Council experiences, as always the case with him, defining his relation to them in a way at the same time complex and direct, intensely personal.

In the first poem, "Ściana" [Wall], the author looks at the wall of St. Peter's basilica, and this leads him to thoughts on man's destiny. These thoughts are continued in "Przepaść" [Abyss], on the basis of a metaphor derived from Psalm XLI: *Abyssus abyssum invocat* [Deep calleth on deep]. Here for the first time he invokes the image of the assembled fathers by the psalmist's reference to the forces of nature on their shoulders: it is they who shift the elements like a boat for the good of all men. In "Murzyn" [The Negro] the poet stresses the many-cultured nature of the Church and expresses his feeling of the essential unity with the Dear Brother, a bishop who has come from another continent. In "Posadzka" [The Marble Floor] by the Apostle's grave he addresses St. Peter, whom he unexpectedly calls "the floor," him who serves the feet of those passing over him "jak skała raciczkom owiec" [as rock serves the hooves of sheep, 9] while "pastwiskiem jest krzyż" [the cross is a pasture, 10]. He continues this thought in the next poem, "Krypta" [The Crypt]. He wishes to descend below the marble floor, into the Apostle's grave, in order "by odkryć człowieka / zadeptanego raciczkami owiec" [to find the man / trampled by hooves of sheep, 2-3] and the crypt will tell him that it is bound with the world which besieges it. It is hard not to be moved by this poem now that John Paul II has been laid to rest in this crypt, only a few meters from the grave of St. Peter.

85

In the next poem, "Synodus," the poet reflects on the Council Fathers and their work, as one of them. Even feeble old men are eager to accomplish their task; robbed by the world, they will remain "biedni i nadzy, a przy tym przejrzyści jak szkło, / które nie tylko odbija, lecz tnie" [poor and naked, and transparent like glass / that not only reflects, but cuts, 6-7] so that the split world might grow together again, lashed by conscience. The poem which follows, "Ewangelia" [Gospel] is a moving hymn in praise of truth: truth does not make man's life easier; it must be painful and difficult to contact, but it lifts man up and, having truth, "patrzymy spokojnie przed siebie, nie dosięga nas przestrach" [we look ahead calmly, fear does not reach us, 12]. This thought is continued in the next poem, "Źródła i ręce" [Sources and Hands] where the poet says that "Mamy / . . . / oparcie w słowach wypowiedzianych kiedyś" [we / . . . / have support in words spoken so long ago, 1] which are still spoken in fear "by nic w nich nie zmienić" [lest they should be changed in any way, 2].

The last poem, "Dwa miasta" [Two Cities] has the character of an epilogue: "Każde z dwu miast" [each of the two cities] — earthly and heavenly, the poet gives us to understand — "jest całością nieprzenośną z serca do serca. / Muszą tak żyć kosztem serca każdego z nas" [is a totality which cannot be carried from heart to heart; / each must live at our hearts' expense, 1-2]. And these reflections he makes above the lights of the Third City — no doubt Rome "które wieczór najbardziej jest sobą, gdy odrzuci całodzienny blichtr" [which is itself best in the evening, when the day's tinsel is cast off, 7]. Thus ended, or was broken off, the most remarkable poetic account of Vaticanum Secundum, an event which for the author was an important and lasting experience, as well as a spiritual journey to the sources of the Church he served and would go on serving.

* * *

The most prolific and consistent thread in Karol Wojtyła's poetry has been connected with the Bible: half a dozen of his poems are, as it were, evolved from events or persons described in either the Old Testament or the Gospels (in one case early Christian tradition). But as Biblical echoes and quotes abound in virtually all his other poems, so here, the Bible can be called a springboard for his ideas and reflections on important aspects of Christian life and doctrine, though used more imaginatively than it would be done by a priest in a sermon. For the most part, though, the Bible-inspired poems of Karol Wojtyła are spiritual treatises imbued with lyrical substance as well, and for this reason they are unique in religious poetry.

Most of the poems on these themes belong to an early phase of his poetry and were published in the fifties in *Tygodnik Powszechny*. If we abide by the Biblical chronology, the third poem to be published there, in 1952, *Myśl jest przestrzenią dziwną* [Thought is a Strange Space], is the only one to deal with an Old Testament subject. "Jacob's fight with the Angel" — as this subject is generally known — becomes the springboard for an entirely modern application in this philosophical poem. This dual aspect is rendered even by the symmetrical structure of the poem, which consists of four parts. The first and third, subdivided into three shorter poems, analyze the fundamental theme of this work; the second and fourth do not have this subdivision: the second part presents, so to speak, "Jacob's problem," while the fourth contains the message and conclusions for the modern man. The word space in the title of the poem, a frequent image in Karol Wojtyła's poems and plays, means the inner space in the mind and soul of man, rather than external physical space, hence the metaphor of the title. The human space in the poem ostensibly applies to Jacob; but in fact the poem's protagonist is modern man who has inherited Jacob's problem and carries it in himself.

The poet begins with a statement that sometimes "stajemy w obliczu prawd, / dla których brakuje nam słów, brakuje gestu i znaku" [we confront truths / for which we lack words, we lack gestures and signs I.1:1-2] because words and gesture will not carry the image, and we must enter it "samotni, by się zmagać podobnie jak Jakub" [alone and fight like Jacob. I.1:5] But our deeds are unable to embrace "wszystkie głębokie prawdy, nad którymi myśleć nam wypada" [all those profound truths which we ought to ponder over, I.1:9]. It may well be — continues the poet — that man suffers so that fundamental changes be brought about (an allusion no doubt to the enforced, sometimes inhuman, social changes introduced in Poland in the Stalinist period when the poem was written). But — he adds significantly: "człowiek najbardziej cierpi z braku 'widzenia'" [man suffers most for lack of vision, I.2:17] because words and gestures (so plentiful and meaningless at the time, we might add), will not carry the image, and we must struggle alone, like Jacob. Man suffers most for lack of "vision," i.e. because he is unable to see the most important things and must force his way through words which resist thoughts.

These statements are made in the second part of *Thought is a Strange Space*, transposed to the image of Jacob the shepherd, who — unlike men today — lived close to the forces of nature, "tak w nich po prostu tkwił" [was embedded in them, II:6]. He was not alienated, had the capacity for vision, understood his thoughts even if he was not articulate and "choć brakowało /mu/ słów" [lacked words to express them, II:8]. When he had sent away his animals, children and wives, "czuł, że ktoś go ogarnia i że nie ruszy się stąd" [in his loneliness he felt he was embraced, II:12] by a higher power, by Him (again the poet does not explicitly use the word God), and that Someone "otworzył jego świadomość do dna" [opened his awareness to the core, II:13]. And this enabled his thoughts "uchwycić w tym wszystkim najprostszą równowagę" [to grasp the simplest balance, II:20] clearly an example to us.

In Part Three of the poem, the author contemplates nature, exemplified in the drops of fresh rain, which focus in themselves "cała zieleń wiosennych liści" [the whole greenness of spring leaves, III.1:2] thus making them surmount their own limitations. And what about the thought of man? The poet addresses it directly, asking it to retain the sense of wonder over matters which it will not embrace in their entirety.

In the last part, entitled significantly "Dla towarzyszów drogi" [For the Companions of the Road] the poet concludes that in order to find the place where Jacob wrestled with the Angel it is not necessary to go to the lands of Arabia, but it suffices to enter into oneself, in silence and solitude. A day will come when appearances and gestures will fall away, "a zostanie w uczynkach naszych tylko to, co naprawdę jest" [and in our deeds only that will remain which truly is, IV.2:4].

The choice of Jacob to epitomize the need for the modern man to discover his awareness and ultimately — truth, is highly significant. Jacob was possibly the only human being to have seen God face to face, won a spiritual fight and received God's blessing. The poem draws the parallel and sets out the example for man today to open immense spaces of spiritual advancement in a poignant and telling way.

* * *

It is not a matter of chance that three of the poems in which Karol Wojtyła wished to express truths concerning the human person have women as their subjects; women who at one time or another came into contact with Christ. We were given some insight into his interest in that subject in bishop Wojtyła's retreat teachings to students at St. Anne's church in Kraków in April 1962:

> What strikes us when we consider the women around Christ, it is above all the fact that all these women, in contact with Christ, gain an inner independence. It is significant too that around Christ there are many fallen women. One such is the Samaritan woman whose conversation with Christ has been noted down by St. John in his Gospel. . . I wonder if you remember that conversation which takes place by a well: Christ asks her for water; she is surprised that he, an Israelite, should ask her for water, her — a Samaritan woman. Then from the natural water, the conversation turns to the supernatural water, the living water which is the drink for the immortal soul. And then, at a certain point Christ tells her: "Go and bring your husband. "I do not have a husband." "You tell the truth saying you have no husband." And then, we observe in the reaction of the woman a kind of liberation. Christ liberated her through truth, through the truth about her situation, through the truth about her life, and he won her confidence. There must have been something in the way he said this to her

because he did not humiliate, shame or degrade her, did not trample on her — but on the contrary, he lifted her up.[9]

Pieśń o blasku wody [Song of the Radiance of Water], published in the *Tygodnik Powszechny* in 1950, is concerned with that change in awareness experienced by the Samaritan woman as a result of her meeting with Christ and of his words to her as well as with the significance of that event for us today. The poem has as its motto the words of Jesus in the Gospel of St. John: "Whosoever drinketh of this water shall thirst again: but he that shall drink of the water that I will give him shall not thirst for ever." In the Gospel Christ continues: "The water that I give him shall be in him a well of water springing up into eternal life" (IV.14). The water in the well becoming the water of life is the symbol of grace that the poet will pursue further in his drama *Radiation of Fatherhood*.

The first of the eight parts of the poem *Song of the radiance of Water* is entitled "Nad studnią w Sychem" [By the Well at Sichar]. It contains a poetic description of the place where the event happened, and the first pointer to its importance for mankind. Turning to Christ the poet says: "w Tobie drży tylu ludzi / prześwietlonych blaskiem Twoich słów" [So many people tremble in you, / transparent by the radiance of your words, I:17-18]. There are so many barren souls, but Christ knows those people in his weariness and with his light. The next part, "Gdy otworzysz oczy w głębi fali. . ." [When You Open Your Eyes Deep in the Wave. . .], continues this theme, transferring it even more openly to the stones of our cities, where "drzwi /otwierają się/ z łoskotem" [doors open with bangs] and only rarely "ściana ludzka / . . . / otwiera się twarzą" [the human wall opens with the face of a passer-by, II:4,6]. The poet appeals that the eyes should "otworzyć się inaczej niż zwykle / I nie zapomnieć widzenia, którym wówczas wzrok się napawał" [open differently / and not forget the vision which filled them, II:23-24). That means one should look deep under the surface in order to see things in a way different from the everyday mundane look. If that happens, all that has been will be experienced and

---

[9] Karol Wojtyła, *Kazania 1962-1978*, p. 184.

enlightened anew. At this point we pass on to the short part three, "Słowa niewiasty u studni, które wypowiedziała odchodząc" [Words Spoken by the Woman at the Well while Departing] where the Samaritan woman confirms her newly acquired knowledge and her affinity with many people gained by her thanks to Christ. In later recollection of the meeting which follows, the Samaritan woman reflects on the uniqueness of Christ: "On poznawał inaczej" [His recognition was different, IV:2]. He was like no other man. He made her aware of her own suppressed thoughts, her shame and pain, "ból, który . . . odmienia się w miłość" [the pain that...changes into love, IV:21-22]. Perhaps the most astonishing is the fifth part, "Rozmowy, które prowadził w niej on i ludzie ze ściany wieczoru" [Conversations He and the People from the Wall of Evening had Within Her]. The inner drama of the Samaritan woman has found here its external expression in a dialogue evocation in which Christ is present, but she herself has been substituted by the human mass — called here the wall of the evening — which was already mentioned in Part Two. Through her He tells them that they are not alone: "nigdy, ani na chwilę nie odłącza się od was mój profil, / który w was staje się prawdą" [never, even for a moment does my profile leave you, / which in you becomes truth V:12-13). They even threaten: "mamy krew / i krwią możemy uderzyć!" [we have blood / and with blood can strike! V:23-24]. But Christ will redeem them with *His* blood. He replies: "Przyszedłem przeważyć krwią. / Przyszedłem szukać znużenia — podobny wam" [I have come to outweigh blood with blood. / I have come to seek weariness, being like you V:25-26]. This dramatic dialogue is followed by reflections of the Samaritan woman, speaking again in the first person the text of the last three parts of the poem. In "Samarytanka" [Samaritan Woman] she states that "Owa studnia złączyła mnie z Tobą" [the well has joined me to You VI:1) and from now on she is enclosed in His eyes. In "Rozważania ponowne"[Renewed Meditations] she gives, herself and us, a detailed account of her great experience and the transformation which happened in her: "O, jakże zostałam dźwignięta. . . Ten ciężar, który ze mnie wyjąłeś — ja rozpoznam dopiero powoli" [Oh how I have been uplifted. . . The burden you have lifted from me — I will sense only slowly VII:11,16]. She begins to speak the hymn of praise and happiness which culminates in Part Eight, "Pieśń o blasku wody" [Song of the Radiance of Water] which is exactly that: her song about the inner happiness she has found when she "przyszłam zaczerpnąć / tylko wody dzbanem /. . ./ O jak dobrze! Nie zdołam Cię całego przenieść w siebie — / ale pragnę, byś pozostał " [came /only/ to draw / water in a jug /. . ./ How good it is! I can never take all of you in me, but I want you to remain" VIII:1-2, 6-7].

As in other poems, philosophical reflection and theological statement are expressed through impressive poetic images. And as always, the Biblical model has for the author a contemporary relevance and reveals his immense understanding and compassion for human weakness, subtly, though not explicitly, pointing the way to purgation of sins through confession.

* * *

On November 1, 1950 Pope Pius XII proclaimed the dogma of the Assumption. Religious celebrations connected with the proclamation in the Archdiocese of Kraków took place on December 8, the Feast of the Immaculate Conception of Our Lady. For the occasion the *Tygodnik Powszechny* devoted its first page to Andrzej Jawień's poem *Matka* [Mother]. The poem may be considered as evidence of how deeply its author felt about the divine — and human — motherhood of Our Lady. The mystery of the Birth of God who was also man is seen here not so much through the mind of a theologian as through the eyes of a poet in a very personal, also unique way. The very concept can be regarded as daring. Of the poem's three parts, the first and third are spoken by Our Lady, who addresses her son Jesus; the second — by the Apostle John, who addresses her.

In the first part "Pierwsza chwila uwielbionego Ciała" [The First Moment of the Adored Body], Our Lady — after the Ascension and before her Assumption — reminisces on the childhood of Christ in a series of beautiful poetic images, recalling the "cisza dalekich uliczek zatrzymana w przestrzeni jak szkło" [stillness of far away little streets, arrested in space like glass, I.1:2] the time when the little Child of God calls out to her like every human child: "Mama — Mama." Those simple days of the childish voice are so far away, she tells her Son, but her first moment of wonder is now as fresh as it ever was. She recalls the moment of Annunciation which was the beginning not only of a New Man, but of her own awareness of things divine. (cf I.2, "Słowa, które rozrastają się we mnie" [Words Which Grow in Me]). She then recalls her great, unceasing astonishment over the Child which was Her own, but was also God's Child; it was the fruit of her life and body, but His light and radiance were not of her (I.3, "Zdumienie nad Jednorodzonym [Amazement Over the Only Child]). Finally, in lines of beauty unparalleled in modern religious poetry, Mary reflects on how the realization of her Son's divinity grew in her and how she gradually matured to the contemplation of his mystery, in which "to ja w Twej tajemnicy cała skupiona trwam" [it is I, wholly attentive, who persists in Your Mystery. "Skupienie dojrzałe," [Mature Concentration, I.4:15]).

In the second part of the poem, the author considers the problem of spiritual motherhood (which later became a major theme in the drama *Radiation of Fatherhood*) via the example of the relation of St. John the Apostle to Our Lady.[10] St. John recalls first the moment of his calling:

> Ja jestem rybak Jan. Tak mało jest we mnie
> do kochania.
> Jeszcze czuję: u brzegu jeziora — pod stopami
> drobniutki żwir —
> i nagle — On.
>
> (II.1:5-8)

> [I am John the fisherman. There isn't much in me
> to love.
> I still feel: on the lake shore, tiny gravel
> under my feet
> and suddenly — He.]

---

[10] . . . And on a non-literary level in his book *Miłość i odpowiedzialność* [Love and Responsibility], Part IV: "Justice with Regard to the Creator," chapter "Vocation," section "Fatherhood and Motherhood."

At Christ's behest, he had called Mary — Mother, so now he asks that she should not withdraw her love (cf. "Prośba Jana" [John's Entreaty, II.1]). Though her Son has now departed, he can be regained through Communion which, though taken in the form of bread, will be for Mary a recollection of the little child's head, hugging her (cf. "Przestrzeń, która w tobie została" [Space which has Remained in You, II.2]).

In the third part of the poem, "Otwarcie pieśni," [Opening of the Song, III.1]), Mary describes symbolically her life and mission on earth as a song. Finally, she reflects on her death here on earth, which for her will be a union with her Son and passing on to a new time. It will also be the beginning of a new song about her Son's life, the Event "które się w każdym człowieku poczyna jawnie i skrycie / — a we mnie stało się ciałem" [which is conceived in every man openly and secretly, / and in me was made flesh, III.2:19-20].

Mother is, indeed, Mary's joyous hymn of praise to her Son, sung at the end of her earthly life. The joy, as the author was to say later in a sermon:

> is the joy of her ultimate motherhood, joy of the motherhood for which she has paid with the suffering and cross of her own Son, it is the joy of motherhood, which is her motherhood for us.[11]

The poem is also a hymn of praise to Our Lady, sung by its author in full command of his artistic powers, a peak, indeed, of Marian poetry in our time.

* * *

The last of the poems about "women around Christ"— *Odkupienie szuka Twego kształtu, by wejść w niepokój wszystkich ludzi* [Redemption Seeks Your Shape to Enter All People's Anxiety] — belongs to the group of Karol Wojtyła's works which

---

[11] Karol Wojtyła, *Kazania 1962-1978*, p. 119. "Birth of Our Lady," Limanowa, 11 September 1966.

were published only after his election to the papacy. The form is characteristic for his later poetry: long lines of free verse, gradually turning into poetic prose of philosophical-religious discourse. The poem broadly concerns St. Veronica and her part in the process of redemption accomplished through the Passion of Our Lord. Like Simon of Cyrene to whom the author had also devoted a poem some years earlier, Veronica found herself on the Saviour's path to the Golgotha. Unlike Simon she was there of her own free will. Her deed — the wiping of the face of the passing tormented Christ — is embedded in Christian consciousness, although the Gospels are silent about her. This is what Cardinal Wojtyła said about Veronica in his Lenten retreat before Pope Paul VI and members of the Vatican curia in March 1976, probably about the time he wrote the poem:

> Tradition has bequeathed us Veronica. Perhaps she is a counterpart to the story of the man from Cyrene. For although, being a woman, she could not physically carry the cross or be called upon to do so, there is no doubt that she did in fact carry the cross with Jesus: she carried it in the only way open to her at the time, in obedience to the dictates of her heart: she wiped his face... There will undoubtedly be many who will ask: "Lord, when did we ever do these things for you?" And Jesus will reply: "Whatever you did for the least of these brethren of mine, you did for me" (cf. Mt 25,37-40). In fact the Saviour leaves his imprint on every single act of charity, as on Veronica's handkerchief.[12]

It is highly significant that Cardinal Wojtyła quotes Matthew's Gospel in respect of Veronica's deed. She literally wiped the Saviour's face but she would do the same, if she were to help any man, thus entering the mystic union with Christ, for "whatever you did for the least of these brethren of mine, you did for me."

---

[12] Karol Wojtyła, *Sign of Contradiction*, translated from the Italian by Mary Smith (Middlegreen, Slough: St. Paul Publications, 1979), p. 189.

This is the thought at the root of the poem. It is as it were, the reverse of Karol Wojtyła's poem *Profile Cyrenejczyka* [Profiles of the Cyrenian] where each and every man has been shown as Simon of Cyrene. Here, however, Veronica's deed, executed once in history, repeats itself many times, as the assistance given to any man is a work for Christ. The poem is divided into four parts. The first two "Weronika" [Veronica] and "Siostra" [Sister] consider Veronica's deed, its meaning for herself and for all men. Thanks to the action of Veronica, our sister, people grow and through the tangles of life find their way to eternity. The poetic images associate the growth of nature and its natural processes with the inner growth and spiritual development of man, In Part Three, "Imię" [Name], the verse changes almost imperceptibly to poetic prose, and the poet traces the emergence of Veronica's name to the "ludzie, którzy naprzód dostrzegali ścieżkę, jaką biegłaś, jaką się przedzierałaś, / idąc z wszystkimi, którzy szli w kierunku miejsca Skazania" [people who first noticed the path you ran, cutting your way. . . to the place of Execution, II.1:1-2]. She wanted so much to have His image in her heart, to feel. "Widzenie jest przestrzenią miłości" [Seeing is the space of love, II.2:5], He says and adds that her cloth expressed the longing of hearts who did not have to grope in the dark, since they saw that her "ścieżka / . . . / jest równoległa / do drogi Skazańca" [path is parallel / to the way of the Condemned Man II.4:4-5]. The poem finds its culmination in the fourth part, "Odkupienie" [Redemption]. Departure of man — the poet says — causes a void in the heart, yearning for closeness, only assuaged by redemption "/które jest/ nieustanną bliskością *TEGO, KTÓRY ODSZEDŁ*" [/which is/ a constant closeness of Him who has departed IV.2:6]) leaving "odbite na płótnie Oblicze" [His countenance imprinted on the linen, IV.3:7). Redemption enters people's anxiety in order to soothe it. . . Thus the significance of Veronica's deed is fully "explained" in the context of the Divine plan of Redemption.

* * *

On March 30, 1958, which happened to be Palm Sunday, the *Tygodnik Powszechny* published a poem by Andrzej Jawień, written the previous year, entitled *Profiles of the Cyrenean,* yet another work inspired by the Passion of our Lord. Reading these poems we are reminded how devoted Karol Wojtyła was since childhood to the *Via Crucis.* It is also clear that while considering Christ's Passion he always contemplated its profound relevance to the entire human family for whom Christ gave his life; particularly the relevance for the confused, insecure man of today. Not by chance Simon of Cyrene, that casual passer-by, forced to help Christ carry the cross to Golgotha, seemed to the poet a figure relevant for our own time. In the same *Via Crucis* meditation during the 1976 Vatican retreat, where he talked about the willing Veronica, Cardinal Wojtyła asked a number of questions regarding the unwilling Simon:

> How long did he go on resenting being forced into this? How long did he go on walking beside this condemned man yet making it clear that he had nothing in common with Him, nothing to do with His crime, nothing to do with His punishment? How long did he go on like that, divided within himself, a barrier of indifference existing between him and the man who was suffering? "I was naked, I was thirsty, I was in prison" (cf. MT 25:35-36), I have carried the cross. . . and: Did you carry it with me? . . . Did you really carry it with me right to the end? (cf. MT 16:24). We do not know.[13]

Again referring to MT 25, he also significantly points to MT 16, where Jesus said: "If any man would come after me, let him deny himself, and take up his cross and follow me." The question of willingness is the crucial one. In *Profiles of the Cyrenean* the poet Wojtyła had attempted to probe into Simon and the aspects of latter-day Simons; that is to say us, since most of us are Simons of Cyrene. We have to carry crosses we do not want to carry, and we rebel against them. How much better it would be if we followed Christ of our own volition, ran up to him, as Veronica had done.

---

[13] Karol Wojtyła, *Sign of Contradiction,* pp. 188-189.

The three-part poem has a symmetrical structure. In Part One, "Zanim jeszcze potrafiłem rozróżnić wiele profilów" [Before I Could Discern Many Profiles] the poet considers the different profiles of man and declares that the profile of the Cyrenean is known to him best. He then contrasts the peace of nature with the bustle of modern civilization where human torment does not even always have a spectacular character; it could, for instance be the toil of "kobiety / piszące na maszynie po osiem godzin codziennie" [women / typing eight hours a day I.2:6-7]. Apart from Simon, he significantly invokes Mary Magdalene, yet another woman, who — like the Samaritan woman, or Veronica — came into contact with Christ, and since then her life was never the same again. Simon is mentioned along with her. Perhaps he, too, having made the first step, will continue. If the way is hard, if you feel you are drowning, just "wtedy / . . . / nadejdzie On i swoje własne jarzmo / przeniesie na twoje barki. Poczujesz, ockniesz się, zadrżysz" [then He will come and put / His own burden on your shoulders. At this, you will awaken I.5).

It is in Part Two, "Teraz już zaczynam rozróżniać poszczególne profile" [Now I Begin to Discern Individual Profiles] that the poet shows the burdens of today's Cyreneans in fourteen examples in as many shorter poems. Even the titles of some depict the burdens their subjects have to carry: "Melancholik" [Melancholic], "Schizotymik" [Schizoid], "Niewidomi" [The Blind], "Dziewczyna zawiedziona w miłości" [A Girl Disappointed in Love]. But there is also "Robotnik z fabryki samochodów" [The Car Plant Worker], whose monotonous work produces that splendid product of our civilization — the motor car; or "Robotnik z fabryki broni" [The Armaments Factory Worker], who says: "Świat, który tworzę nie jest dobry — / lecz ja nie tworzę złego świata!" [Though the world I create is not good / the world's evil is not of my making II.10:12-13]. But even a seemingly gorgeous profession like "Aktor" [The Actor] can be a cross. He creates so many people, but "czyż ten, który ze mnie ocalał, może patrzeć na siebie bez trwogi?" [can the real man who survives in him look at himself without fear? II.4:7]. Even Dzieci [Children] — a natural state of human beings, who "dorastają znienacka przez miłość" [grow unawares through love, II.6:1] and then have to go through all the vicissitudes of the

98

human condition, strive to differentiate between good and evil, and take upon themselves the destiny of generations. There is also Mary Magdalene, who must painfully adjust her body to the transformation her spirit has undergone already. We find also more general reflections on the hardships of men: "Myśli człowieka" [Man's Thoughts] and "Rysopis człowieka" [Descriptions of Man]. Such profiles as "Człowiek emocji" [Man of Emotion], "Człowiek intelektu" [Man of Intellect], "Człowiek woli" [Man of Will] all signify that qualities regarded as positive can become a burden, as when the "man of will" complains that for him "Nie ma miejsca na serce i myśl, / jest tylko ten moment, który wybucha / we mnie jak krzyż" [there is no place for heart and thought, / only the moment exploding in me, / the cross II.14:12-14]. It follows that we cannot sacrifice with impunity some positive qualities for others, emotion for intellect or vice versa. In that cycle of fourteen poems there is no room for all of today's Cyreneans, and it was not the poet's intention to recite a catalogue of all misfortunes, ailments, crosses, difficult qualities or professions. But there is a cross-section, considered with precision and felt with compassion.

We are thus led to the conclusion in Part Three of the poem, entitled "Szymon z Cyreny" [Simon of Cyrene] which has exactly the same length as Part One. It defines a kind of synthesis of the problem of the Cyrenean in our time. He wants to be left in peace, without offending anyone, without being broken into by "nędzarz, skazaniec ni Bóg" [a beggar, condemned man, or God, III:5]. He wants to be self-sufficient. Still, he wants "to be just," so he bargains with the tormentors "over that Man" (III:6-7). But he cannot be just. He thinks himself too weak, and his small world too insignificant in God's great world. He reproaches God with the power to smash his little world, but admits:

> każdy człowiek się mieści /w Tobie/
> / . . . /
> Ledwo stoję na progu,
> skąd widać nowy świat!
> / . . . / wszyscy krążą na granicy Boga.
> / . . . /
> Sprawiedliwość domaga się buntu

— lecz przeciw komu bunt?
                                    (III:31,32-33,36)

[all men are contained in You.
                    / . . . /
I only stand on a threshold,
glimpse a new world
/ . . . / Everyone gropes near God's frontier
                    / . . . /
Justice demands rebellion
            — but rebellion against whom?]

These closing lines epitomize the dilemma of the modern man, who
has lost his way, and in whom good and evil are so entwined. Thus
in Karol Wojtyła's poem the profiles of modern Simons, carrying
their burdens with reluctance, form the complex face of tormented
humanity, in their unconscious search for God.

                            * * *

        At the end of the second session of the Vatican Council in
which he had taken part, bishop Karol Wojtyła went with a number
of other bishops of various nationalities on a pilgrimage to the Holy
Land (December 5-l0). On his return he several times commun-
icated his impressions in public and as capitular vicar of the Kraków
archdiocese (soon to be nominated metropolitan archbishop) issued
also a lengthy letter to its priests, entitled "Two weeks in the Holy
Land." Apart from detailed descriptions of the places seen and
events witnessed, he explained the reasons for his, and his fellow-
bishops' trip:

        We feel that working in the Council on the
        regeneration of the Church, we must turn directly to
        Our Lord himself, whose Mystical Body the Church
        is. Hence the desire to visit the places where He was
        born, where He lived, taught and worked, where He
        also suffered, died on the cross, rose from the dead
        and ascended into heaven. . . I did not regard my

> participation as a personal or private property, but as
> the grace given me by Providence also for others.[14]

That is the reason, he says, why he wants to share his experiences and reflections with his brethren in the priesthood. In the letter he describes the role of the places he has visited in the life of the Saviour and their significance for Christians today.

No wonder that, as his participation in the first session of the Council the year before, so now the equally profound experience of Holy Land found, apart from pastoral, also its artistic expression. In the June, 1965 issue of *Znak* there appeared, under the cryptonym A.J., the poem *Wędrówka do miejsc świętych* [Journey to the Holy Places], similar in its form to *The Church*. On the example of this poem we can observe how fluid in the work of Karol Wojtyła is the borderline between poetry and philosophical-theological reflection with literary flair. The poem consists of five parts. Halfway through the second part, the author's characteristic long-line blank verse and its rhythm change into poetic prose. As far as the content is concerned, *Journey to the Holy Places* is by no means a geographic or illustrative description of external observations but — which is something not at all surprising with this author — a journey to the interior of the human soul, as it were. In confrontation with the places visited the dominating factor is reflection on their meaning for Christians. The places themselves, though existing in reality, are also signs of the events that created our faith, and symbols which are to strengthen it in us, today.

Already in Part One, entitled "Oliveti," the poet, while looking at the Mount of Olives, addresses Christ recalling "fragment ziemi widziany wciąż jeszcze przez Ciebie" [a fragment of earth still seen by you, I:4] and because of that "każde spojrzenie od tysiąc dziewięciuset lat / przechodzi w to jedno spojrzenie, które się nigdy nie zmienia" [every gaze since one thousand nine hundred years / passes into that one gaze that never alters I:7-8]. This thought is developed in Part Two, "Pustynia Judzka" [The Desert of Judea]: the poet contemplates this land, which in itself is not beautiful, but it was in it that "Ten, który Jest, stał się nam Ojcem"

---

[14] Karol Wojtyła, quoted in Boniecki, pp. 206-207.

[He who Is became Father to us II:28]; a land bound to Him for ever. In the longest central part, called "Tożsamości" [Identities], the author analyzes the identity of the places of two thousand years ago as our own "pilgrimage to identity."[15] It is not a pilgrimage to stones, houses or streets. "Jest tożsamość odnajdywania się w krajobrazie. Do niej pielgrzymuję. To miejsce jest święte" [It is the identity of finding oneself in the landscape. I am on a pilgrimage to it. This place is holy, III:9]. In the identity of the places at the roots of our faith we find our identity in faith. The fourth Part, "Jedno drzewo" [One Tree] traces the rise of religion from the Biblical wanderings of Abraham, "widomy początek nowego Adama" [the visible beginning of the new Adam, IV:1] to the rise of Christianity, the development of man through the tree of the Cross, which for us has become the "studnia Jakuba" [well of Jacob, IV:9]— the water of life. The final Part, "Miejsce wewnętrzne" [The Inner Place], defines the place of man: "Miejsce moje jest w Tobie. Twoje miejsce jest we mnie" [My place is in You. Your place is in me, V:1], he writes. The external places where God used to walk on earth, where he died, but where he also established the sacrament of the Eucharist, lead us to understand and define the inner place "w którym Siebie udzielasz a mnie przyjmujesz" [where You give yourself and accept me, V:5]. It is highly significant that this concluding part of the poem is also a prayer. Reading this work of the poet-philosopher we understand best how true the words of the bishop were in the already quoted letter to priests that the stay in the Holy Land "took us into what is the most vital and holiest in that land."[16]

* * *

Karol Wojtyła's deep attachment to his native Poland is well known. It has always been based on the equally profound conviction that the country's development is intrinsically connected with its Christian roots and spirit. Adherence to it made the country great; departure — made it fall into difficulties and cause its

---

[15] *Pielgrzymuję do tożsamości* [I am on a pilgrimage to identity], the poet declares in III:9]

[16] Karol Wojtyła, quoted in Boniecki, p. 210.

eventual downfall. This thought underlies his poems on Polish themes, except that in the earliest of them the emphasis is somewhat different, as the work is devoted to social issues; but even there the Christian awareness of the problem is of paramount importance.

In the June 1957 issue of the monthly *Znak* a poem signed "Andrzej Jawień," entitled *Kamieniołom* [The Quarry] was published. Its theme — workers and physical labor. It was written in 1956, a significant date. In June 1956 workers in the city of Poznań demonstrated in the streets, demanding their basic rights and an improvement of working conditions. Tanks were brought out by the Communist authorities, and over fifty people lost their lives. The Poznań events could well have contributed to the poem having been written in that year, yet it is not an overtly political work. Let us recall the title: "The Quarry." During the German occupation of Poland in World War Two, from 1939 to 1944, the young Karol Wojtyła was employed as a physical worker in the Solvay chemical works near Kraków — early on as an assistant blasting rocks at the quarry. A dozen or so years later he referred to those experiences in order to express his innermost feelings with regard to physical work and the men engaged in it. It is amazing that in spite of such a long lapse of time, his memory of those days produced images so direct, and emotional commitment of such intensity. As in many of his poems, the subject described is seen both directly and is the focus of a grand metaphor. Drawing on his experience of work in the quarry, to the Stalinist axiom that the present generation of workers should sacrifice everything for the good of future generations, the author opposes the Christian view that every man is a unique person and must not be exploited in this way.

Above all, however, "The Quarry" is a hymn in praise of human labor, its value and meaning. In Part One, "Tworzywo" [The Material], the poet defines the nature of work in a quarry, shows how human energy cuts and shapes the stone for the use of man. But he adds that "cała wielkość tej pracy znajduje się wewnątrz człowieka" [the whole greatness of this work is within man I.1:5]. And although the electric current is useful, it is not it that "rozwiązuje ich /. . . / moc" [unbinds / . . . / the strength, I.2:7] of the stones, "ale ten, co ją nosi w swych dłoniach: / robotnik" [but he who carries it in his hands: / the worker I.8-9]. The poem abounds

103

in images of striking beauty, like one of "dłonie /które/ są krajobrazem serca" [hands /which/ are the landscape of the heart I.3:1]. This particular image is then connected with the main theme, that of manual labor.

Part Two, "Natchnienie" [Inspiration], analyzes the motivation behind human toil. "Przez pracę dojrzewa człowiek / ona bowiem niesie natchnienie trudnego dobra" [Man matures through work / which carries the inspiration of a difficult good II.1:8-9], but love which should be at the basis of work finds its supplementation in anger (this may be a veiled reference to recent events in Poznań). Part Three, "Uczestnictwo" [Participation], a superb sequence of eight quatrains, while continuing a dissertation on the essence of labor, expresses also the poet's enduring solidarity with his fellow-workers, subtly pointing to the different tasks allotted to different people:

> Znam was, wspaniali ludzie, ludzie bez manier
>   i form.
> Umiem patrzeć w serce człowieka
>   bez obsłon i bez pozorów.
> Czyjeś ręce należą do pracy, czyjeś ręce należą
>   do krzyża.
>   / . . . /
> Młodzi szukają drogi. Wprost w moje serce
> uderza droga wszystkich.
>   (III:13-16; 19-20)

> [I know you, magnificent people, people
>   without manners of pretence.
> I know how to look into men's hearts
>   without disguise.
> Some hands are for toil, some belong to the cross.
>   / . . . /
> The young search for a road. The roads of all
> drive straight at my heart.]

The final part of the poem, dedicated "pamięci towarzysza pracy" [to the memory of a fellow-worker] brings a vivid description of a worker's death: "kamień / . . . / miażdżył mu skroni / i / . . . / przeciął komór serca" [the stone crushed his brow / and cut the ventricles of his heart IV.1:4-5], his being carried away by other workers: "wzięli ciało, szli milczącym szeregiem" [They took his body, walked silently in single file, IV.2], "złożyli go milcząc plecami na płachcie żwiru" [they laid him down in silence, his back on a sheet of gravel IV.5:3], the coming of the bereaved family: "przyszła znękana żona i wrócił ze szkoły syn" [came the despondent wife, the son returned from school, IV.5:4], and the conclusions

> Czy jego gniew ma się tylko na innych przelać?
> Czy nie dojrzewał w nim samym własną miłością i prawdą?
> Czyż mają go jak tworzywo zużyć pokolenia
> i wyrzuć z treści najgłębszej, jedynej i własnej?
>   (IV.6:1-4)

> [Is his anger only to spill over onto others?
> Had it not grown in himself with his own love and truth?
> Is he to be used only as raw material for other generations,
> deprived of his profoundest substance, uniquely his own?]

But it should be remembered, the poet adds, that in the "wewnętrzną strukturę świata" [world's inner structure] he has taken with him, "miłość tym wyżej wybuchnie, im większy nasyca ją gniew" [love will explode the higher, the greater the anger that permeates it, IV.7:4].

An actual event remembered from the time when he himself worked in a quarry may be taken to have inspired a dirge for the workers killed in Poznań. But, like the rest of the poem, it is universal in its appeal. Both in its intellectual substance and on its artistic level, "The Quarry" is an outstanding work in the body of poetry devoted to human labor. It is also proof of how fruitful and meaningful in its human sense the heavy physical work which he had of dire necessity to engage in during the war was for its author. He had the strength, the will and the capacity for full commitment to it, like to so many other tasks he undertook in the course of his life. At a time when he wrote the poem as a young priest it was a personal and fully credible statement and a comment on the abuses of the enforced Marxist approach to labor in his country. Later his voice sounded just as genuine when he talked about problems of human labor and social justice at the Vatican and in the course of his travels to so many countries.

* * *

In the April 1966 issue of *Znak*, the then metropolitan of Kraków, Karol Wojtyła, published under the cryptonym A.J. his second longest poem (*Song of the Hidden God* is the longest), entitled *Wigilia wielkanocna 1966* [Easter Vigil 1966]. The date in the title was highly significant. It was the millenary year, celebrated in Poland with solemnity but, unfortunately, with a duality characteristic for a Communist-ruled Christian country. The authorities celebrated the thousandth anniversary of the Polish state; with her celebrations the Church reminded us that this was also the millennium of Christianity in Poland and that the country's history, even though today's rulers would rather forget this, was from its beginnings bound with the history of the Church. The poem was Karol Wojtyła's offering for the millennium and will remain as one of the most impressive literary monuments for that occasion.

In a striking manner, *Easter Vigil 1966* combines meditation on the mystery of Christ's Resurrection with a view of the history of Poland from the perspective of the millennium. Associations of this kind have a long tradition in Polish literature. It is enough to recall that the action of Stanisław Wyspiański's drama *Akropolis* takes place — as its author tells us — at the Wawel castle in Kraków "on the great night of Easter." In Polish Romantic poetry, Poland, as "Christ of the Nations," buried by her enemies, was to rise from the grave like the Saviour. It would be wrong, though, to suppose that in his poem Karol Wojtyła follows a traditional Romantic "messianism." His is rather a philosophy-of-history kind of poem, in which the poet, tracing the course of human history, in this case the history of his country, aims at discovering the deeper sense of man beyond history: man in God.

The poem consists of seven parts which subdivide into sections. In the four poems of Part One, "Inwokacja" [Invocation] the poet defines his attitude, as that of a modern man, to the visions of old chroniclers and historians. He then analyzes the transience of man on earth against the background of history written by God, and asserts that although the "ciało ludzkie w historii umiera częściej niż drzewo, umiera wcześniej / Trwa człowiek poza progiem śmierci" [human body in history dies more often and earlier than the tree, / man endures beyond the threshold of death II.2:1-2], endures in God. Through history he searches for the image and presence of the Man-God, Christ.[17]

In the second part, "Opowieść o drzewie zranionym" [Tale of the Wounded Tree], the poet goes back to the beginnings of the Polish state, evokes a striking vision of its first ruler Mieszko — who introduced Christianity to Poland — planting his orchard for future generations.[18] The poet develops from this a grand metaphor about the growth of the wounded tree in his country — symbolizing the development of Christianity, tracing its beginnings to the Holy Cross. In the next part, "Spojenie" [Welds, or Joints], the poet traces further the spiritual development of the nation which gave the world Copernicus, who altered our vision of the universe. The great fact of his discoveries did not in any way cancel the inner meanings which had been imbued centuries before by the baptism of the Polish tribes, meanings which gave them Fatherhood, Word, Love and the Sign. In the fourth part, "Rozwój języka" [Development of Language], the poet asserts that the human language had developed from the simplest words and meanings to complex ones, but it was God who "wielości słów przyniósł jedność" [brought unity to the multiplicity of words, IV:22].

In Part Five, "Echo pierworodnego płaczu" [Echo of the Firstborn Cry], the poet considers in an illuminating way the problem of freedom, so well known to his countrymen. He points out the abuses of freedom which after a thousand years resulted in

---

[17] John Paul II considered his reflections on history in the poem *Easter Vigil* so important that in the last book published in his lifetime, *Pamięć i tożsamość* [Memory and Identity] he quotes extensively from the "Invocation." See pp. 159-160 of the original Znak edition.

[18] It is worth noting that Easter Saturday (Easter Vigil) 1966 was the one thousandth anniversary of Mieszko's baptism, which took place on 14 April 966.

"bogactwo klęsk" [riches of defeats, V.1:10]. In the name of freedom violent and unjust deeds were also committed, until in the end freedom "pozostawała wielką próżnią do wypełnienia" [remained a great vacuum to be filled, IV.2:5], and hope for that was placed in "Twój Znak" [Your Sign, IV.2:6] — the Cross. When reading this part of the poem one is reminded of its striking affinity to a passage in the homily delivered by Pope John Paul II at the shrine of Our Lady of Częstochowa at Jasna Góra on June 13, 1987:

> The difficult gift of freedom, which makes us exist between good and evil. Between salvation and rejection.
>
> But freedom can turn into license. And anarchy — as we know also from our own history — can mislead men with the fiction of "golden freedom."
>
> We witness all the time how freedom becomes the nucleus of various "captivities" for man, people, societies. . . Man can only be truly free through love. Love of God above all and love of men: brethren, neighbors.[19]

The sixth part. "Obrzęd"[Ritual] is a great hymn of praise of our earth which for the poet "stała się obrzędem" [has become a ritual, VI.1:1], all-embracing, life-giving and leading man, through his seeming transience, to eternal Wisdom. Man then acquires the one Light which the earth cannot give him. The short final part is entitled, like the entire poem, "Wigilia wielkanocna 1966" [Easter Vigil 1966]. The tangled history of man, considered in the poem, finds its resolution on Easter night,

---

[19] John Paul II, *Trzecia pielgrzymka do Polski — Przemówienia, homilie* [The Third Pilgrimage to Poland — Speeches, Homilies] (Kraków: Znak, 1987), p. 170.

gdy czuwając przy Twoim grobie,
    najbardziej jesteśmy Kościołem —
jest to noc walki, jaką toczy w nas rozpacz z nadzieją:
ta walka wciąż się nakłada na wszystkie walki dziejów.
                                                    (VII:1-3)

[when keeping watch by Your grave we are the Church
    more than ever —
it is the night of struggle between despair and hope within us:
a struggle imposed on all struggles in history.]

Everything now falls into place because:

Tej Nocy obrzęd ziemi dosięga swego początku.
Tysiąc lat jest jak jedna Noc: Noc czuwania
    przy Twoim grobie.
                                                    (VII:6-7)

[On this Night the earth's ritual reaches its beginning.
A thousand years is like one Night: the Night
    of keeping watch by Your grave.]

    In this prayer-like conclusion the poet gives us to
understand that it is in the mystery of Christ's death and
resurrection that the meaning of a millennium of history is made
clear. His view of history, like his poetry — so concerned with the
lot of man — is above all — theocentric.

* * *

    In a sense, two further poems which remained unpublished
until after Cardinal Wojtyła's election to the papacy continue the
thoughts of *Easter Vigil 1966*. In *Myśląc ojczyzna. . .* [Thinking my
Country], written in 1974, poetry is again combined with philosophy
and meditation. Through poetic images he expresses his feelings
and thoughts relating to his native country, his roots. The six parts
are in turn very short lyrical poems and longer reflections with a
historiosophic slant. The poem expresses its author's love for the

109

land where he was born and his great concern with its proper development.

In the introduction the poet receives his country into himself like a treasure, but is also concerned with increasing it. In the second part, "Gdy dokoła mówią językami. . ." [All Around They Speak Tongues. . .] he analyzes the significance of his native tongue, which identifies and distinguishes his people among the nations of the earth, though at the same time limits them in human space, as it seems to be "za trudna" or "zbędna" [too difficult or superfluous, II:10] to others. But thus enclosed within one speech his people exist deep into their roots, waiting for the fruit of ripeness and crises.

Ogarnięci na co dzień pięknem własnej mowy, nie czujemy goryczy, chociaż na rynkach świata nie kupują naszej myśli z powodu drożyzny słów.
/ . . . /
Lud żyjący w sercu własnej mowy pozostaje poprzez pokolenia tajemnicą myśli nie przejrzanej do końca.

(III:2-4)

[Embraced every day by the beauty of our language we do not feel bitter that on the world markets our thought is not bought because of the high price of words.
/ . . . /
A people living in the heart of its own speech remains for generations a mystery of the thought unfathomed to the end.]

In the very short third part he lyrically evokes the landscape and life of his native countryside. In Part Four, "Docieram do serca dramatu. . ." [I Reach the Heart of the Drama] the author amplifies his earlier thoughts on the history of his country where the abuse of liberty led to captivity and to the struggle for true freedom. "Ojczyzna: wyzwanie tej ziemi rzucone przodkom i nam, by stanowić o wspólnym dobru" [Our country: a challenge of this land

110

thrown to our ancestors and to us to determine our common good"
IV.2:1]. The poet asks for forgiveness of other peoples who had
connected their freedom with ours and were disappointed. After the
lyrical "Refren" [Refrain] on the search for a road "kiedy myślę:
Ojczyzna" [when thinking: my country, V:1], in the last part of the
poem, "Myśląc ojczyzna, powracam w stronę drzewa. . ." [Thinking
my Country I return to the Tree], the author reflects — as he had
done in *Easter Vigil* — on the history and all-important meaning of
Christianity in his country. Good and bad grew in the country's
history, but history cannot "popłynąć przeciw prądowi sumień"
[flow against the current of conscience VI.1:4]. The poet goes on to
these significant observations, whose validity has been tested over
and over again, before and since:

> Nie możemy godzić się na słabość.
> Słaby jest lud, jeśli godzi się ze swoją
> klęską, gdy zapomina, że został posłany, by czuwać,
> aż przyjdzie jego godzina. Godziny wciąż powracają
> na wielkiej tarczy historii.
> Oto liturgia dziejów. Czuwanie jest
> słowem Pana i słowem Ludu / . . . / Godziny
> przechodzą w psalm nieustających nawróceń:
> Idziemy uczestniczyć w Eucharystii światów.
> (VI. 3:4; 4:1-2)

[We must not consent to weakness.
Weak is the people that accepts its defeat, if
it forgets that it has been sent to watch until its hour
comes. The hours keep returning on the great clock
face of history.
This is the liturgy of history. Vigil is the
word of the Lord and the word of the People. . . The
hours pass into the psalm of continual conversations:
we go to partake of the Eucharist of the worlds.]

The poet ends with an apostrophe to earth, the "ziemia naszych
upadków i zwycięstw, która wznosisz się we wszystkich sercach
tajemnicą paschalną /. . . i / nie przestajesz być cząstką naszego

111

czasu" [earth of our falls and victories, which is in our hearts as a paschal mystery /and/ remains part of our time, VI.5:1-2]. Throughout the history of the earth, the author concludes, we learn new hope and, on the way to the new earth, we raise the old earth "jak owoc miłości pokoleń, która przerosła nienawiść" [as the fruit of the love of generations that outgrew hate, VI. 5:3].[20]

It can easily be discerned that *Thinking my Country*, far from being limited to one people's problems, opens up to all humanity, and its direct message is pertinent to any people, any country, though particularly to those that have had more than their share of suffering.

* * *

It is fitting that the last published, perhaps also the last written, poem by Cardinal Karol Wojtyła concerns St. Stanisław, Bishop of Kraków. The author was his successor at that bishopric. On May 7, 1972, the nine-hundredth anniversary of Stanisław's appointment to the see of Kraków, Cardinal Wojtyła initiated the seven-year long preparations for the celebration of the nine hundredth anniversary of his martyrdom, and it was for that purpose that, now as Pope John Paul II, he visited his native country in June 1979. In his homily in Warsaw, on June 2, the first day of his visit, he had this to say:

> Is not my pilgrimage to my country in the year in which the Church in Poland celebrates the nine-hundredth anniversary of the death of St. Stanisław, a particular sign of our Polish pilgrimage through the history of the Church. . . The millennium of Poland's Baptism, whose first ripe fruit is St. Stanisław — the

---

[20] In the chapter of his last book *Pamięć i tożsamość* [Memory and Identity] entitled "History," John Paul II quotes long excerpts from *Thinking my Country*, which proves that this poem too retained its validity for him to the end. See the Znak edition, pp. 78-80.

millennium of Christ in our yesterday and today — is
the main reason of my pilgrimage.[21]

These and many other pronouncements stress in a
significant way his personal attitude to bishop Stanisław
Szczepanowski, and his view of a close connection between the
drama that took place nine hundred years earlier and the history of
the nation as well as the Church in Poland. This drama has long
been the subject of debate between some historians who argued that
the bishop conspired with the king's enemies, was tried and
executed and others who maintained that the king killed Stanisław,
enraged by his admonitions regarding his immoral behavior. The
conflict between the Bishop and the King fueled those ideologists
who stressed the irreconcilable antinomy between Church and State.
The "manipulators" intended to divide the people, but the result was
the opposite — a spiritual unity of the people around the
anniversary celebrations, just as centuries ago, according to legend,
the miraculous growing together of St. Stanisław's severed limbs
forecast the territorial unification of Poland, then divided into
regional dukedoms. Karol Wojtyła saw very clearly the ever valid
model of St. Stanisław as a "spokesman of true freedom and
creative synthesis, achieved in the soul of a believer, between the
loyalty with regard to his country on earth and the faithfulness to
the Church."[22] But he has always seen also the strange interrelation
of the two protagonists: Stanisław and Bolesław. The mission and
martyrdom of the one, the crime and penitence of the other both
have influenced the history of the Polish people and can be
somehow considered positively. As a well-known Kraków
theologian, and Karol Wojtyła's collaborator, put it, the country
"acknowledges them both. The King, after all, remains someone
from Poland. And the Bishop is Someone from Poland. They
remain in history as two great warning signs."[23]

---

[21] John Paul II, Homily during Mass at the Victory Square in Warsaw, on 2
June 1979. *Słowo Papieża*, p. 64.
[22] John Paul II, Speech to foreign guests, Kraków, June 9, 1979. *Słowo
Papieża*, p. 64.
[23] Rev. Prof. Józef Tischner, Speech at the Congress of Solidarity. *Tygodnik
Powszechny* XLII:1708, 18 October 1981.

This is also the view adopted by Karol Wojtyła as author of the poem *Stanisław*, his third — after *Easter Vigil* and *Thinking my Country* — poetic comment on the deep affinity between the history of the Polish nation and the history of Christianity in Poland. The poem is divided into two parts of equal length. The first opens with a significant statement:

Pragnę opisać Kościół —
mój Kościół, który rodzi się wraz ze mną,
lecz ze mną nie umiera — ja też nie umieram z nim.

(I.1:1-3)

[I want to describe the Church —
my Church, which is born with me,
but does not die with me — nor do I with it]

For, as Cardinal Wojtyła said in his homily on May 7, 1972 at St. Stanisław's birthplace, Szczepanów, opening the seven-year preparation period:

Nine hundred years have passed, so many generations have passed, but the Church is the same. The people of God are the same. . . For such is the mystery of the Church as the community of God's children; such is the mystery of the Church as the communion of saints that a man grows with it and of it, grows into that community of people of God, through his earthly life and then — as it particularly applies to St. Stanisław, through eternal life.[24]

In the poem the author states that he wants to describe his Church "w człowieku, któremu dano imię Stanisław" [in the man whose name was Stanisław I.2:5]. He then describes the very moment of martyrdom, the blow which struck when — as tradition has it, St. Stanisław was saying Mass. The poet speculates on the King's thoughts, which strangely enough, may have been that "Kościół /.../

---

[24] Karol Wojtyła, *Kazania*, p. 60.

narodzi się z krwi rozlanej" [the Church /. . ./ will be born of the spilled blood, I.5:1,4]. In his last moments, on the other hand, Stanisław may have thought that if "Słowo nie nawróciło, nawróci krew" [the word did not convert, the blood will, I.6:5]. The sword and the blood both fall "na glebę naszej wolności /. . . / Który ciężar przeważy?" [on the soil of our freedom. Which will weigh more? I.7:2-3).

The second part begins with a lyrical invocation of the Polish land, which "przebiega w zieleniach, jesieniach i śniegach" [rushes by in greens, autumns and snows II.1:4], and its contemplation prompts the poet to ponder on "ziemia trudnej jedności. Ziemia ludzi szukających własnych dróg" [the land of hard unity. The land of people seeking their own roads II.2:1]; the land where freedom was first abused, then lost, torn from the maps, but "ziemia poprzez rozdarcie zjednoczona w sercach Polaków / jak żadna" [the land through having been torn apart united in the hearts of Poles / like no other, II.2:6-7]. The poet concludes by wondering about the name, "to imię" [that one name, II.3:5] given for him, for the episcopal see in Kraków, for King Bolesław, for the twentieth century...

Thus, with nine hundred years of history bridged in a flash, ends *Stanisław* and possibly, the poetry from the pen of Karol Wojtyła, before a new phase opened in the life of its author. But Karol Wojtyła, who in his youth played the part of King Bolesław in a clandestine war-time performance, and on his appointment as cardinal celebrated Mass at the exiled King's grave, considered his poem important enough when, after two decades on the throne of St. Peter, he referred to it in one of his latest books and reprinted its first part, which constitutes three quarters of the work.[25]

* * *

It would have been a reasonable assumption that after 16 October 1978 there could be no room for poetry in the life of John Paul II. And yet we would be wrong. For twenty-four years into his

---

[25] John Paul II, *Wstańcie, chodźmy* [Arise, Let us Go] Kraków: Św. Stanisława BM, 2004.

pontificate he did not publish any new poems, but some of his official statements were written in the form of poetry and occasionally even had poetic content. During his first foreign trip — to Mexico in January 1979 — the new Pope presented his Prayer to our Lady of Guadalupe in the form of a poem. And so were some of his other pronouncements, such as the Urbi et Orbi message at Christmas 1982, or the Prayer for the Jubilee Year at Easter 1983. In those "poetic prayers" there might not be metaphors, but there was the intensity and spirit of poetry. And then, in the quarter-centenary year of his astonishing pontificate, John Paul gave us *The Roman Triptych*, the first, and only poem so signed. This fact was also a symbolic confirmation, if one were needed, that its author — the pontiff — remained a poet as well. We must not be put off by the *Triptych's* description on the title page as *medytacje* [meditations]. In his penultimate book *Arise, Let us Go*, the author describes *The Roman Triptych* as "meditations." In fact, it is both a poem and a meditation, and the same can be said for the fourteen long poems constituting Karol Wojtyła's mature work in the genre. Moreover, in the *Triptych*, in spite of a long lapse of time, he preserves the characteristic qualities of his poetry and brings its main themes to their culminating point, as a thinker and as a poet.

The main theme of Pope John Paul II's poem is man's spiritual journey to God through Redemption. In the first part, "Strumień" [The Stream], the author refers to nature as God's creation, shows its importance for man, but also the basic difference between them. Nature exists unawares. Like everything in nature, man's life is short in earthly time. But unlike nature, man is amazed, that is to say — *thinks*, and in his passing — he halts before the Everlasting Word which — as we know — was in the beginning. And in the meeting with the Word "to przemijanie ma sens" [the passing makes sense I.1:40]. This phrase is repeated by the author three more times. He reiterates his thoughts expressed in his poem *Meditation on Death*. In the brief section two, "Źródło" [Source] the author makes an important statement that one must not flow down the stream, but "iść do góry, pod prąd" [walk up, against the current, I.2:4] in order to reveal the secret of the beginning and find the source. From the source springs the water of life.

If the structure of Part One is based on the image of a mountain stream and its source, Part Two — the longest and most complex — "Medytacje nad «Księgą Rodzaju» na progu Kaplicy Sykstyńskiej" [Meditations on the Book of Genesis on the Threshold of the Sistine Chapel] impresses with the scale of its symbolism. The Book of Genesis is after all, at the source of the Word. And nature connects here with art, which is the most perfect expression of man's "zdumienie" [amazement]. Section I — "Pierwszy Widzący" [The First Who Sees] — begins with words spoken by St. Paul at the Areopagus in Athens. "For in him we live, and move, and have our being." Then the author asks: "Who is *He*?" and replies that He is the Creator — the everlasting Word. He is in fact the creative force.

After a beautiful ode to the Word which is everlasting, "Słowo przedwieczne, jak gdyby / próg niewidzialny / wszystkiego co zaistniało, istnieje i istnieć będzie" [as if an invisible threshold of all that had existed, exists and will exist, II.1:21-23] standing at the entrance to the Sistine Chapel the poet refers again to the Book of Genesis. He says that even though the story of creation would be easier to tell in words the Book of Genesis waited for an image. He invokes Michelangelo, as well as "was wszystkich «widzących» wszechczasów" [all those of you who saw at all times, II.1:33] — the artists. In the analysis of Michelangelo's great work which follows he turns attention to the ever important fact — for himself and all men — that even more telling than the beginning is the End, "droga, którą wszyscy przechodzimy — / każdy z nas" [the road which we, all of us, everyone of us, takes, 1.59-60]."

The second section of Part Two, "Obraz i podobieństwo" [Image and Likeness] is connected with a long cycle of the Holy Father's teachings at general audiences years ago, on the theme "male and female He created them" (GEN 1.27). Quoting the verse "And they were both naked. . . and were not ashamed" (GEN 2.25) he asks: "Czy to możliwe?" [was that possible?] and gives a strange reply: "Współczesnych o to nie pytaj, lecz pytaj Michała Anioła" [Do not ask today's people, but ask Michelangelo, II.2:5-6]. I see it as a momentary doubt, if confused (also in matters of sex) people today are able to answer this. Yet, immediately after, he adds in

117

parentheses "a może także współczesnych!?" [but perhaps also ask today's people, II.2:7]

In sequences that follow ("On" [He] "Człowiek /Ja/" [Man /I/], "Michał Anioł" [Michelangelo], "Oni" [They]) the author reflects on the content of the Sistine Chapel frescoes, on creation and the history of man on earth, the good with which he had been endowed and the evil he commits. He quotes Genesis: "And God saw everything that He had made, and, behold, it was very good" (GEN. 2.31). But then the poet asks:

> Czy temu nie przeczą dzieje?
> Choćby nasz wiek dwudziesty! I nie tylko dwudziesty!
> A jednak żaden wiek nie może przesłonić prawdy
> o obrazie i podobieństwie.
>
> (II.2:35-37)

> [Does not history contradict this?
> for instance our twentieth century!
> And not only the twentieth!
> But no age can obscure the truth
> about God's image and likeness.]

Although man disturbs the beauty created by God, it still exists, like He, the Creator of all that is.

In Section Three, "Prasakrament" [Pre-sacrament] is contained humanity's gift from God and it becomes a "wzajemne obdarowanie / . . . / w Nim" [mutual gift /. . . / in Him, II.3:16-17]. And when they become one body, by the same token they reach the source of life which is in them. Thus is fatherhood and motherhood born: "wiedzą, że przeszli próg największej odpowiedzialności" [They know that they have crossed the threshold of the greatest responsibility, II.3:34]. Unexpectedly the author makes a personal statement. He quotes a Latin inscription on the need for purity[26] and says: "słowa te czytałem codziennie przez osiem lat, / wchodząc w

---

[26] *Casta placent superis; pura cum veste venite, / et manibus puris sumite fontis aquam* [Those divine are pleased with things chaste; enter adorned in purity / and take of the fountain waters with pure hands]. A citation from Tibullus, "Quisquis adest, faueat: fruges lustramus et agros," lines 13-14.

bramę wadowickiego gimnazjum" [I read these words every day for eight years / when walking through the gate of my high school in Wadowice, II.3:24-27].

In the next sequence — "Spełnienie-*Apocalypsis*" [Fulfilment-Apokalipsis] and in Section Four — "Sąd" [The Judgment], the author contemplates the Last Judgment as depicted by Michelangelo and the dilemma which for a man is the end of his life. The words "z prochu powstałeś i w proch się obrócisz" [From ashes you were born and to ashes you will return, II:Spełnienie, 14] he counters — most interesting this —with a quote from Horace: *non omnis moriar* [I do not die completely] and the translation: "To co we mnie niezniszczalne, / teraz staje twarzą w twarz z Tym, który Jest!" [What is indestructible in me remains / stands now face to face with Him who Is, II.4:7-8].

An unusual conclusion of the *Triptych* is the third part — "Wzgórze w krainie Moria" [A Hill in the Land of Moria] which refers to an important event described in the Old Testament. The childless Abraham obeyed the Voice which told him to move from Ur in Chaldea and was rewarded by offspring. (1. "Ur w ziemi chaldejskiej" [Ur in the Land of Chaldea], 2. "Tres vidit et unum adoravit" [Three he saw and One adored]). When the Voice demanded of him to sacrifice Isaac, his long-desired son, Abraham in spite of his immense suffering was ready to obey. He trusted God and was not disappointed. (3. "Rozmowa ojca z synem w krainie Moria" [Father's Discourse with his Son in the Land of Moria]). God revealed through Abraham that he too would sacrifice his son for the benefit of all mankind. (4. "Bóg przymierza" [God of the Covenant]):

O Abrahamie — tak bowiem Bóg umiłował świat,
że Syna swojego dał, aby każdy, kto w Niego uwierzył,
miał żywot wieczny.

(III.4:12-14)

O Abraham — God so loved the world,
that He gave His Son so that everyone who believed in Him,
should / have eternal life.

Because of God's sacrifice and His Covenant with man, our inevitable end in death will also be our beginning.

So closes *The Roman Triptych*. It is not a treatise or a papal text "ex cathedra," but a very personal, even intimate statement by its author. It is also — we realize it now even more than two years ago when the poem was published — that it is also the poetic testament of John Paul II. The pre-figuration of Christ's Passion on behalf of mankind and each and every one of us was for John Paul II a matter of great importance. The last chapter of his book *Arise, Let us Go* published in 2004 is entitled "Abraham and Christ." He writes there: "I returned to Abraham recently in a poetic meditation" and quotes a fragment pertaining to his address directed at his brethren in the episcopate. Abraham had to leave his country at God's behest. John Paul II writes:

> I am speaking from the place to which I was led by love of Christ the Saviour, demanding of me that I should leave my land and bear fruit — fruit that is to last, in another place. . . Repeating the words of our Master and Lord, I direct to each of you, dear Brethren in the Episcopate, the call "Arise, let us go!" Let us go with confidence in Christ. He will accompany us on our way to the goal which only He knows.[27]

At the end of Part Two of *The Roman Triptych* the author has placed an Afterword, in fact a moving ending not of the poem, which it is not, but thoughts on his own life and mission here on earth coming to a close. The continuation will be — now is — elsewhere:

> I tu właśnie u stóp tej przedziwnej sykstyńskiej polichromii zbierają się kardynałowie —
> wspólnota odpowiedzialna za dziedzictwo kluczy Królestwa.
> Przychodzi właśnie tu.
> I Michał Anioł znów ogarnia ich widzeniem.

---

[27] John Paul II, *Wstańcie, chodźmy*, p. 164.

/ . . . /
Sykstyńska polichromia przemówi wówczas Słowem Pana:
Tu es Petrus — usłyszał Szymon syn Jony.
«Tobie dam klucze Królestwa».
Ludzie, którym troskę o dziedzictwo kluczy powierzono,
zbierają się tutaj, pozwalają się ogarnąć sykstyńskiej
        polichromii,
wizji, którą Michał Anioł pozostawił —

Tak było w sierpniu, a potem w październiku
        pamiętnego roku dwóch konklawe,
i tak będzie znów, gdy zajdzie potrzeba,
po mojej śmierci.
/ . . . /
Postanowiono człowiekowi raz umrzeć, a potem
Sąd!

Ostateczna przejrzystość i światło.
Przejrzystość dziejów —

Przejrzystość sumień —
/ . . . /
Ty, który wszystko przenikasz — wskaż!
On wskaże. . .
        (II.Afterword. 1-5, 11-19, 24-27, 30-31)

[And here at the foot of this wonderful Sistine fresco
the cardinals gather
the community responsible for the heritage
        of the keys of the kingdom.
They come here
And Michelangelo again surrounds them with his vision.
/ . . . /
The Sistine fresco will speak then with the Word of the Lord:
Tu es Petrus — Simon son of Iona heard this.
I will give you the keys of the kingdom.
Men to whom the care of the heritage of the keys
        was entrusted

gather here, they let themselves be embraced
            by the Sistine fresco,
the vision left by Michelangelo —
Thus it was in August, then in October
            of the memorable year of two conclaves,
and so will be again, when necessary,
after my death.
                    / . . . /
It has been decreed that man dies, and then
—judgment

The ultimate clarity and light,
Clarity of history —
clarity of consciences —
                    / . . . /
You who permeate all — show!
He will show. . .]

Karol Wojtyła, Playwright
HAROLD B. SEGEL

The late Pope John Paul II was well known for his enthusiasm for everything related to the stage. This manifested itself very early in life so that by the time he matriculated as a student at the Marcin Wadowita Gymnasium in 1934 in his native Wadowice, he was only too eager to take part in as many plays as he could. When he traveled to Kraków to enter the Jagiellonian University in the fall of 1938, that enthusiasm was part of his baggage. There is ample anecdotal (and other) evidence to suggest that before the German invasion of Poland in September 1939, he had already given serious thought to making the theater his life's career. The war changed all that, as it did so many other things. It was during the occupation, in December 1939, that Karol Wojtyła is believed to have written his first play. This was a dramatic poem on the Biblical subject of David, but it was rooted in Polish history as well. This pattern of combining Biblical and Polish historical motifs would reappear in his subsequent playwriting. The grim realities of war and occupation were to shape not only the future Pope's outlook on physical and spiritual existence, but also his decision to enter the priesthood. They were also destined to shape, to a considerable extent, the kind of dramatic writing that he would undertake.

The German occupation imposed severe limitations on Polish cultural activity. Unable to continue as a university student during that period, Karol Wojtyła went to work in a quarry and then in a chemical plant. With the end of the work day, he pursued academic studies and cultural activity in the extensive underground operating in Kraków at the time. Theatrical conditions were obviously rudimentary — funds, costumes, settings, and appropriate performance venues were in extremely short supply—but Wojtyła and his fellow enthusiasts were undeterred. They came together in private homes and apartments, gave readings, and kept theater alive to the best of their ability.

Wojtyła's entry into the priesthood did not bring down the curtain on his involvement in theatrical art, although it could no longer play a dominant role in his life. In October 1942, he became a student of theology at the clandestine Faculty of Theology of the Jagiellonian University. By then he had also entered the equally clandestine Seminary of the Kraków Diocese.

Karol Wojtyła's first extant play, *Hiob* [Job], subtitled *Drama ze Starego Testamentu* [A Drama from the Old Testament] is dated "Kraków, Lent 1940" and thus predates his affiliation with the Faculty of Theology. Although the fertile literary and theatrical history of the story of Job must surely have been a part of his intellectual and artistic formation, the future Pope brought his own interpretation to the main character. The play is set in different time periods: *W Starym Testamencie — przed pryjściem Chrystusa —* [In the Biblical period, that is before the coming of Christ]; *za dni dzisiejszych* [in Our Days], *czasu Hiobowego* [In Job's time], *Polski i świata* [For Poland and the world] and finally in the

> Czasu oczekiwania,
> Błagania o sąd,
> Czasu tęsknoty
> za testamentem Chrystusowym,
> W cierpieniach Polski i świata[1]

> [Time of expectation, /Of imploring judgment, /In the time of longing for Christ's testament,/ Worked out/ In Poland and the World's Suffering]

The political context, that is, the German invasion and subsequent occupation of Poland, obviously determined Wojtyła's appreciation of the timely relevance of the Biblical narrative. Job's anguish at his catastrophic downfall, his loss of family and property, is meant to echo the calamitous defeat of Poland in war. And the

---

[1] All translations are based on the texts of the plays as they appear in *Poezje i dramaty* [Poems and Plays] *Karol Wojtyła* (Andrzej Jawień, A. J., Stanisław Andrzej Gruda, Piotr Jasień) (Kraków: Znak, 1979). English translations of the plays and theater writings of Karol Wojtyła appear in *The Collected Plays and Writings on Theater. Karol Wojtyła.* Translated with introductions by Bolesław Taborski (Berkeley: University of California Press, 1987).

impassioned question to which he demands an answer from God —
why such a fate befell him, a truly good man — was one that could
have issued from the mouths of countless Poles between 1939 and
1945. By crafting the drama as he has, Wojtyła has at once yoked
the Christian view of the New Testament as the fulfillment of the
Old Testament and the legacy of Polish Romantic messianism
elaborated so compellingly in the nineteenth century by such poets
and dramatists as Adam Mickiewicz, Juliusz Słowacki, and
Zygmunt Krasiński. That Wojtyła would have naturally assimilated
this view of Poland as the chosen nation in Christian terms in his
early schooling, is a given. One need go no further than Witold
Gombrowicz's explosive novel, *Ferdydurke* (1938), to appreciate
the tenacious hold of the Romantic legacy on young Polish minds.
Because he *is* deserving, Job is informed by Elihu, God's
messenger, that he has been divinely chosen to understand the
purpose of Christ's sacrifice on the Cross and to see therein the
fulfillment of prophecy:

ELIHU
On jest nazwany Syn Człowieczy —
On urodzony jest z Niewiasty —
On niesie w sobie Zakon Słowa —
—Baranek idzie z niebnych pastwisk —

JOB
On idzie — wiem — ja wiem, że żyje.
Żyje On — Jasny, co rozjaśni,
co mi z mych pęt uwolni szyję,
co wskrzesi mię po mojej kaźni. —
Z ciebie — Elihu — we mnie zeszło —
Widzę, że żywie Odkupiciel,
/ . . . /
że z Nim powstanę nowym bytem
oglądać, jak On zło pokruszy.[2]

[ELIHU: He is called the Son of Man — /He is born of

---

[2] *Hiob*, in *Poezje i dramaty*, 312.

Woman —/ He bears in Him the Testament of the
Word — / —The Lamb is coming from heaven's
pastures —// JOB: He is coming — I know — I know
He lives. / He lives — the Bright One who brightens
all, / who will rid my neck of its fetters, / who will
resurrect me after my torment. — / From you —
Elihu — has it descended unto me — / I see that the
Redeemer lives. (...) / that I will rise with Him in new
life / To behold how He will crush evil.]

Thus, the related motifs of divine selection and
resurrection, in this case of Job, in the broader context of Poland,
underscore the central tenets of messianic thought.

The future Pope's theatrical experiences also played a
pivotal role in his appropriation of Romantic messianic philosophy.
The preference on Wojtyła's part for a combination of blank and
rhymed verse in short lines of eight or nine syllables — unlike the
longer lines and more prosaic rhythms of his later plays — recalls
the poetic drama of Młoda Polska [Young Poland], as the period of
Polish neoromanticism is commonly known. The critical
engagement of this drama in the issues central to the Polish
Romantic movement, above all Poland's destiny as a nation and the
messianic heritage, was also bound to incline the future Pope to the
interweaving of metaphysics and national history in his wartime
plays.

Karol Wojtyła's next play, *Jeremiasz: Drama Narodowe
we Trzech Działach* [Jeremiah: A National Drama in Three Acts],
dated Kraków 1940, is the most national of his dramatic *oeuvre*.
While limiting the Biblical element of *Jeremiah* to a lesser role than
in *Job*, the plot reiterates the condemnation of the pride, arrogance,
and wantonness of the Polish nobility articulated so abundantly in
the political literature of the Polish Renaissance (Andrzej Frycz-
Modrzewski, Łukasz Górnicki, Piotr Skarga, and others).[3] This said,
however, the question arises as to why Wojtyła would have chosen
to write such a play early in the war. What resonance would a

---

[3] On this, see my *Political Thought in Renaissance Poland: An
Anthology in English* (New York: PIASA Books, 2003).

ringing denunciation of the arrogance and selfishness of powerful noble families in sixteenth- and seventeenth-century Poland have in the year 1940 in a country already suffering under brutal German occupation? Except, perhaps, to underline the pattern of rise and fall, of grandeur and humiliation, and of ultimate rebirth across the broad sweep of Polish history and thereby advance belief in the inevitability of national regeneration. The prophetic visions of the Mickiewiczian Father Piotr in *Jeremiah*, alas, come true and Poland faces destruction for the ways of the nobility. Only Piotr's steadfastness and the great sacrifice of Hetman Stanisław Żółkiewicz at the battle of Cecora against the Turks hold out hope of redemption. But how do we bend the analogy to the Polish situation in 1940? Was it really Karol Wojtyła's view that the German invasion in 1939 was in some way a divine retribution for Poland's waywardness, Poland's fall from grace, in the interwar period? This would be a difficult thesis to defend. Rather, it seems that in a sense Wojtyła was following a certain natural progression from *Job* to *Jeremiah*. The future Pope's first play uses the Christian grafting on the Biblical story of Job to imply at least a limited endorsement of the messianic interpretation of Poland. Viewed in terms of the year 1940, Job's incredulity at the misfortunes visited on him, and his ever shriller demands for justice and fairness, easily accord with the plight of the Poles during the war. When Job's anguish is finally transposed from the Hebraic sternness of the Old Testament to the redemptive promise of the New Testament, a beacon shines through to the Poles in the darkness of their wartime situation. Ultimate victory will be theirs and Poland will rise phoenix-like from the ashes. Absent in Wojtyła's play is the hubristic Romantic messianic conception of Poland as the Christ of nations destined to achieve the redemption of other nations under Christ. Poland *will* be reborn if she remains faithful to her Christian origins; but the salvation of Poland through Christ is not necessarily equated with the salvation of European Christendom.

Polish messianic philosophy and Polish Romantic drama were not the only Polish literary influences on the shaping of *Job* and *Jeremiah*. The legacy of the foremost dramatist of Młoda Polska, Stanisław Wyspiański (1869-1907), also left its traces on the play. Wyspiański's fondness for animating inanimate figures and assigning them speaking roles in a play is a hallmark of his dramatic style. The statues of Greek gods and goddesses in *Noc listopadowa* [November Night, 1904], the Masks and the statue of Genius with whom Konrad contends in *Wyzwolenie* [Liberation, 1903], and the figures from ancient tapestries in the Wawel Castle in Kraków that come alive in *Akropolis* [Acropolis, 1904] represent a series of powerful, and unforgettable, images in Polish modernist drama. Even absent his interest in theater, Karol Wojtyła would most certainly have been conversant with these plays. But the depth of his interest opened him to the influence of this prominent feature of the writing of his illustrious predecessor. Two white angels, likened to pillars, preside over the altar at the beginning of *Jeremiah* and, in turn, present a tableau of sculptures from the carved altarpiece of the chapel, all representing such Biblical figures as Jeremiah, Joakim, king of Judah, several ministers of the king, and Passur [Pashur], the priest of Yahweh. This part of the play brings to mind not only Wyspiański but also the tradition of the Polish *szopka*, essentially a puppet show in which Biblical and contemporary everyday figures intermingle. Wyspiański made this the structural lynchpin of the most resonant of his plays, *Wesele* [The Wedding, 1901]. But in Wojtyła's play, the "Phantoms" appear, speak their lines, and retire from the stage before the appearance of the historical characters. There is, in fact, no real interaction between the real and imaginary as in Wyspiański's *November Night, Acropolis,* or *The Wedding.*

The likely influence of Wyspiański on Karol Wojtyła's dramatic writing also ought to be set in the broader framework of the tradition of Młoda Polska Biblical drama.[4] Encouraged by the metaphysical proclivities of Młoda Polska modernism, as well as by the renewed interest in early Christian history and the historical Jesus in Europe as a whole at this time, writers often favored plays with Biblical settings. Among the best, in Poland, were Jan

---

[4] On the Biblical drama of Młoda Polska, see *Dramat biblijny Młodej Polski* [The Young Poland Biblical Drama] ed. by Jan Błoński, Janusz Degler, Jacek Popiel, and Dobrochna Ratajczak (Wrocław: Wiedza o kulturze, 1992).

Kasprowicz's *Na Wzgórzu śmierci* [On The Hill of Death, 1898] and *Uczta Herodiady* [The Feast of Herod, 1905]; Lucjan Rydel's *Betlejem polski* [The Polish Bethlehem, written in 1903, published in 1906], a *jasełka*, or Christmas play, in 3 acts; Karol Hubert Rostworowski's *Judasz z Kariothu* [Judas Iscariot, 1912], by far the most ambitious, and impressive, of the group and one in which Karol Wojtyła himself had acted in his last school performance in his native Wadowice;[5] Kazimierz Przerwa-Tetmajer's *Judasz* [Judas, 1917]; Antoni Szandlerowski's *Maria z Magdali* [Mary Magdalene] and *Tryumf* [Triumph], both written in 1906 but published for the first time only posthumously in the 1914 edition of the author's collected works, and *Paraklet* [Paraclete], written in 1908 and also included in the posthumous collection of Szandlerowski's works. As we can see, Wojtyła's Biblical plays could draw on a robust tradition. With the exception of the lesser known Szandlerowski, the other writers were all major representatives of Młoda Polska.

After his two Biblical plays with their World War II Polish referentiality, Wojtyła wrote the curious historical drama, *Brat Naszego Boga* [Our God's Brother], which arose during the period 1945-1950 when the future Pope was already an ordained priest. Rejected by the journal *Znak* in the early 1950s, it was finally published in the Christmas 1979 issue of *Tygodnik Powszechny*. The play dramatizes salient moments in the career of Adam Chmielowski (1845-1916), an erstwhile combatant in the Polish January Uprising [Powstanie Styczniowe] of 1863 against Russia. Chmielowski later became a well-known painter and eventually a monk under the name of Brother Albert and the founder of the Congregation of Albertine Brothers. A figure of strong personal appeal to Karol Wojtyła, Chmielowski is depicted in *Our God's*

---

[5] On Karol Hubert Rostworowski's *Judasz z Kariothu* in particular, see especially Jacek Popiel, *Sztuka dramatyczna Karola Huberta Rostworowskiego* [The Dramatic Art of K.H.R.] (Wrocław: Wiedza o kulturze, 1990) and the same author's introduction to the Biblioteka Narodowa edition of Rostworowski's selected plays, *Karol Hubert Rostworowski, Wybór dramatów* [A Selection of Plays] (Zakład Narodowy imienia Ossolińskich: Wrocław, 1992), V- CXLIV.

Brother at that turning point in his life when his social consciousness, his deep concern for the plight of the poor and homeless, compromises his commitment to art. This shift in the future Brother Albert's outlook on painting is effectively realized in the debate in Act I with fellow artists, all of whom represent prominent figures in Krakow's art milieu at the time. No matter how hard they try to turn Chmielowski away from the path he seems about to embark on, he becomes progressively more involved in social activism. He is also encouraged along the way by a shadowy figure identified only as Nieznajomy [The Stranger] and obviously intended to represent a Marxist revolutionary. Wojtyła's depiction of the downtrodden, in a manner worthy of Maxim Gorky, is neither flattering nor wholly sympathetic, though far removed from the grotesque satire of Luis Buñuel's classic film of 1961, *Viridiana*. They are coarse, quarrelsome, demanding, and cynical. However, nothing can dissuade Chmielowski from his commitment to doing whatever he can to alleviate the misery he sees so prevalent around him. But The Stranger presses his conviction that the lot of the poor will only change through a revolution of the masses. As conceived by Wojtyła, The Stranger is neither caricature nor parody, but rather the embodiment of true revolutionary zeal. Once his metamorphosis from artist to monk is complete, Chmielowski, now Brother Albert, heads a monkish order of men dedicated to a life of utter poverty, with Christ as their ideal. Many of his fellow monks have in fact been recruited from among the very people he had been trying to help. Although some of them grumble about their vows of poverty and alms gathering, they ultimately remain steadfast in Brother Albert's service. Near the end of the play, as the monks pray in the Angelus service, they are interrupted by reports of disturbances in the city. Public transportation has been shut down, people have quit work, and many have taken to the streets marching and chanting slogans. The revolution prophesied by The Stranger has erupted. Although at the very end Albert declares that he knows for certain that he has chosen a greater freedom, meaning the liberation of the spirit through Christ, he speaks with no rancor about the revolution. As he tells the doubting Brother Antoni: *Wiedziałem o tym od dawna. To musiało przyjść* [I have known about this for a long time. It had to come]. When

Brother Collector [Kwestarz] asks him what it is that he has known, he replies *O gniewie. O wielkim gniewie. — Słusznym. / . . . / A cóż? Przecież wiecie, że gniew musi wybuchnąć. Zwłaszcza jak jest wielki*[6] [About anger. About great anger. Just anger. / . . . / And you know, after all, that anger has to erupt. Especially if it is great].

Our God's Brother is perhaps Wojtyła's theatrically most viable play, despite the stage directions clearly intended for reading (a feature, in general, of his dramatic style). At its core is the crisis taking place within the future Brother Albert's heart and mind as he seeks a resolution to the dilemma of art vs. social consciousness. It is not enough for him to transform his beliefs into art; he must take an active part in lifting his fellow men from poverty and degradation. The debates between Chmielowski and his fellow artists in their Kraków salons, between Chmielowski and The Stranger, and between Brother Albert and his fellow monks are convincing and stageworthy. The seeming acceptance by Brother Albert, as the play reaches its finale, of the inevitability, and even necessity, of great social upheaval would seem to be a bow in the direction of The Stranger. It is not necessarily artistically motivated. But in light of the time frame of the play's composition, 1945-1950 — the immediate post-World War II years when the Communists were consolidating their power in Poland — Brother Albert's final words on the turmoil taking place around him at the end could be interpreted as Wojtyła's way of heading off possible political censorship, or worse. Man of the church or not, Wojtyła, as a creative writer, with a long history of involvement in theater, would surely have wanted to see his play brought to life on stage, if at all possible, or at the very least published. Indeed, there is little reason to believe that politics were not the reason behind *Znak*'s rejection of the play in the 1950s. Even then, notwithstanding the apparent political correctness of Brother Albert's final words, the rejection by *Znak* may have convinced Wojtyła of the prudence of confining the play to a drawer until times had changed.

Wojtyła's next play, *Przed sklepem jubilera* [The Jeweler's Shop], appeared (in *Znak*) for the first time in 1960, ten years after he had completed *Our God's Brother*. It is a very different kind of

---

[6] *Brat naszego Boga,* in *Poezje i dramaty,* 182.

work than its predecessor. Subtitled *Medytacja o sakramencie małżeństwa przechodząc chwilami w dramat* [A Meditation on the Sacrament of Matrimony, Passing At Times into a Drama], it is a thoughtful play about the institution of marriage and its place in God's scheme for man. Divided into three acts and five scenes per act, the play is primarily a series of narrative monologues exchanged between several sets of characters: Teresa and Andrzej, a young couple about to be betrothed; Anna and Stefan, a couple with three children on the verge of the breakup of their marriage; Anna and Adam, the latter a kind of raisonneur who prophesies a reunion between Anna and Stefan and who may also be viewed as a spiritual presence in the drama; and Krzysztof and Monika. The action of the third and last act is set farther in the future: Andrzej has died in the war, and Krzysztof is the son he has left behind. Monika is the daughter of Anna and Stefan. The union between Krzysztof and Monika heralds, as it were, a reconciliation between Anna and Stefan. Aware that his "Meditation on the Sacrament of Matrimony" could be regarded as a kind of *Lesestück*, or play intended solely for reading, Wojtyła wanted it understood that he did think of his work as dramatic in nature, even though this might perhaps not be immediately obvious. And so, wryly, he spoke of it also having moments of drama, as indeed it does.

Besides the principals already mentioned, other voices are heard in the play. The first act is expository in nature as the monologues of Teresa and Andrzej establish the history and nature of their relationship and the reason for their coming to the jeweler's shop to buy a ring. The jeweler's shop serves as the structural nexus between the different sets of couples. It is the focus of their relationships. They come there either to buy a ring, thereby signaling their desire to unite in holy matrimony; or they come there to get rid of a ring, thereby signaling their desire to sunder a marriage. The other voices heard in the play are those, for example, of a chorus in Act I which like the chorus in classical drama comments on the action and the decision of Andrzej and Teresa to enter matrimony; a chance interlocutor; the figure of the mysterious Adam; and the chorus again in Act II which is devoted to establishing the background to the breakup of the marriage of Anna and Stefan. In this tonally contrastive act, which offsets the joy of

Teresa and Andrzej by means of the gloom and uncertainties hovering over the relationship of Anna and Stefan, the almost supernatural presence of Adam serves as an antidote to despair, a beacon of hope. The various threads of the narrative are brought together in Act III. This is when the impending marriage of the son of Teresa and the now dead Andrzej, and the daughter of the estranged Anna and Stefan, bring the jeweler's shop back again into focus. During the wedding ceremony, Adam takes the place of Krzysztof's father since Adam served alongside Andrzej during the war and was the last person to see him alive.

Notwithstanding a certain moral and philosophical obviousness, and its undeniably static quality, *The Jeweler's Shop* is not uninteresting as a dramatic text. "Poetic" by virtue of its uneven, generally long, lines of blank verse, broken up on occasion by the recitation (in Act I) of excerpts from letters exchanged between Teresa and Andrzej, the lines of the chorus, and the brief interjections by the other men in Act II, the play has no temporal boundaries. It moves unobtrusively from present to past, to future, and back to present. The characterization of the play as a meditation is immensely important as the work addresses not just the place of holy matrimony in God's plan for man, but invites meditation on the nature of love. The characters in *The Jeweler's Shop* are anything but puppets, mere spokesmen for the author's ideas. They are complex human beings, drawn by Wojtyła with deep understanding and compassion. Avoiding a pat solution at the end, he shows instead a contrite and repentant Stefan, willing at last to acknowledge responsibility for the demise of his marriage to Anna. The meaning of Adam's earlier words acquire particular resonance at this point:

Czasem ludzkie istnienie wydaje się za krótkie dla miłości. Kiedy indziej jest jednak odwrotnie: miłość ludzka wydaje się za krótka w stosunku do istnienia — a może raczej za płytka. W każdym razie każdy człowiek ma do dyspozycji jakieś istnienie i jakąś miłość — jak z tego uczynić sensowny całokształt? [7]

---

[7] *Przed sklepem jubilera*, in *Poezje i dramaty*, 225.

[Sometimes human existence seems too short for love. At other times, however, the opposite appears to be the case: human love seems too short in relation to existence — or perhaps too trivial. Be that as it may, every person has at his disposal an existence and a love. How, then, to build a sensible structure from them?]

The Jeweler's Shop was followed by Karol Wojtyła's last play, Promienowianie ojcostwa [Radiation of Fatherhood], which is closely linked intellectually with it, in a sense growing out of it. Although Radiation of Fatherhood had been written somewhat earlier, it was published only in 1979, in the November issue of Znak, after Wojtyła had already been elected Pope. Wojtyła designated the play a misterium [mystery], thereby harking back to the medieval tradition of the mystery play so-called because of its intended use as a vehicle for the illumination of mysteries of the Christian faith. But Wojtyła had no need to return directly to medieval drama as his source. European neoromanticism had opened up a new chapter in the history of the drama that lasted at least well into the late 1920s. The stage for the development of the modernist neomystery was set by the brooding and haunting plays of the Belgian Maurice Maeterlinck (1862-1949), the author of the internationally celebrated Pelléas et Mélisande. Metaphysical tragedies designed to suggest the world beyond the external, Maeterlinck's plays served as vehicles for his ideas on static drama. External action was kept to a bare minimum; dialogue was equally minimalist, repetitive, even incantatory. The emphasis was not on the here and now but on the hereafter. The Belgian's impact on the theater was extraordinary; before long followers began springing up from one end of Europe to the other, as much attracted by his philosophical views as his dramatic writing. Closely related to the metaphysical drama of Maeterlinck was the neoromantic mystery play, a throwback of course to the Middle Ages but modified in keeping with the outlook and aesthetics of the Symbolist movement. Popular in its day, it was also well suited to the contemporary marionette theater which began enjoying a great revival in Europe in the late nineteenth century as witness, for example, the two-volume collection, *Mystères bibliques et chrétiens* [Biblical and Christian Mysteries, 1920], written by Maurice Bouchor (1855-1929) for production by Henri Signoret's Parisian marionette theater, the Petit-Thèâtre.[8] Writers as divergent as Karl Wolfskehl (1869-1948), one of the leading members of the circle grouped around the high priest of contemporary German symbolism, Stefan George, and the Soviet journalist and novelist, Ilya Erenburg (1891-1967), wrote mystery plays. Wolfskehl took a particular interest in the genre and wrote two small mysteries, *Orpheus: Ein Mysterium* [Orpheus: A Mystery] and *Sanctus*. Both were published separately in George's journal *Blätter für die Kunst* (1908/1909), with which Wolfskehl collaborated closely. The works are short, but *Orpheus*, with its extensive use of the shadow motif and a chorus of shadows, would perhaps have been the more probable candidate for production by the renowned Munich shadow theater, the Schwabinger Schattenspiele, founded by Alexander von Bernus (1880-1965) in 1907. Von Bernus was himself the author of a volume of mystery plays under the title *Sieben Mysterienspiele* [Seven Mystery Plays, 1957]. Wolfskehl believed in the compatibility of shadow theater and mystery play and most likely composed his mysteries with performance by the Schwabinger Schattenspiele in mind.

It would be fair to assume that Wojtyła was familiar with the early twentieth-century interest in the mystery play, if not specifically in the adaptation of the mystery for performance either as marionette or shadow play. In writing *Radiation of Fatherhood* his purpose was not modernist theatrical experimentation or novelty, but rather the formulation of complex, even arcane philosophical and theological thought within what he considered to be a poetic dramatic structure.

As in the works of Maeterlinck and other turn-of-the-century dramatists, *Radiation of Fatherhood* exhibits little concern for external action. The entire thrust of the play relates to the drama

---

[8] On Bouchor, Signoret, and related developments, see my book *Pinocchio's Progeny: Puppets, Marionettes, Automatons, and Robots in Modernist and Avant-Garde* Drama (Baltimore and London: The Johns Hopkins University Press, 1995).

135

taking place within the soul of Adam as he grapples with the essential meaning of life and fatherhood. *Radiation of Fatherhood* has three speaking parts, including a chorus. The characters have been carried over from *The Jeweler's Shop*: Adam — the central moral and philosophical voice of *The Jeweler's Shop*; Monica, here a child; and the generically designated Woman [Niewiasta], also called Mother. The opening soliloquy is spoken by Adam who expresses the focal problem of the drama — his quest for his own personality. As he declares:

> Od tylu już lat żyję jak człowiek wygnany z głębszej mojej osobowości, a równocześnie skazany na to, by ją zgłębiać. W ciągu tych lat docierałem do niej w nieustającym trudzie, często jednak myślałem z przerażeniem, że ja gubię — że oto zaciera się pośród procesów historii, gdzie decyduje ilość, czyli masa. [9]

> [For many years I have been living like a man exiled from my deeper personality, yet at the same time condemned to probe it. In the course of those years I have sought to reach it in unceasing toil, but have often thought with horror that I would lose it, that it would be effaced among the processes of history, where what matters is number, or mass.]

Viewing himself as a common denominator for all men, Adam then enters into a lengthy *analiza samotności* [analysis of loneliness]. In the fourth section, *Między Spotkaniem a Spełnieniem* [Between Meeting and Fulfillment], Adam understands that God did not want him to be a father until he became a child, perceiving this in Christian terms: *Dlatego właśnie przyszedł na świat Twój Syn. Jest On całkowicie Twój* [10] [It is for that reason that Your Son came into the world. He is entirely Yours]. Woman appears and explains to Adam the meaning of the "radiation of fatherhood:"

---

[9] *Promieniowanie ojcostwa,* in *Poezje i dramaty,* 228.

[10] *Promieniowanie ojcostwa,* in *Poezje i dramaty,* 232.

Macierzyństwo jednak stanowi wyraz ojcostwa. Musi zawsze powracać do ojca, by zabrać z niego to wszystko, czego jest wyrazem. Na tym polega promieniowanie ojcostwa / . . . / Trzeba wejść w promieniowanie ojcostwa, w nim dopiero wszystko staje się rzeczywistością. [11]

[Nevertheless, motherhood is an expression of fatherhood. It must always go back to the father, to take from him all that it expresses. The radiation of fatherhood depends on this / . . . / One must enter the radiation of fatherhood, for it is only there that everything becomes fully real].

In the next part of the drama, Adam appears as a father, and his child is now named Monika. The first three sections, *Album* [The Album], *Rezerwat dziecka* [The Child's Sanctuary], and *Ojcze, bądź moją Drogą, bądź Źródłem!* [Father, Be My Way, Be My Source!] are written in poetic prose and serve an essentially expository purpose as father and child discuss, and discover, the meaning of their relationship. Making their way through a forest, they come upon a stream in which Monika undergoes a baptismal rebirth:

Oto we wszystkie komórki na nowo wstępuje życie.
Ach, gdy się rodzę na nowo z tego leśnego potoku,
wtedy proszę: bądź dla mnie wodą!
proszę: bądź wodą dla mnie! [12]

[Life enters anew into all the cells of my being. / Ah, as I am being born anew from this forest stream, / I ask: Be water for me! / I ask: Be water for me!]

The experience is indeed mutually illuminating, for daughter and father alike. She understands what it means for her to have been

---

[11] *Promieniowanie ojcostwa,* in *Poezje i dramaty,* 234.
[12] *Promieniowanie ojcostwa,* in *Poezje i dramaty,* 243.

given birth by him, and he understands what it means for him to find himself in her. The dominant figure in the third part of the drama is the Mother who attempts to transmit to Adam the metaphysical meaning of her seemingly dichotomous words: *Promieniowanie Ojcostwa i obumieranie ojcostwa Ja skupiam: we mnie stanowią jedno* [I gather the Radiation of Fatherhood and the dying of fatherhood: in me they become one]. When Adam, at the end of the play, asks the question *Czy tego nie można było już dawno odczytać? / Czyż to nie tkwiło zawsze na dnie wszystkiego, co jest?* [Could this not have been learned long ago? Has this not always been at the core of everything that is?], the Chorus repeats his words. After a brief silence, the Mother's voice is heard in answer: *Mylisz się Adamie! Mylicie się wszyscy! / We mnie przetrwa dziedzictwo wszystkich ludzi zaszczepione w śmierci Oblubieńca*[13] [You are wrong, Adam! You are all wrong!/ In me will survive the heritage of all men that is imbedded in the Bridegroom's death]. The reference to Christ is obvious.

It would be difficult to imagine a text as intellectually complex as *Radiation of Fatherhood* performed, or performable, on a stage, with the possible exception of those passages in the second part where Adam and Monika enter the forest on their journey of spiritual discovery. Much of the play assumes the character of a philosophical treatise. Dialogue, within the context of rhythmic prose, occurs mostly only in the second part. The appearance of a chorus consisting of people who circle around Adam at certain points in the play and either repeat words he utters or comment on events, such as the descent of Monika and Adam into the forest stream, introduces the element of mimed action in the play. But this minimal theatrical enhancement is insufficient to elevate the text as a whole from the level of a *Lesestück*.

However distantly it may recall Maeterlinck, the slight external action in *Radiation of Fatherhood* is not analogous to the Belgian's style. In Maeterlinck, the drastic downplaying of physical activity is accompanied by a unique kind of dialogue that creates a portentous mood well suited to the metaphysical intention (and pretensions) of the play. Strange sounds of uncertain origin, the

---

[13] *Promieniowanie ojcostwa,* in *Poezje i dramaty,* 258.

misty, doomlike ambiance of the Maeterlinckian text work in unison toward the construction of a specific mood. These theatrical elements are lacking in Wojtyła's *Radiation of Fatherhood* which, in the final analysis, remains, as its author no doubt intended, an exemplar of the word-dominant style of the Rhapsodic Theater with which he was closely involved throughout the period of his dramatic creativity. This necessarily modest undertaking, established in wartime Poland by Mieczysław Kotlarczyk (1908-1978), a boyhood friend of Wojtyła's with whom he maintained a long personal relationship, began its activities on August 22, 1941.[14] The privations of war and the absence of appropriate performance venues imposed a distinct asceticism on the five members of the young troupe. Unable to employ the conventional devices and techniques of theater, the Rhapsodic Theater, could develop only as a theater of the word. In this instance, necessity evolved into a theatrical creed.[15] The basic premise of the Rhapsodic Theater accorded with, and accommodated, Karol Wojtyła's purpose with *Radiation of Fatherhood.* Its poetic, "rhapsodic" style notwithstanding, the drama — to the extent that it can be intellectually assimilated or intuited by the uninitiated — can succeed only as declaimed text. That Wojtyła thought of casting this no doubt long germinating treatise in a type of poetic theatrical form, as he understood it, attests of course to his continued fondness for theater and his conviction that his ideas might achieve greater resonance if they were presented in a more engaging, even provocative form than that of the usual prose treatise. When all is

---

[14] Karol Wojtyła's friendship with Kotlarczyk and his association with the Rhapsodic Theater are discussed by Bolesław Taborski in his introduction to *The Collected Plays and Writings on Theater. Karol Wojtyła*, 5-16.

[15] For English translations of Karol Wojtyła's own writings on the Rhapsodic Theater — its philosophy of theater and certain major productions — see "On the Theater of the Word" *[1952]*, "Drama of Word and Gesture" *[1957]*, "Rhapsodies of the Millennium" *[1958]*, "*Forefathers' Eve* and the Twentieth Anniversary" *[1961]*,"On the *Divine Comedy*" *[1964]*, and "Forward to Mieczysław Kotlarczyk's *The Art of the Living Word*" *[1974]*, in *The Collected Plays and Writings on Theater. Karol Wojtyła*, 371-95.

said and done, in reviewing the future Pope John Paul II's life in art it becomes obvious that, just as his central character in *Our God's Brother*, Karol Wojtyła stood at a crossroads at an early juncture in his career. The great strength of his faith, hardened by years of war, inclined him away from a life in theater, despite his attraction to it, to a life in the service of his Church. When his responsibilities as a cleric began mounting after his ordination as a priest in October 1946, less time remained to him for dramatic creativity. Nevertheless, it was during the period 1945 to 1960 that he was able to write his two best (and most performable) plays, *Our God's Brother* and *The Jeweler's Shop*, and the philosophically challenging *Radiation of Fatherhood*. Karol Wojtyła's extraordinary achievements as Pope John Paul II command universal respect and admiration. But we may be certain that his innate humility would not have negated a desire to be remembered as well for his place in the artistic culture of his native land during one of the most difficult periods of its long history.

Our God's Other Brother: Karol Wojtyła, Adam Bunsch, and St. Brother Albert on Stage

CHARLES S. KRASZEWSKI

When a literary scholar considers the extraordinary life of Adam Chmielowski, St. Brother Albert, his first association is with Karol Wojtyła's play *Brat naszego Boga* [Our God's Brother], composed between the years 1945-1950 and recently filmed (1997) by Krzysztof Zanussi. But there exists another, equally interesting, dramatic work on the career of St. Brother Albert, virtually forgotten by the public and ignored by critics, despite its aesthetic value, which is not insignificant. I am speaking of the play *Gołębie Brata Alberta* [Brother Albert's Pigeons].[1] The author of this drama, published in Glasgow in 1943 under the pen name of Andrzej Wart, is no less intriguing than the young priest, the reigning Pontiff, who brought out *Brat naszego Boga* under the pen-name of Andrzej Jawień. He is Adam Bunsch (1896-1969), professor at the ASP in Kraków, one of the giants of contemporary Polish painting. Both he and Wojtyła seem to have been drawn to the character of Chmielowski by a similar attraction.[2] It has often been pointed out that Karol Wojtyła, a young actor and poet affiliated with the Teatr Rapsodyczny, underwent a vocation-experience compatible to Chmielowski's, both abandoning, or at least sublimating, their artistic lives in favor of service to Christ and His Church. Bunsch, likewise, while not abandoning his art, employed it in large measure in service to the Church. His position as one of the greatest religious artists of the twentieth century can

---

[1] *Gołębie Brata Alberta* has to rank among the worst titles of all time. Quite natural in Polish, it is impossible to be turned into English without sounding saccharine, *The Doves of Brother Albert*, or ridiculous: *Brother Albert's Pigeons*. The author himself subsequently changed the title to *Przyszedł na ziemię święty* [A Saint Appeared on Earth], under which it was produced at least thrice.

[2] It is interesting to note that the future Pope was aware of, and admired, *Gołębie Brata Alberta*. In 1947, in the Belgian College in Rome, the third act of this play was produced under the direction of two young priests: Alfred Delmée and Karol Wojtyła. Vide Teresa Dudek-Bujarek, et al. *Adam Bunsch: 1896-1969* (Bielsko-Biała: Muzeum Okręgowe w Bielsku-Białej, Muzeum Diecezjalne w Katowicach, Muzeum Śląskie w Katowicach, 1991), p. 31.

be witnessed to by many works, of which we will mention but two: the mosaic Stations of the Cross in the Church of St. Hedwig in Chorzów, and, especially, the fabulous, gigantic polychrome of *Christ Stilling the Sea*, which towers over the main altar in the church of Divine Providence in Katowice.[3]

Yet to those who are familiar with the biography of Adam Chmielowski, St. Brother Albert does not seem like the perfect candidate for dramatization. Except for his heroic, and tragic, participation in the January Uprising, in which he lost a leg as a cavalry officer, his life was one of intense spiritual activity, and his conflicts were played out on an inner stage. Both Wojtyła and Bunsch acknowledge this in their particular works, which consequently are quite in the tradition of the Monumental Drama. The former poet, who calls his work a *próba przeniknięcia człowieka* [an attempt at penetrating a man][4] confines the action of his play to that period of agonized searching, during which the young painter, friend and fellow student of Maks Gierymski and Stanisław Witkiewicz, was drawn to abandoning his career as a promising painter of the Munich School in the upper reaches of Cracovian society, in favor of living amongst the poorest of the poor in the *ogrzewalnia miejska*, the municipal almshouse. Wojtyła's treatment is more a of a philosophical tract, a Platonic dialogue, than a drama per se, and can best be described as an intense psychological mapping.[5]

---

[3] Bunsch also served the poor through his art. To give just two examples, in 1932 he participated in an exhibition of paintings for the sake of the unemployed, and in 1947, *Przyszedł na ziemię święty* was produced for the third time at the national offices of Caritas in Kraków. (The two earlier productions that year were in Rome, directed by Delmée and Wojtyła, and the national premiere in Częstochowa).

[4] Karol Wojtyła, *Brat naszego Boga* in *Poezje i dramaty* [Poems and Plays] (Kraków: Znak, 1979), p. 109. All citations come from this edition of the text; all translations into English are my own.

[5] In his relation of the Cracovian premiere of the play, Stanisław Edward Bury speaks of the *teatr wewnętrznej przestrzeni* [theatre of inner spaces]. *Teatr*, nr 3, 1.II.81. Likewise, Stanisław Żak refers to the influence of the Monumental Drama of the Polish Romantics, and the *wielka indywidualność samego bohatera, który przecież toczy olbrzymią walkę w sobie z sobą* [grand individuality of the protagonist, who after all wages a gigantic war with

Bunsch, on the other hand, reveals himself to be more consciously an artist than his great colleague. *Gołębie Brata Alberta* is a tripartite work. Each act is dedicated to a significant third of the protagonist's life. We see Chmielowski as soldier, painter, and finally, servant of the poor. In each of these acts, Chmielowski must overcome a different sort of spirit: the *ignis fatuus* of narrow militant nationalism, the chimera of effete hypersensitivity to art, and at last a false appreciation of Christianity. His struggles with each of these ghosts leads him ever closer to contact with the only spirit that matters, the Holy Ghost, who calls and seals the protagonist to his proper vocation.

It seems that the first of these specters, that of *służba narodowej sprawie* [service to the national cause], was the most difficult for the author himself to lay. The first act of *Gołębie Brata Alberta* is played out in a Russian field hospital, after the failed January Uprising, where Adam awaits his amputation. The atmosphere is ultra-patriotic throughout, in the high style of the proud, brooding romantics. At one point, Adam asks his pretty nurse her name:

ANNA: Hanka. . . Anna mi dano na imię.

ADAM: Anna czy Hanka? To wielka różnica! bo Anna to może być także Rosjanka. Po polsku mówisz doskonale, ale w rosyjskim szpitalu /. . . / Może Polka za Moskalem. Może z naszych „białych", co zgodę z szatanem utrzymać zdołali i teraz płacić chce drobny podatek obywatelski przegranej sprawie. A może prowokator do badania polskich jeńców w gorączce, czy czegoś nie zdradzą...[6]

---

himself, within himself]. "Między Konradem a Pankracym," ["Between Konrad and Pankracy"] *Przemiany* [Transformations] nr 4, April 1981. See also Teresa Sorska, "Filozoficzny dialog na teatralnych deskach," ("A Philosophical Dialogue on Stage") *Głos Nowej Huty* [Voice of Nowa Huta], nr 2, 15-21 V 1981.

[6] Adam Bunsch, *Gołębie Brata Alberta* (Glasgow: Książnica Polska, 1943), p. 7. All translations into English are my own. Bunsch was the author of quite a

[ANNA: Hanka. . . Anna is my given name.

ADAM: Is it Anna or Hanka? There's a big difference! 'cause Anna might also be a Russian name. You speak Polish perfectly, but in a Russian hospital / . . . / Maybe you're Polish, but you married a Russian. Maybe you're one of our "whites," who were able to keep their pact with the devil, and now want to pay a little civic tax to the lost cause. Maybe you're an *agent provocateur* sent to watch over Polish POWs, to see if they might not betray something in their fevered mutterings. . .]

This is laying it on a bit thick. But it must be remembered that the play arose during a period of great suffering in Poland, and from the pen of a soldier in exile. Bunsch was among some 3,500 Polish soldiers evacuated to the town of Biggar, in Lanarkshire, Scotland, in the summer of 1940 after the fall of France (the Biggar Museum, parenthetically speaking, contains some of Bunsch's paintings from this period).[7] More than just a literary artefact, Bunsch's play is something of a *cri du cœur* in places like this, a fossil-record of emotions caught *in flagranti*. This explains, perhaps, and to some extent excuses, the more purple patches of patriotic kitsch, such as these cries which escape Adam in his fevered dream with which the drama opens:

ADAM: Andrzej gdzie ty?! Jędrek gdzie ty?! Idą! Idą! O moja noga! Moja noga! Jędrek zniszcz mapy i rozkazy! Idą Moskale! (*cisza*) Koń ma rozpruty brzuch. Gdzie moja torba z rozkazami? Widzisz co? Ja nic! Gdzie moja torba? Idą!

---

few dramatic works, which were produced at various times in Poland. In 1974, a collected volume of his *Dramaty* was published.

[7] Bunsch was a decorated veteran of three wars, having served with the Austrian Army during World War I, the Polish Army during the Polish-Soviet War, and the Polish Army again during the Second World War. In this last conflict he was a colonel of the First Armored Division under the command of Gen. Stanisław Maczek.

Prędko! Podrzeć i zjeść! Tego nie mogą dostać! . . .
(*pauza*). Jędrek wstawaj! /. . . / Te twoje bawole
oczy. . .! Co Tobie jest? Czemu się one nie mrużą
wcale? Jezus Maria! Trup! Trup!

(5)

[ADAM: Andrzej where are you?! Jędrek where are
you?! They're coming! They're coming! O my leg!
Jędrek, destroy the maps and the orders! The
Russians are coming! (*quiet*) My horse's belly is
ripped open. Where is my bag with the orders? Do
you see anything? I don't! Where is my bag?
They're coming! Quick! Tear them up and eat
them! This can't fall into their hands! . . . (*pause*)
Jędrek get up! / . . . / Those eyes of yours so
round...! What's with you? Why don't you blink at
all? Jesus and Mary! You're dead! You're dead!]

However, Bunsch is too much an artist to wallow in the *O ma
patrie!* swill for too long. What is more, outbursts such as these
already noted must be understood in the same way as Konrad's
frothing accusation of God as "not the world's Father, but its
Tsar!"[8] Bunsch's Adam, like Mickiewicz's Konrad, is possessed.
This is brought out in scenes heavily redolent of the spectral
visitations of the great Romantics such as the incubus scenes in
Dziady [Forefathers' Eve], the whorish maiden nightmares in the
Nie-boska komedia [The Undivine Comedy] of Krasiński, and the
temptation scenes in *Kordian*, in which the eponymic hero of
Słowacki's drama is led by fiends to the brink of becoming an
assassin.

It is not coincidental that these patriotic visitations in Act I
of Bunsch's play arise during a high fever, that is, a period during
which the hero's intellect is ill. Like *Brat naszego Boga*, *Gołębie
Brata Alberta* is a play which moves from confusion to knowledge,
or, more aptly, from hallucination to enlightenment.

---

[8] From the Great Improvisation in *Dziady III*. In Konrad's defense, we must
note that the last word was spoken, not by him, but by one of the demons who
had been tormenting him, after Konrad had passed out.

When Sister Anna is in the room—whether she is Polish or Russian is immaterial, what is important is that she is firmly grounded in Christian realism, and will point Adam the way to a proper understanding of the world—Adam is relatively secure from chimeras. But when she leaves for a moment, that he might get some rest, they return. This time, he is confronted by the ghosts of his dead comrades, Jędrzej Sierakowski and Leon Frankowski:

ADAM: Sierakowski! Jędrzej. Ty żyw? ! Przecież sam widziałem jakeś się przewracał na trawie, a trawa nie wszędzie była potem zielona. . . Dziwne! Komu dziś wierzyć, jeśli swoim oczom wierzyć nie można!

(13)

[ADAM: Sierakowski! Jędrzej. You're alive?! But I saw with my own eyes how you were rolling around on the ground, and the grass wasn't all green after. . . Strange! Whom might one believe today, if one can't trust one's own eyes!]

The reference to eyesight, in a play that deals with an artist, in a play written by an artist, is an important one. The ghost of Frankowski—whether a ghost indeed, or a figment of Adam's fevered imagination—takes up this hint a few lines on and builds his temptation around it. From sight as instrument of recognition we move on to consciousness of one's appearance: *being* a sight for others to recognize:

FRANKOWSKI: Fason! Rozumiesz chłopcze?! Mazgaić się to nie sztuka. Fason i gest! Na gest stać uczciwego nieboszczyka! A to nie jest bez znaczenia dla historii, jaki przybierzesz w trumnie gest! Ubieraj się! Pójdziemy razem. Nie bój się nic. Przez tych łapiduchów cię przeprowadzę. Nie będziesz przecież konał w szpitalnych gaciach z termometrem pod pachą, kiedy na kołku wisi kurtka powstańcza i rogatywka z kokardą! / . . . / Miałeś talent artysty. Tembardziej nie wypada ci spaskudzić ładnie podmalowanego obrazu. O! to rozumiem! Kokarda ci do twarzy! to są rzeczy, które zostają! Właściwie to tylko z nas zostaje tutaj. I to wrogów straszy. No niech ci kto taką kokardę odstrzeli, jeśli ją nosi duch.

ADAM: Tak, rzeczywiście! Nie pozostaje nic jak zostać bohaterem! Jednym z wielu—jak każdy z was. Ale przeszkoda jedna wielka! Jednego buta wdziać nie mogę.

FRANKOWSKI: Nie szkodzi. Piękny chłopak jesteś i z tym bandażem, bez buta. Niejedna dziewucha się obejrzy i zapamięta na wieki.

ADAM: Czemu na wieki?

FRANKOWSKI: No, bo doczesność twoja dla wszystkich dziewuch świata skończona. Zostaje kokarda i do tej kokardy dorobiona legenda. Powinieneś ułatwić robotę temu, co będzie robił legendę.

(14)

[FRANKOWSKI: It's all about style! Understand, boy?! It doesn't take any talent to be a crybaby. Style, and *geste*! An honest corpse can afford a *beau geste*! And it's not without meaning for history, what sort of posture you assume in your coffin. Get up! We leave together. Don't be afraid of anything. I'll lead you through these stretcherbearers. You're not going to die in bed, wearing a hospital smock, with a thermometer under your arm, as long as that rebel's coat and four-cornered cap with the cockade hang there on the hook! / . . . / You had a painter's talent. All the more so then, you shouldn't mess up a pretty picture! Now, that I understand! The cockade

147

suits you! That's the sort of thing that lasts! As a matter of fact, that's all that remains behind us. And it fills our enemies with fear. There! Let somebody shoot that cockade off you now, if it's a ghost that bears it!

ADAM: Yes, you're right! There's nothing left but to become a hero. One of so many—like each of you. But there's only one problem, and it's a big one! I can't get one of my boots on.

FRANKOWSKI: No problem. You're a good looking fellow even with that bandage, bootless. More than one lass will look twice at you, and remember the sight forever.

ADAM: Why forever?

FRANKOWSKI: Because you're finished with girls now forever. The cockade will remain, along with the legend. You ought to make his work easier, the one who'll create your legend.]

As the seriously-ill Adam Chmielowski is tempted from his sickbed by the ghosts of militant nationalism, we wonder what would have become of him had not Anna—the personification of cold realism (she is a medic) and warm Christian virtue—intervened and returned him to bed. His fanciful expedition would certainly have ended in his death, and a life filled with real service to real people would have been pre-empted in favor of a half-life as a nationalist legend—Prince Józef Poniatowski in the waves of the Elster, Pułaski falling at Savannah.

What is worse, any real action that Adam may have undertaken under the influence of his spectral visitors would have been simply horrid. We read on:

ADAM: A dokąd prowadzisz tym razem i poco? Czy jest jeszcze dla nas jakie zadanie?

148

FRANKOWSKI: Znajdzie się po drodze. Może wydusimy we śnie kilku naszych oprawców. Wykonamy wyrok sprawiedliwości. Byłoby to w każdym razie podciągnięcie świata do „Królestwa Bożego na ziemi" choć o mały cal. Idziemy! (*wychodzi nucąc*) Zgasły dla nas nadziei promienie...

(15)

[ADAM: And where are you leading me this time, and for what? Does any mission yet remain for us?

FRANKOWSKI: We'll find one on the way. Maybe we'll strangle a few of our tormentors in their sleep. We'll exact some just retribution. At the very least, it will be dragging "God's Kingdom on Earth" an inch closer. Let's go! (*he exits, singing*) The rays of hope for us extinguished. . .]

The blasphemous nature of Frankowski's proposition (so strongly reminiscent of the Devil's words about strangling the Tsar in the surreal III:5 of *Kordian*), when seen in the light of Brother Albert's later career, is so obvious as to require no explanation. All of the spectral visitors in the monumental dramas of Mickiewicz, Słowacki, Krasiński, tempt real people laboring under some psychic illness, to their ruin. Bunsch's Frankowski is true to type. It is not coincidental that the ghost's last words on stage are a snippet of a song expressing the one unforgivable sin of despair. Fortunately, Anna, a real person, who, like Mickiewicz's Father Piotr, can assess the sick man's situation rightly, enters to stop Adam from fulfilling his "orders" of murdering his fellow patients in their sleep.

In speaking of this martio-nationalistic Act I, it is to Bunsch's credit that he avoids the naive, patriotic cheerleading that would be understandable, and perhaps even defensible, considering the period in which his work was written. Instead, the ideological motor of the play is the existence of two worlds, two realities, the temporal and the eternal, the earthly order and that of God, between which Adam finds himself. His story is that of a journey from the earthly order to that established by Christ, and it is Bunsch's realization of this that allows him to look at the history of his country, and its military traditions, from a more detached point of view:

ADAM: / . . . / Idiotyczne to wszystko „Rewolucja moralna", „Za waszą wolność i naszą". „Misja narodowa, sprawiedliwość i równość, ład społeczny, zbratanie warstw narodu"!—Święty Krzyż, Opatów. . . Małogoszcz. . . Hymn bohaterstwa wyśpiewany publiczności siedzącej w wygodnych fotelach! Europa platonicznie wzdycha, bo ją to nie boli. Kto wziął decyzję? Kto jest odpowiedzialny? Nic nie przygotowane! Bez planu, bez broni, bez organizacji! Należę do grupy ludzi, którzy okazali się niegodnymi wspólnego stałego miejsca na ziemi!!!

(10)

[ADAM: / . . . / Idiotic, all of it. "The Moral Revolution," "For your freedom, and ours." "The Mission of the Nation, Justice and Equality, Social Order, the Fraternity of all the Nation's Classes"! — Holy Cross, the Abbots. . . Małogoszcz. . . The hymn of brotherhood sung to a public sitting in comfortable chairs! Europe sighs platonically, 'cause it doesn't cause her any pain! Who made the decision? Who is responsible? Nothing prepared! No plan, no weapons, no organization! I belong to a group of people who have proven themselves unworthy of a common, permanent place on earth!!!]

In these lines Adam expresses his realization that his entire nation was, like Krasiński's Henryk, chasing after a dead whore in the guise of a maiden by ingesting the unreal, unrealizable myths of the *długie nocne rodaków rozmowy* ("the long conversations of one's countrymen at eve"). The gulf between the ideal proffered and the real material which was to bring it about is just too wide, too

150

unbridgeable. It's hard to conceive of a more damning summary of Romanticism, and the wonderfully ironic thing is that it is based on the *individual*—one of the bastions of the Romantic *Weltanschauung.* Although it is a bitter cry, it is also an epiphany—a realization of what one might expect of this world, which can be summed up in the words of Lech Janerka: *nie nastąpi już żaden cud—cudów nie ma* [There'll be no miracle now—there are no miracles].[9] And why? Because when God does wish to intervene in history, He works His miracles through historical material: men and women. And these men and women must be up to the task. It is not enough simply to proclaim Poland "Christ of the nations;" through their concrete virtues and willingness to sacrifice, Poles must all, on an individual level, become Christ-like.

Thus, in rejecting the romantic/nationalistic quick-fix approach to reality, under which he had been operating up till now, Chmielowski is ready to turn his gaze inward, and concentrate on the perfection of his own self:

> ADAM: Każdy z osobna bohater albo artysta albo święty. A wszyscy razem — kupa idiotów i niedołęgów. Dlatego grozi nam rozproszenie. Wy — o wy! I ci z zachodu też: każdy z osobna może być płazem przyziemnym, albo ordynarnym łajdakiem, ale razem są: wojsko, albo związek, albo państwo!
>
> (10)

> [ADAM: Each one alone is either hero or artist or saint. But all together—a bunch of idiots and cripples. And that's why we're faced with dispersion. You — oh, you! And those in the West too: each one alone can be either a beast crawling on his belly, or a vulgar bastard, but together they become: an army, or a union, or a nation!]

---

[9] Lech Janerka, from the song "Dobranoc."

The catalogue of individual virtues, with which this speech begins (and which, coincidentally, mirrors the career of Brother Albert himself), must be read as a two-fold statement. Firstly, everyone pretends to be hero, artist or saint, but when it comes time for action, these cloaks are cast off and their professors' true individual natures are shown to be quite far from the promised goods, whereas the Russian army and state, or that of Prussia in the "West," may be made up of beasts and villains, but they *work*. Now, the next step must be taken. Adam is calling for a regeneration of individuals, an authentication on a personal level, if you will, which will lead in turn to the regeneration of Poland. By becoming heroes, artists, saints individually and actually, Poland becomes a nation to be reckoned with once these actual strengths are united. We are reminded of Stanisław, the narrator of Ferdynand Goetel's *Z dnia na dzień* [From Day to Day], who smirks:

I ja ubrałem się w żakiet i wraz z innymi współdziałałem dokoła puszczania w społeczeństwo dreszczów państwowości. Wypadło lepiej niż się spodziewałem. Wszystkiego było w miarę, a hymn państwowy zagrano tylko raz jeden. I nikt nie przypomniał, że „Polska to wielka rzecz". Chwała Bogu, bo może stanie się nią naprawdę, gdy już raz skończymy z tą dewizą.[10]

[I myself dressed up in a tux, and along with others, cooperated in the dissemination of patriotic shivers through society. Actually, it turned out better than I had thought. Everything was done modestly, and the national anthem was played only once. And no one admonished us that "Poland is a grand thing." Thank God, because maybe she'll actually become so, when we finally put that slogan away.]

---

[10] Ferdynand Goetel, *Z dnia na dzień* (London: Orbis/Księgarnia Polska, 1957), p. 80.

The idea mentioned above of two worlds, two realities to choose from, and the fact that following the higher road, the road of Christ, can lead to a bettering of the one below, that heroic self-sacrifice can conquer miserable self-centeredness, is given broader treatment toward the end of Act I, in the words of Anna:

ANNA: Są światy na tym świecie. Przegrana bitwa, czy wojna nie jest przegraną człowieka. Utrata broni w jednym świecie nie jest rozbrojeniem człowieka. Fortepianu Szopena boją się wrogowie więcej niż polskich armat.

ADAM: Zwłaszcza, gdy ich niema. Ale cóż ja? Bliższy byłem zdobycia armat, niż fortepianu.

ANNA: Któż to może napewno wiedzieć? Mnie się wydaje, że na czole twojem wypisane są dziwne rzeczy.

(17)

[ANNA: There are different worlds in this world. A lost battle, or a lost war doesn't equal a lost man. The loss of a weapon in one world does not mean the disarming of the man. Our enemies fear Chopin's grand piano more than Polish cannon.

ADAM: Especially when there are no cannons. But I? I was closer to capturing cannons than grand pianos.

ANNA: Who can know that for sure? It seems to me that strange things are written on your forehead.]

Anna, as we have earlier remarked, is a real person, an antidote to the hallucinatory specters of Adam's military past. And as they would lead him to his ruin, body and soul, according to the dictates of the romantic, nationalistic siren-song, so Anna seeks to lead Adam out of his "possession," exorcising these ghosts, and turning him towards other, real, and realizable human goals. It is worth noting that the road she seems to be pointing him towards does not lead directly to the religious life, but to art, to his first transformation, from soldier to artist. For even though her words are—unconsciously, perhaps—a leading forth from the national-messianic tradition of Mickiewicz and Słowacki toward the ideal of the Christian artist as exemplified by Norwid, and even though there will occur a somewhat Franciscan "betrothal" scene in which Adam and she will exchange the Crosses their mothers had given them, to make Sister Anna of the Tsarist field hospital into Anna the Prophetess of Luke's Presentation in the Temple scene, would be to ruin the entire ideological thrust of Bunsch's play. For Adam is not being directed by a spirit, or a spiritualist—he is being guided by a real person, a woman of flesh and blood. She takes him to the next stop on his journey; he will only arrive at his destination thanks to the Holy Spirit.

Wojtyła's play, for reasons of dramatic focus, ignores this first transformation of the protagonist from soldier to artist. The dramatic tension of *Our God's Brother*, and here some have seen an autobiographical motif) centers on the transformation from artist to religious. In the first act of the future Pope's play, aptly entitled *Pracownia przeznaczeń* [The Workshop of Destinies], a good amount of stage time—ten whole pages of text—pass before Adam even comes on stage. Characteristically, while all present are discussing aesthetics, Adam, in whom the leaven of metanoia is already at work, directs his first words—his first in the entire play—to some beggars offstage whom he has led home:

> (*Drzwi otwierają się szybko.*
> ADAM. *Mówi jeszcze przez drzwi do kogoś z drugiej strony:*)
> —A więc to tutaj. Zapamiętajcie sobie dobrze. Numer domu. Piętro. Drzwi. Możecie przyjść dziś wieczór. Będzie można się przespać.
>
> MAKS: (*do otaczających*) Te historie stają się coraz częstsze. Coraz mniej tu pracowni malarza, coraz więcej przytułku dla żebraków.
>
> (120)

154

[(*The door opens quickly.*
ADAM. *He speaks to someone on the other side of the door:*)
—So this is it. Remember it well. The number, the floor, the door. You can come this evening. You'll be able to sleep here.

MAKS: (*to the others*) This sort of thing happens ever more often. This place is becoming ever less of a painter's atelier, and ever more of a beggars' shelter.]

Krzysztof Zanussi, who made a film of the play, calls *Brat naszego Boga* "relatively the most dramatic" of the Pope's plays, because in it, as nowhere else in his dramatic corpus, we have the "opposition of antagonistic points of view."[11] In the latter, socially-oriented parts of Wojtyła's play, Adam's foil will be the "Stranger," a Communist agitator limned in broad Leninist lines. In this first portion of the drama, the role of antagonist is played in the main by Maks Gierymski, and the battle concerns the role and intrinsic value of art:

MAKS: Uważam, że powinieneś malować za wszelką cenę. Powinieneś sobie zadawać gwałt.

ADAM: Na to by trzeba jeszcze wierzyć w sztukę, tak jak ty![12]   (126)

---

[11] See the next item in this book, the conversation with Krzysztof Zanussi, pp. 195-196.

[12] Wojtyła's play is quite faithful to what we know of Brother Albert's biography. In 1930, writing, at the behest of the Albertines, his memories of his friend, Andrzej Szeptycki, Metropolitan Archbishop of Lwów, notes: *W świecie jednak bywał i gorąco uczestniczył w dyskusjach artystycznych /. . . / Ale nie tylko o malarstwie dysputował Brat Albert. Zaczynał i religijne dyskusje. W tym świecie malarzy i literatów, którzy go wszyscy bardzo kochali, śmiało poruszał żywotne pytanie religii* [Yet he was in the world and took part enthusiastically in artistic discussions /. . . / In this world of painters and writers, all of whom loved him greatly, he boldly moved important religious

155

[MAKS: I think that you should paint, at all costs. You should force yourself to paint.

ADAM: To do that, I'd still have to believe in art as you do!]

Seen from the perspective of this little exchange of words from Act I, it might be said that there is little, if any, dramatic movement in *Brat naszego Boga*. Adam's fate is sealed from square one, and our interest is concentrated on the hows, whys, and whens of his transformation into servant of the poor; there are no "ifs," and in this sense, our dramatic experience of Wojtyła's play is similar to a lecture of the latter chapters of St. Augustine's *Confessions*, in which we wait, with the future saint agonizing between two wills, for the grace that will break the infinitesimal chains holding him back from Christ. However, as in the case of the *Confessions*, the experience is engaging, and one is pleasantly surprised at the artistic maturity of the young priest, who constructs so beautiful a metaphorical context around one of the play's central visual images: Brother Albert's magnificent, unfinished canvas, the *Ecce Homo*:

ADAM: /. . . / Jestem głęboko przeświadczony, że to wszystko razem to nic innego jak ciągła ucieczka.

STANISŁAW: Ucieczka?

ADAM: Tak. Ucieczka.

STANISŁAW: Przed kim?

ADAM: W pewnym znaczeniu przed sobą samym. Ale nie. (*snuje*) Przecież Maks także jest sobą, Maks także żyje w tym samym świecie, co ja, co każdy z

---

questions] Ks. Arcybiskup Andrzej Szeptycki, Metropolita Lwowski Obrządku Grecko-Katolickiego, *Ze wspomnień o Bracia Albercie* [From my Memories of Brother Albert], in *Tygodnik Powszechny* (Kraków, 9 September 1984, XXXVIII/37), p. 1. Archbishop Szeptycki's memoirs first appeared in a 1934 edition of the *Przegląd powszechny* [Universal Review].

nas. A Maks nie musi uciekać, nie ma poczucia, że
jest ścigany... A zatem to nie jest... ucieczka przed
sobą samym.

MAKS: Oczywiście, zapewne ucieczka przed
odpowiedzialnością. Tak? Ciekaw jestem, w jaki
sposób ja mogę być odpowiedzialny za obywatela,
który zmarnował swoje życie i teraz jest na dnie?

ADAM: Ty ciągle myślisz, Maks, że układ ludzkiej
nędzy odpowiada układowi kary...
No, mniejsza. Ale to nie jest tylko ucieczka przed
odpowiedzialnością. To jest ucieczka przed czymś, a
może raczej przed kimś w sobie i przed kimś w
tamtych wszystkich ludziach.

(125)

[ADAM: / . . ./ I am firmly convinced, that all of this
is nothing more than a constant escaping.

STANISŁAW: An escape?

ADAM: Yes. An escape.
STANISŁAW: From whom?

ADAM: In a certain sense, from myself. But no. (*he
ponders*) After all, Maks is himself, Maks lives in
the same world as me, as all of us. And Maks isn't
escaping. He doesn't feel as if he's being pursued...
And so this isn't... an escape from myself.

MAKS: Of course. It's an escape from responsibility,
right? But I'm curious. How can I be held
responsible for a citizen who's ruined his own life,
and now finds himself on the bottom?

ADAM: You're always thinking, Maks, that poverty
is some sort of penalty. But less of that. At any rate,

it's not only an escape from responsibility. It's an escape from something, or rather someone, in myself and in all those people.]

This motif of seeing Christ in the poor is carried throughout the second act of Wojtyła's play, *W podziemiach gniewu* [In the Undergrounds of Anger]. On a stroll with the supremely interesting character known only as "Tamten" (i.e. "That One," a tempter figure which, we can never be sure, either exists on his own, or is a projection of Adam's persona), "they" pass by a homeless man helplessly leaning on a lamppost:

ADAM: / . . . / Jest w nim coś więcej niż żebrak oparty o latarnię.

TAMTEN: Czyżby? Nic o tym nie wiem.

ADAM: A właśnie. W nim jest obraz.

TAMTEN: Ach tak, dla ciebie wszystko ma wartość obrazu. Jesteś malarz.

ADAM: Obraz pozamalarski. Obraz nieuchwytny mojemu oku, a który trawi od dawna moją duszę.

TAMTEN: Nie poddawaj się. Odstąp. Zapomnij.

ADAM: (*jakoby nie dosłyszał*). Obraz i podobieństwo.

(141)

[ADAM: / . . . / There's something greater in him than just a beggar leaning against a lamppost.

THAT OTHER: Oh, yes? I know nothing about it.

ADAM: Of course. In him, there's an image.

158

THAT OTHER: Oh, sure. For you, everything has value as a picture. You're a painter.

ADAM: Greater than a painting. An image my eye can't see, but which has tormented my soul for so long.

THAT OTHER: Don't give in. Step back. Forget it.

ADAM: (*as if he didn't hear that*). The image and likeness.]

This is the determining scene, the recognition scene, if you will, in the Pope's drama. Hoisting the helpless man onto his shoulders, Adam smiles *No chodź. Uratowałeś mnie* [Come on then. You've saved me], and in the scene which follows, Wojtyła closes the magnificent extended metaphor with Adam's monologue before the *Ecce Homo* canvas:

> Ty musisz przybrać dla mnie ten kształt.
> Ten kształt, który obejmuję duszą, i te plamy barw
> na płótnie — i Ty w tylu ludziach — to jedno —
> (*Z wysiłkiem:*)
> —To jedno!
> (*Odstępuje na krok:*)
> Przecież tak Cię utrwalę w tylu, tylu ludziach.
> (143)

> [You must take on this form for me.
> This form, which I embrace with my soul, and the splashes of color on the canvas—and You in so many people—are the same—
> (*With effort:*)
> —The same!
> (*He moves back a step:*)
> This is how I will set You, in many, many people.]

One of the differences in the second transformation of Adam Chmielowski into Brother Albert that we find in the plays of Wojtyła and Bunsch can be formulated this way. For Wojtyła, although the change of orientation from painter to religious seems doomed from the start, the decision itself seems to possess a soul-shattering weight. For Wojtyła's Adam, it is truly a religious decision. As we have seen in a previously cited fragment, the choice is between believing in God and believing in art. This perspective rests on deep biographical bedrock, as we read from the following excerpts of Chmielowski's correspondence. In 1873, writing to his friend and patron Łucjan Siemieński, he states:

> I malarz i zakonnik poeta. . . czy sztuce służąc, Bogu też służyć możem? Chrystus mówi, że dwóm panom służyć nie można. Choć sztuka nie mamona, ale też nie bóg, bożyszcze prędzej. Ja myślę, że służyć sztuce, to zawsze wyjdzie na bałwochwalstwo, chyba jak Fra Angelico sztukę i talent, i myśli Bogu ku chwale poświęcić i święte rzeczy malować.[13]
> [Both the painter and the monk are poets. . . now, serving art, can we also serve God? Christ tells us that one cannot serve two masters. Although art is not Mammon, it's not a god either, more like an idol. I think that the service of art always ends in idolatry, unless perhaps like Fra Angelico one devotes one's art and one's talent, one's thoughts, to God and paints holy things.]

Seven years later, in a letter to Helena Modrzejewska, his tone is even more plain:

> Choć nie wiem, czy talent mam, czy tylko talencik, to wiem jednak z pewnością, że jestem w drodze do

[13] Cited by Tadeusz Chrzanowski in "Adam Chmielowski — św. Brat Albert, czyli pomiędzy sztuką a świętością." [Adam Chmielowski — St. Brother Albert, or Between Art and Sanctity] in *Kraków: dialog tradycji* [Kraków: a Dialogue of Traditions], ed. Zbigniew Baran (Kraków: Znak/Międzynarodowe Centrum Kultury, 1991), p. 103.

powrotu z nad samego brzegu tej rzeki, a wieluż ich pochłonęła, tych nieszczęśliwych topielców i wieluż wciąż pochłania. Sztuka i tylko sztuka, byle jej uśmiech albo cień uśmiechu, byle jedna róża z wianka bogini, bo z nią sława i dostatek i osobiste zadowolenie—mniejsza o resztę: gubi się w szalonej gonitwie rodzinę, moralność, związek z Bogiem, gubi wszystko co dodatnie i święte—lata uciekają, organizacja fizyczna niszczeje, a z nią i talent tak zwany—poza tym śmierć—ale żebyż tylko śmierć i nicość, ale i to nie, bo dusza nie umiera nigdy. . .[14]

[Although I don't know whether I have a real talent, or just a lick of a talent, I do know this for sure, that I am on my way back from the very edge of that river [*this is a citation from Słowacki's* Kordian I:ii, 359-60, *talenta są to w ręku szalonych latarnie / ze światłem idą prosto topić się do rzeki:* "talents in the hands of the mad are lanterns; / they follow the light right into the river, to drown"] and many it has swallowed, these unfortunate drowned souls, and it swallows them constantly. Art and nothing but art, her smile, or just the shadow of her smile, at least one rose from the garland of the goddess, for she brings fame and fortune and personal satisfaction—who cares about the rest: one loses in an insane chase one's family, morals, one's union with God; one's physical powers are destroyed, and with it one's so-called talent—and then there's death—but if it were only death and nothingness, but no, 'cause the soul never dies. . .]

Bunsch, perhaps because he was a painter himself, and thus free of the gawking awe of the neophyte for the artist-as-prophet, under which so many outsiders labor, has his Adam look at painting as a craft:

---

[14] Cited by Chrzanowski, p. 103.

HRABIANKA: (*podchodzi do okna zamyślona*) A czego tam ludzie szukają teraz pod drzewem?

ADAM: Tam śmietnik.

HRABIANKA: Śmietnik? ! Tak, teraz dopiero widzę jaki tam brud. Boże! A wszystko tak przykryte kwieciem. Piękne to przeznaczenie: przykrywać wszystko co brzydkie na świecie! I jaki — mimo wszystko piękny jest ten świat, wiosną przez kwiaty a zawsze przez sztukę!

ADAM: (*odkłada pendzle i wstaje*) Czy to ironia? Czy tak pani naprawdę sądzi?

(21)

[COUNTESS: (*moves over to the window, in thought*) And what are those people looking for, under the tree?

ADAM: That's a garbage dump.
COUNTESS: A dump?! Yes, now I see how dirty it is there. God! And everything covered with blossoms. What a beautiful destiny: to cover over everything that's ugly in the world! And how — despite it all — how beautiful is the world; beautified in spring by flowers, and for all time by art!

ADAM: (*setting aside his brushes and rising*). Are you being ironic? Or do you really think so?]

Thus, in Act II of Bunsch's drama, Adam will have a second ghost to lay. Expressed by the coquettish countess, who visits him in his atelier (and is something of a second love interest, after Anna), it is the exaggerated notion of the artist's special aura, his mission to the world, his being set apart from the common rout, for which English lacks the edgy descriptive word we find in the Polish *pięknoduchstwo.* As can be seen from the above-cited exchange, Adam doesn't share this mannerism at all. Where the blinkered countess can only see the blossoming tree, Adam sees the garbage beneath it; her love of art as escapism, as the "beautiful destiny" of covering all that is ugly in the world with a beautiful veneer, shocks Adam, who wonders if she is not mocking him.

Because Bunsch's Adam looks at painting, more or less, as a job like any other, and because he also has a realistic approach to appraising the world, this "ghost" of effete aestheticism will not be that difficult for him to exorcise. The loving, human approach to others which will see him through to his self-sacrifice on behalf of the poor will not be a conversion, but rather an awakening of something that has lain dormant in him. Later, in this same scene, when a fight breaks out between some people squabbling over rags at that garbage dump, we see this clearly:

> HRABIANKA: / . . . / O! Niech pan spojrzy! Tam się teraz biją dwa dziady. O co oni się biją?

> ADAM: Biją się dwaj ludzie — rzeczywiście. To śmieciarze.
>
> (24)

> [COUNTESS: / . . . / Oh! Have a look here! Two bums are fighting now. What are they fighting over?

> ADAM: Yes, two people are fighting. They're ragpickers.]

Where the Countess sees "two bums," Adam counters immediately with "two people"—two human beings. The definition of "ragpickers" that he adds is not a scornful evaluation like "bums" — it is an answer to her second question. This is what they do—as we see later in the play—they try to make a living out of the materials tossed aside by those better off than they, and this is at the root of their quarrel.

If Wojtyła's Adam is like St. Augustine, Bunsch's Adam, the painter, is more like Aeneas. He needs no "conversion" to make the final transformation from artist to servant of the poor—he needs

163

a reawakening, a reminder of his responsibility to Christian love for his brothers. He needs the sudden appearance of a messenger from God to awaken him from his quiet, well-fed life, as Wojtyła's hero puts it, *na małej wysepce zbytku* ("on his little island of luxury," 122), with a rousing *Quid struis? aut qua spe Libycis teris otia terris?*[15]

In Adam's case, Mercury to his Aeneas will be played by a little homeless boy from the municipal almshouse, who shatters his artistic musings by slinging a stone through the window of his atelier. The stone will pierce a canvas that Adam had been contemplating, a portrait, and after his first rush of anger is spent, Adam's heart will be moved with pity for the hungry urchin whom the policeman leads into the garret for punishment. He will feed the child, and accompany him to the almshouse, where he will come face to face with the needs of the poor, and his final transformation will be effected.

Before we move on to that, however, we should point out that the portrait destroyed was that of Anna. These are Adam's thoughts just before the rock tears through the portrait:

ADAM: (*siada przy oknie przy sztalugą i patrzy w obraz kobiety*). Anna jej było na imię. Siostra Anna! I więcej nie dowiedziałem się nic. . . Gdzie ty teraz jesteś Anno? Może to dobrze, że nie widzieliśmy się więcej! Nie zmieniony jestem do dziś w twoich oczach i ty nie zmieniłaś się dla mnie.

(25)

[ADAM: (*sitting down by an easel at the window and gazing at the painting of a woman*). Anna was her name. Sister Anna! I learned nothing else about her... Where are you now, Anna? Maybe it's better that we never saw each other again! To this day I remain unchanged in your eyes, and you have not changed for me.]

---

[15] Virgil, *Aeneis*, IV: 271 [What is it you're arranging here? In hope of what are you lazing about in Lybia?]

The last line, spoken just before the vandalism, is more than a sticky sweet for the sentimental. It has just as deep a philosophical resonance in this play as the *Ecce Homo* metaphor does in *Brat naszego Boga*. For as we have said at the outset, the journey of Bunsch's Adam Chmielowski is from chimeras to flesh and blood, from empty slogans and spiritualism to spiritual reality. Anna, the person of flesh and blood who saved Adam from the martial specters threatening to destroy him, has become idealized, spiritualized, falsified in turn by Adam's painting her portrait *in absentia*; by eternalizing her on his canvas he has killed her, set her up as a muse, made her into just another spirit to lead him through, if not actually away from, the real world. Thus, there is a deep philosophical and poetic meaning to the fact that it is *her* portrait, her false image, which is destroyed by the second great, salvific incursion of reality into Adam's life—the brusque entrance once again of flesh and blood, in the person of the little boy.

The scenes in the municipal almshouse, which constitute the final third of both plays, are perhaps the most realistic of all. It seems that both authors, Bunsch and Wojtyła, were after the same thing: the last specter to be dealt with, the last mirage to be wafted away, is the false image of the poor, and with it, a false understanding of Christianity and Christian sanctity. In neither *Brat naszego Boga* nor *Gołębie Brata Alberta*, is Adam Chmielowski shown as a sweet pastel-hued saint from a holy card. Instead, in both plays we have a real man, doing real, holy work, among real people.

We have seen how Wojtyła expands the image of *Ecce Homo* into a metaphor of suffering humanity in general. One of the strongest scenes in his play occurs when Adam enters the *ogrzewalnia* with alms and cast-off clothing for the poor. We, like he himself, do not expect the reception he receives there. Mocked, rejected by the people he had come to help, it is in this scene that he most resembles Christ—Christ at the pillory:

[JEDEN Z BIEDNYCH]: He, ty! Słuchaj no, dobrodzieju od dobroczyńców, zabieraj się z tym wszystkim! / . . . / No, słyszysz, zabieraj się, mówię, bo wstanę. Zabieraj się, pókim dobry. / . . . / Mówię ostatni raz. A wy rozumiecie, hołoto?! Jak wam kto w gębę napluje, to też weźmiecie. Siedzi to draństwo po pałacach, wygrzewa się, baluje, kpinkuje, przepija od czasu do czasu likierem; a jak im od czasu do czasu wyobraźnia taka przyjdzie, to ci rzucą ochłap. Szmatę znoszoną albo spleśniały chleb. A ty się kłaniaj, nazywaj dobrodziejami i całuj ręce.

A to jest wszystko jedna niesprawiedliwość i krzywda. Rozumiecie?

Za co tamten chodzi w garniturze i pod krawatem — a ja nie mam czym grzbietu zasłonić? Dość, dość. Niech lepiej znika z oczu. / . . . / Więcej to warta niż pierwszy lepszy strzęp.

(138-39)

[/ONE OF THE POOR/: Hey, you! Listen here, your do-gooder from do-gooders, get out of here with all that stuff! / . . . / Do you hear? Out, I say! Don't make me get up! Get out while I'm still in a good mood. / . . . / I'm telling you for the last time. And you, you rabble, do you understand?! Even when they spit in your mouths you take it. Rascals like this sit in their palaces, warming themselves, dancing, joking, tippling liquor from time to time; and when the mood strikes them, they toss you their offal. Their worn-out rags or their moldy bread. And you bow low, call them benefactors, kiss their hands.

And all of this is one big injustice and wrong. Understand?

How come that one there walks about in a suit and tie—and I don't have anything to cover my back with? Enough, enough. Let him get out of here. /.../ That's worth more than the best rag in the lot.]

Zanussi speaks of the challenge of portraying an *uduchowiony* (soulful, spiritualized) hero in a way that should not make him seem emasculated.[16] By opting for so realistic an image of poverty over the saccharine image of the strong shepherd greeted with open arms by an innocent, grateful flock—as many a Victorian catechist might have written the scene—Wojtyła gets right at the heart of Adam's greatest example of courage. For in this beautiful scene, this horrid, powerful scene, Wojtyła shows us that the difficulty with the poor is not feeding them, it is loving them. It is loving them and continuing to help them despite their rejection of us, despite their—perhaps justified—anger. How easy it would have been for any of us, greeted in a similar fashion, to wash our hands of the whole situation, to shrug and turn our back on the ungrateful poor with a self satisfied pat on the back: "Well, I've tried. They wanted nothing of it." But Adam is ready not only to see Christ in others, but to let others see Christ in him as well. He will not only be servant to the poor, he will endure imitating the Suffering Servant. This is the sense of the following exchange, upon his return to the almshouse:

A: A, to on.
B: Jeszcze mu się nie znudziło?
C: Powinno mu było wystarczyć . . .

ADAM: /. . . / Tak, mnie wystarczyło.   Nie wystarczyło Jemu.

(147-48)

[A: Oh, it's him.

B: He's not bored with it yet?

C: One would think he'd had enough . . .

ADAM: / . . . / Yes, I've had enough. He hasn't.]

---

[16] See the conversation with Krzysztof Zanussi, p. 197.

In Bunsch's play, we have a similar situation, only here the isolation of Adam as the Suffering Servant, as Christ at the pillory, is even more intense. As in Wojtyła's play, Bunsch's Adam is rejected and mocked by the inhabitants of the poorhouse:

> SIERAK: Gość! Czego tu właściwie u nas chce? Artykuł do gazetki po pięć centów od wiersza, czy scenka do powieści, czy smutny obrazek na wystawę? / . . . / Albo misjonarz w cywilu nawracać grzeszników!
>
> (35)

> [SIERAK: A guest! What exactly does he want with us? An article for the paper at five cents a line, a scene for a novel, or a sad picture for an exhibition? / . . . / Maybe he's a missionary in mufti, looking for converts!]

One of them even takes the opportunity to steal his wallet. When the crime is discovered and the perpetrator found by a police agent making his nightly rounds in the almshouse, Adam, like the bishop in Hugo's *Les misérables* when confronted with Jean Valjean's theft of his silver, lies to protect the offender: *To ja dałem właśnie. . . aby rozdzielić między potrzebujących tej ogrzewalni. . . tak przed świętami zapomogę. . .* ("I gave it to him . . . to distribute among the needy in this poorhouse . . . alms at the holidays. . ." 38). Of course, the agent doesn't believe that by a long shot, and his parting words, spoken as something of a soliloquy, are key to our understanding of Bunsch's Adam as Christ at the pillory:

> AGENT: / . . . / Dobranoc! Taki zakład powinien być lepiej izolowany. Spotkać dziwaka takiego, to lepiej żeby czarny kot przebiegł drogę. . .
>
> (38)

> [AGENT: / . . . / Good night! An institution like this ought to be better isolated. It's better to have a black

cat cross your path than meet with a weirdo like
that...]

Like the Countess earlier, the police agent would like to see the
almshouse—one of the "ugly" things in the world—better isolated,
out of view, out of the reach of "weirdos" like Adam. Most
important, however, is the thrust of his disparaging approach to
Adam. He thinks Adam to be a crazy person, perhaps even more
dangerous than the despairing inhabitants of the poorhouse. And
with this—his rejection by the "better" classes of society,
represented by the guardians of social order—as well as by the
extremely poor, for whom that society has little, if any, place, Adam
is isolated even more perfectly than in Wojtyła's play, and thus
becomes all the more similar to the Saviour.

Just as the Countess' views on art represent the chimera of
aestheticism, so do the actions and words of the police agent
express a chimerical understanding, a false understanding, of
Christianity and Christian sanctity. Surely the police agent, and the
officer who accompanies him, as well as nearly the entire upper
echelons from which Adam himself descends in turn of the century
Austrian Kraków, would call themselves Christians, and await,
piously and smugly, an eternal reward in heaven—a heaven without
poorhouses. But are they really Christian? And will their brand of
Christianity—dare I say our brand—lead them, necessarily, to that
eternal palace where, from time to time, they'll relax over a nip of
liquor, after a dance? We get the impression that if it were Christ
Himself, instead of Adam, standing before the police agent, He
would be rejected nonetheless by this upright Christian man, who
would leave the almshouse with the same words, twirling his fingers
at his temple.

Towards the very end of Bunsch's play, Christological
references abound. We have allusions to Mary Magdalene, the
Raising of Lazarus, and Doubting Thomas. But there is no more
moving scene in the entire play than Adam's final transformation
into a religious, which is expressed in such a way that it
foreshadows his elevation to the altar.

In Wojtyła's *Brat naszego Boga*, Adam wins the heart of
the poor by his unflagging determination to serve them, practically,

which is emphasized in contrast to the fiery exhortations of the Communist Stranger, who can only offer them promises and a promised land that they will never see. Similarly, in Bunsch's play, Adam's undeterred desire to help wins his acceptance into the circle that had earlier pushed him away. His entrance into religious life is handled by the author in a marvelous manner. Just like the novice's entry into religious life, Adam receives a new name—Albert—bestowed on him by the almshouse inhabitants' faulty memories—a name he accepts. From now on he will be theirs; from now on he will be Albert. There then occurs the vows and *indutus habitu* scene:

ADAM: / . . . / Tu już na zawsze zostanę. Przyszedłem przed dwunastą, aby nie wybiła dwunasta nigdy. Będę jak wy spał i jadł, żebyście widzieli, że nie jestem stolikowym duchem.

GARBUS: (*podchodzi i dotyka go*). Jeśli chcesz z nami zostać na zawsze to dobrze; bądź naszym hersztem. Kuba już nam się sprzykrzył, a jest od ciebie słabszy. Zresztą często siedzi i wtedy w norze porządku niema. Ale z koca zrobię ci habit mnisi, bo tak ubrany jeszcze żaden święty nie chodził po ziemi i potem na ołtarz nie przyjmą klechy (*wraz z Kuternogą okrywają go kocem robiąc rodzaj habitu. On pozwala im na to i stoi cichy, spokojny. Postać jego w habicie w mroku na tle bladych promieni światła nabiera nieziemskiej powagi, wszyscy w milczeniu zbliżają się jak urzeczeni do postaci*).

SIERAK: Kto jest między nami? Czy to ten sam? Czy to pan?

ADAM: Brat.

SIERAK: Czyj brat?

ADAM: Człowieka brat.

SIERAK: Powiedz bracie, co wiesz jeszcze o świecie. Powiedz wszystko co wiesz.

ADAM: Nic wam już więcej nie powiem, tylko jedno, a to będzie wszystko co jeszcze wiem: że Ojca mamy w niebie i że do niego mówi się tak: (*klęka*) Ojcze nasz który jesteś w niebie (*wszyscy klękają*).

(48)

[ADAM: / . . . / Now I'll always remain here. I've come before midnight, so that midnight will never strike. I'll eat with you and sleep with you, so that you know I'm more than just a ghost at the nightstand.

GARBUS: (*comes close and touches him*). If you want to stay with us forever, all right. You can be our boss. We're tired of Kuba, and he's weaker than you anyway. What's more he's always in the clink, and then there's no order here in the den. But first let me make you a monk's habit from this blanket, 'cause no saint ever went around dressed like you, and later the black robes wouldn't set you the altar (*Along with Kuternoga, he covers him with a blanket as if it were a monk's habit. Adam permits it, standing quietly, peacefully. His figure, covered in the grey habit, in the darkness, against the background of the rays of light, takes upon itself an unearthly gravity. All approach him in silence, as if charmed.*)

SIERAK: Who is this among us? Is this the same person? Is this you?

ADAM: Brother.

171

SIERAK: Who's brother?

ADAM: The brother of man.

SIERAK: Then tell us, brother, what you know of the world. Tell us everything you know.

ADAM: I won't tell you anything more than this, and this is all I know: that we have a Father in the heavens, and one addresses him like this: (*he kneels*) Our Father, who art in heaven (*all kneel*)]

He has taken upon himself an "unearthly gravity" in a tableau that once again calls the *Ecce Homo* canvas to mind, but this is not to suggest that it is "unreal." Just the contrary is true: Adam has fought through all the illusions, exorcised all of the ghosts (of nationalism, effete aestheticism, surface Christianity) and realized that other, overarching, only *real* reality—that which Gerard Manley Hopkins calls man's "inscape"—identification with Christ.[17] Never was there a more real Adam Chmielowski than now, as Albert. The fact that this transformation comes at the hands of the poor—they rename him, they accept his vow and present him with his habit—is the strongest expression of real sanctity found in any piece of literature that I have read.[18] For it shows us that sanctity is not to be attained simply by reading holy books and binding our hands in rosaries so tightly that they cannot be moved when reached out for by the weak—saints, like Brother Albert, Isidore of Seville, St. Joseph, Henry Garnet, Maksymilian Kolbe,

---

[17] Vide Gerard Manley Hopkins, "As Kingfishers catch fire. . .", 11-14: *[man] acts in God's eye what in God's eye he is—/ Christ. For Christ plays in ten thousand places, / Lovely in limbs, and lovely in eyes not his / To the Father through the features of men's faces.*

[18] Equaled only, perhaps, by the wonderful scene in Sienkiewicz's *Quo vadis?* in which a Christian father accepts as a brother the man who had tormented his daughter, after he has confessed his sin and become a Christian himself.

become sanctified *through* contact with everyday reality, not by escaping from it.[19]

Finally, it is worth noting that both Wojtyła and Bunsch affirm that there is no shortcut to sainthood. It is Christ one must imitate, not Brother Albert. In both plays, a character who wishes to follow in Adam's footsteps is gently dissuaded from doing so. In *Brat naszego Boga,* the young musician Hubert is turned away with the words:

> BRAT STARSZY (ADAM): Trudno pomyśleć, ażeby dwóch ludzi miało iść tak blisko siebie tą samą drogą. Czy to by godziło się z Jego bogactwem? Pan Bóg bogaty jest w swoich drogach.
>
> (176-77)

> [THE BROTHER GENERAL (ADAM): It's hard to think that two people should tread the same path. Would that agree with His wealth? The Lord God is wealthy in His paths.]

Similarly, Bunsch's Adam turns the little boy, whom he had first rescued from a life of homelessness, away from him and back into the world when he decides to enter the religious life, the almshouse, for good: *Ty pójdziesz do domu prostą drogą. Tą drogą, którą ci pokazałem. Ty nie możesz mi wszędzie towarzyszyć* ("You go right home. By the road I've showed you. You can't accompany me everywhere," 42). These are not rejections, they are directions to the paths each must take toward an eventual reunion. For every

---

[19] Interesting in this regard are the words of Archbishop Szeptycki: *Nie uderzał świętością—a jednak wszyscy ci, którzy się do niego zbliżali, odczuwali to, co tak doskonale określił / . . . / ks. Henryk Jackowski SJ. Mawiał o Bracie Albercie: „Nie lubię ludzi za życia kanonizować, ale to pewne, że Brat Albert robi takie dzieła, jakie tylko święci umieją robić." / . . . / Tymi drogami tylko Duch Boży może człowieka prowadzić* [He did not strike one as particularly saintly, and yet everyone who came to know him felt what Fr. Henryk Jackowski, SJ described in this regard when speaking of Brother Albert: "I don't like to canonize people during their lifetimes, but it is true that Brother Albert did such works as only saints know how to do." / . . . / Such are the roads along which only the Holy Ghost can guide a man. Szeptycki, p. 1.]

Christian is called to sanctity, but not all are called in the same way. There is, as Anna puts it early on in *Gołębie Brata Alberta,* "something strange written" on all of our foreheads, and each sign is different, yet alike. But whatever path the Christian takes to sanctity, it will not lead to illusions, however pretty. The Christian moves toward his Master with his feet firmly planted on the good solid earth.

Our God's Brother: a Conversation
KRZYSZTOF ZANUSSI and CHARLES S. KRASZEWSKI

Charles S. Kraszewski. In his introduction to the play, Karol Wojtyła calls his work not a drama, but an "attempt at penetrating a man." This seems to be something of a generic statement. Do you look at your film in a similar way, i.e. "It's not a movie, but a..." and if so, how would you fill in the blank?

Krzysztof Zanussi. Yes. I would say that it's not a film. Rather, it is theatre filmed. This doesn't have much in common with the Author's comment, which to me is a bit pretentious, in the spirit of that style of writing, directly derived from his awe for Wyspiański, on whom he was raised. (And here I'll boldly state that, for me, Wyspiański himself is pretentious.) Now, this "attempt at penetrating a man" is a goal quite compatible with dramatic form in general. For what else is a drama, if it doesn't "penetrate" the characters it presents? Perhaps that comment was an apology of sorts for the lack of dramatic construction in the work—that's possible, but the same thing can be said for the entirety of Wojtyła's dramatic works. Dialogue wasn't his strong point—his plays are monologues. He develops a line of thinking, but he doesn't oppose two antagonistic points of view. In this sense, *Our God's Brother* is, relatively speaking, the most dramatic of them all, for here the antagonist is the "Stranger."

CSK. There is relatively little "action" in Our God's Brother. *You keep very close to the text of the Pope's play, and that text is somehow closer in form to the dialogues of Plato, or, to get closer to our own time, the "trialogues" of Czech philosopher Rio Preisner, than a drama per se. It seems to me that this decision to let the deep dialogues of the text carry the dramatic tension of the film required a great deal of courage, especially from an artist like yourself, who has spoken several times of how the image has in a certain sense superseded the word.*

KZ. Did that really require courage? The very fact of my deciding to film the play of an Author, whose fame is derived not from artistic achievements, but rather from his public activity, placed me in quite an uncomfortable situation. For I set myself up as a target for charges of being opportunistic, and if there was any courage required at all, it was the courage to brush aside this sort of sniping and say: "this play is worth filming despite its imperfections, because of its important intellectual content. I would compare it to the dramatic works of other Polish Catholic writers of the forties: Zawieyski, Kossak-Szczucka—and against their intellectual background Wojtyła has the advantage. But even people from circles close to him don't like to acknowledge this. For example, I refer to the harsh commentary on the film (or rather, on the drama, really) from the pen of Fr. Adam Boniecki, the editor-in-chief of the *Tygodnik Powszechny*, and the similarly harsh review in the Catholic magazine *Znak*. George Weigel, in his *Witness to Hope*, succumbed to such opinions, openly appealing to sources close to the Pope. I see in this sort of thing a pettiness; people who confess to the Pope's greatness stress, with relish, that he wasn't anywhere near an accomplished writer, and they do it carefully, as proof of their independence, in fear of otherwise being considered uncritical.

CSK. *I've heard your film described as a "document" and as an "encyclical on film." But as far as dramatic movement is concerned—do we have the right to say that the film, like the text on which it is so closely based, elevates all of the action out of the temporal world and onto an eternal plane of decision? Would it be fair to say that the action of* Our God's Brother *takes place entirely in the soul of Adam Chmielowski?*

KZ. Even if we assign the entire transformation which occurs in the film to the soul of the protagonist, still and all the expression of this transformation is to be found in the dramatic decisions which we witness with our own eyes. Somebody gives up his art, undergoes a psychic turmoil, founds a community and is faced with a rebellion of his subordinates

176

(just like in the case of St Francis)—all of these things are external manifestations of the drama which takes place in his soul. Thus, you can't say that this is just an "encyclical for several voices" (although that's not a bad advertising slogan, and it was used in that way by my producer). On the other hand, I think that the coincidence of the thoughts expressed in this youthful work with the encyclicals written by the older man is striking.

CSK. Why does Modrzejewska appear in Our God's Brother? *Granted, Adam knew her, just as he knew Witkiewicz and Gierymski. But does the author use her as Adam's "dark sister", that is, like Maks, an artist turned in upon herself, unlike Adam, who seems tormented from the very start of his story with a need to serve others?*

KZ. As far as Modrzejewska's concerned I can only offer hypotheses. From an historical point of view, Adam was in love with her (as was Sienkiewicz and many others; she did not reciprocate). Do we have in her character a hidden autobiographical theme touching upon the Author himself, who, it seems, while associated with the Teatr Rapsodyczny favored one of his female friends with his affection, who for her part was in love with another writer? The emotional life of the future Pope, who set out on his road to the religious life relatively late, must have existed. But if our guess is correct it is still completely meaningless.

CSK. Several scenes pass in the Pope's play before Adam, the titular protagonist, comes on stage. What does this delay in introducing the main character signify? Almost eleven pages of text (in the Znak edition of Wojtyła's poetry), full of people talking about Adam, precede his entry. Why?

KZ. I think that the very "stagy," that is strongly theatrically prepared *entré* of Adam is an effective dramatic coup. His character has no chance to express the motives of his behavior by himself, so the characters of his friends do it for him. This is, of course, quite static, but at the same time it heightens our interest in the hero who, when he finally enters in action, has already been defined.

CSK. *O.K., but why do you, in an otherwise startlingly faithful treatment of the play, have Adam enter our ken before his entrance in the Wojtyła script? Of course, the audience should be filled in on his life, and the scene „in the wings" (not to mention the battle scene) is very welcome in a film that will be so dialogue-based. But it seems to me very important that the first words we hear Adam speak in the play are not about art, but charity, and directed not to his painter friends, but to the homeless: "Here it is. Remember the door. . . You can sleep here tonight."*

KZ. The entire frame (the vignette, which I added at the start) serves to explain the theatric character of the film, and to present the audience with necessary historical information. The reference to the January Uprising is addressed to the foreign spectator. A soulful or spiritualized hero might make a rather emasculated impression on one, and yet Adam Chmielowski's biography (how heroically he undergoes the amputation) bears witness to his virility. The change of address in the monologue seemed immaterial to me. It arose, simply, from the structure of the film script.

CSK. *When Adam finally does enter the atelier, an interesting conversation commences between himself, Maks, Madame Helena et al., in which Adam's position seems to be that art by itself cannot change the world. To Maks' statement "I think you ought to paint, at all costs," Adam responds, "To do so I'd still have to believe in art as you do." This seems to be the message of the Pope's play. Adam, in giving up his art, finds himself; he begins to play the role in salvation history destined for him by God. And yet the Pope uses art to deliver this message which, if not anti-art, certainly sees art as trivial in comparison to the service of love. I'm not arguing with that point of view, but this somewhat reminds me of a poem by*

Günter Grass, "In Ohnmacht gefallen," in which the poet laughs at protest songs "powerless, with a guitar," by. . . writing a protest song.

KZ. I see both the inconsistency, and the wisdom that arises from it. The wisdom is the recognition of the "many paths"—for Maks, the art of painting will be his path to a full life, whereas for Adam, it will not. Every fate, or every vocation, is different. I think that here we find the greatest biographical consistency between Adam and the Author. Wojtyła abandons his art, just like Adam, in the scene where he states that one cannot serve two masters. This resignation is painful, but not radical—sometimes art will return, but it will not be the main current of their lives. For this reason I can't see a reason for calling art as trivial in comparison with love. Art can bear love, but in the case of Adam (and the Author) another mission is more important than love. I am reminded here of an anecdote about one of the great mystics, who wrote that, if in the course of the greatest exaltation you notice that your brother has a fever, pause your prayers and give him some water.

CSK. *Your characterization of the Stranger (played by Wojciech Pszoniak) makes this character terribly similar to the historical person of Lenin. Do you find this in the text? If not, where did you get the idea for the identification?*

KZ. Whether the Stranger is Lenin or not is not a polite question! As long as Leninism was alive, and Lenin was "eternally alive," it was not proper to notice this, even though it's obvious. According to a well-known legend, Chmielowski met Lenin in Poronin—the Author knew the story—and at the Albertine convent in Kraków hangs an anonymous painting (from the sixties) which presents that scene. No character in the Pope's play has a deciphered name, despite the fact that we don't hesitate to recognize Modrzejewska in Helena and Gierymski in Maks. The type of realism presented by the Author is not strictly chronological and historical. Thus I felt that I'm not going too far in presenting the Stranger's character in this way. But I didn't want to do it pedantically, thus Pszoniak wears a different sort of beard from the classical Lenin type.

CSK. *The scene in which Adam, bearing gifts, is rejected, mocked, threatened even, by the inhabitants of the almshouse, is a marvelous one. It seems that here more than anywhere else Adam becomes Christlike. Here he undergoes his own scourging at the pillar.*

KZ. The rejection scene is also one of the most "theatrical," because it contains a conflict of intention and event and is *a*sentimental—it smashes the candied stereotype of the grateful poor, and presents something of the mechanism of revolutionism. Anger directed towards the benefactor. Adam turns the other cheek. Like Christ.

CSK. *Let's talk a little bit about the scenes with "the Other." In Krystyna Skuszanka's version, which brought the play to the stage for the first time in Kraków in 1980, these scenes hew quite close to the Pope's text. I mean, we see two actors on stage (Jan Frycz or Jerzy Grałek as Adam, Romuald Michałowski as the Other), both similar in appearance, yet still visibly two. How did you and Scott[1] arrive at the decision to do these scenes as a kind of split internal monologue? I'd like to state here that this scene is one of the strongest in the film, and really shows Scott's talents to good effect. But aren't you somewhat simplifying a consciously complicated scene? I mean, in Skuszanka's stage version, we're not quite sure just who this tempter, this Other, is. Is he a side of Adam's personality (his intellect as opposed to his heart, or the personification of his nervous condition) or someone outside of him—a diabolical tempter, in truth? In the film, it seems that only the former possibility is acknowledged.*

---

[1] Scott Wilson, the American actor who portrays Brother Albert in the film.

KZ. I remember Skuszanka's version, but in composing my adaptation I was convinced that this must be a monologue, not a dialogue, that it takes place in the protagonist's, Adam's, soul, and that just as a second actor "fits" in the conventions of the stage according to the "willing suspension of disbelief," in film, a literal treatment would create some dissonance. It is a fact that this scene was a *tour de force* for the actor, and if it wasn't for Scott I don't know what I would have done with this scene.

CSK. Another beautiful scene has Adam before the Ecce Homo *painting. At the start of his prayer he says, in near despair, "They don't need me. No. I'm convinced of that." But he ends "This is the way I'll capture you, in so many, so many people." This means that he will train himself to see, as G.M. Hopkins puts it, the Suffering Christ as the "inscape" of humanity, and treat people accordingly. So, even though he will stop painting, does Adam ever cease to be an artist?*

KZ. I will permit myself a completely irresponsible digression at this point. I look at the Author as a person who grew from theatre and who contemplates the world "theatrically." And this explains his failures sometimes. The creative eye of the portraitist sometimes outpaces the model. There are people who state that many of the Pope's unfortunate appointments arise from the fact that he often sees people like Adam—not as they actually are, but as their imagination of the artist makes them to be. And from this sometimes arise disappointments.

CSK. To speak in terms of Westerns, we have a showdown of sorts between the Stranger and Adam one evening in the almshouse. The poor reject the Stranger, and embrace Adam, it seems, because all the Stranger wants to do is exploit their anger, whereas Adam treats them as human beings. The Stranger can only offer them theory, whereas Adam helps them in a real, practical manner. What then is the sense of the revolutionary context of the final scene of the film (and the play), in which the workers go on strike, and it appears that the Stranger will finally win out after all? And how, especially, do you explain Brother Albert's seeming acquiescence to the revolution? that it „had to come about, when there is so much anger, so much just anger?" Does he approve of the revolution? His final words: „and yet I know that I've chosen the greater freedom" seem to have a ring of defeat to them.

KZ. The relationship to revolution of the young author, stirred by the postwar changes, is a fascinating theme for conjecture. I sense Wojtyła's ratiocinations as a union of opposites. Revolution is, on the one side, a punishment meted out to a soulless, merciless world which has established its order in such a way that only the demon of destruction might shake it. But a better solution would be love. As far as the scene in the asylum for the poor (the *ogrzewalnia*) is concerned, I'd like to recall an episode from the life of Rosa Luxemburg who, in moving away from Kreuzberg, the proletarian section of Berlin, said "I can give up my life for the workers, but I can't live among them any more." And she did give up her life. The Christian doctrine of love anticipates the identification of my neighbor with Christ, and therefore with me as well. I must find the face of God in my neighbor, just as I look for it in myself. The Stranger proposes the practical solution: revolution, which is perhaps even more effective than the solution proposed by Adam. But Adam becomes one of them, one of the beggars, while the Stranger says "there's no reason for me to identify myself with them."

CSK. *In the scene with the rebellious Brother Antoni, what is the distinction that Brother Albert draws between being a mendicant and being a beggar?*

KZ. I think that in this scene too the distinction is freedom. By accepting poverty, the beggar is poor by his own free choice and that does not bring discredit on his dignity. He accepts it in the name of something higher, and not as a consequence of helplessness. Christians say "love the Cross." Poverty is a cross.

CSK. *Towards the end of the film there is a very eloquent scene with beggars and a cross. I'm speaking of the "rebellion" of Brother Antoni. If, in this scene with Antoni, the somewhat beaten Brother Albert feels that he has failed to help Christ "penetrate deeply enough" into Antoni's soul (before the crucifix he says, "Who's to blame? Not Christ, not you /Antoni/, maybe me?") why does he refuse to sow the seeds on fertile soil, so to speak, when Hubert arrives at the poorhouse?*

KZ. The story of Hubert (Roztworowski) is for me most explicitly a personalistic parable. Hubert wishes to follow in Brother Albert's footsteps and is turned away because what he wants to do is take a short cut. Everybody must mature to his or her own vocation. Imitation is forbidden. Imitation leads to the reduction of the human person, its reduction to being just a portion of a crowd, deprived of freedom. Even should that crowd race after the Saint, it will not be racing in the direction of salvation, because that is a matter between each human person and God. A crowd can't be saved, only a person can. And Hubert wants to hide in someone, sink into someone; he's looking for his own crowd and he meets with a cruel rejection. Maybe harsh is a better word than cruel.

CSK. *Speaking of Hubert, I like the shift of location for his scene. Instead of at the almshouse, Hubert accosts Brother Albert at a salon. This approach seems more believable, more logical than that of Wojtyła's text. For Hubert seems to broach the idea on the spur of the moment in the film, which allows for Brother Albert's words about finding one's own road to sanctity sound more natural. In the text, the very fact that Hubert's come to the almshouse makes his resolve seem all the more strong, and Brother Albert's response all the more harsh.*

The name Hubert appears at least twice in your films. Of course, giving the name "Hubert" to the young musician in Our God's Brother *was the Pope's choice. But Hubert is also the name of the little boy in your semi-autobiographical film* At Full Gallop *(Cwał). Is this just a coincidence? Or do you at some level identify with the character from the Pope's play?*

KZ. In "At Full Gallop" I had to avoid my own first name because the film is only three-quarters autobiographical. Thus "Hubert." There might be some connection between the two, because in Wojtyła's play he is the character I can identify with most, or maybe the character that expresses sentiments closest to my own.

CSK. *I'm not sure I like the scene in the mayor's office, another departure from the text. Why the change? Just to make use of the wider "geographical" horizons enjoyed by cinema, unmatched by the stage?*

KZ. Yes, the mayor is only spoken of in the play, whereas I felt in the film that by getting out of the long scene in the garret I might cinematize the monotonous first act a bit.

CSK. *Along with* From a Far Country, Our God's Brother *is your second "Papal" film. Which of the two was more difficult to do?*

KZ. *From a Far Country* was a film that I had to construct, and it was an impossible film, because it is impossible to write the biography of a living, important person. *Our God's Brother* was an already existing, dramatic structure, and in this sense it was easier. I've also directed Wojtyła's *Hiob* (Job*)* on stage in Italy.

CSK. Brat naszego Boga *was not the first play written about Saint Brother Albert. It was preceded by a few years by Andrzej Wart's (Adam Bunsch's)* Gołębie Brata Alberta [Brother Albert's Pigeons] *published in Glasgow in 1943. Do you know if the Pope read this very different play before writing his own? Have you ever read it?*

KZ. I know that Bunsch's text exists, but I hadn't read it, and I assume that Wojtyła hadn't either. Nor did I ever ask him, because it would have been a bit awkward, as if I were nosing around after so many years to see if he'd borrowed anything.

184

CSK. *You are a good friend of Krzysztof Penderecki, who composed the musical score for Skuszanka's world premiere of the play in 1980, and Wojciech Kilar, who composes the music for all your films, including* Our God's Brother. *Can you tell us anything about the different musical settings, how Kilar's differs from Penderecki's and why?*

KZ. The difference is not merely between Penderecki and Kilar, but we also have a difference of twenty years, in which much has changed in music. Modernism has become something barren, exhausted; the neoacademism of the avant-garde. Kilar, like Penderecki, has moved away from Modernism. *The Gates of Jerusalem* are quite different from *A Threnody for the Victims of Hiroshima.*

CSK. *I am a big fan of Scott Wilson's; as you know, his performance in* A Year of the Quiet Sun *is very meaningful to me. I have heard that, if Scott didn't agree to take this role, you wouldn't have gone on to shoot the film. What was it about Scott that told you, "this, and no one else, is my Brother Albert?" Whatever it was, you certainly hit the nail on the head. After the screening of the film in the Vatican, the Pope was moved by Scott's deep understanding and skillful interpretation of the saint's character, and said "Now I cannot imagine my play's protagonist with any other face."*

KZ. I can verify the Pope's words you cite. Scott himself didn't hear them too well because he was overcome with emotion. There was a time when it seemed that we'd be doing this film as something purely Polish. In that case we were considering another actor about whom I wasn't quite convinced—I had already imagined Scott in the role and I understood that only he could play the part as I had dreamed it.

CSK. *I must say that of all the Pope's dramas, I like* Job *the best. There is a somewhat Young-Polish, ritualistic feel to that biblical drama (although as you've said above, Young Poland doesn't really speak to you). Now, you've done* Our God's

185

Brother *to great acclaim; several years ago* Before the Jeweler's Shop *was realized in English with Olivia Hussey and Ben Cross; do you see any chance of* Job *being produced, perhaps for the smaller format of television?*

KZ. My *Job* was filmed by Italian TV (*en plein air*). Idziak did the camera work (he was nominated for an Oscar this year for his work with Ridley Scott's film).[2] Unfortunately, the recording was destroyed in montage. No one knows, was it fate, or sabotage. Lots of money were tossed in the muck. There is no film. That was 1984, I think.

PR. *You are one of the giants of the contemporary authorial cinema genre. What was it like to be working from a script that you yourself did not write?*

KZ. To me, someone else's script means a vacation from half of my responsibilities. I've only adapted Wojtyła and Max Frisch, and I collaborated as a writer with Szczepański. At one time I also did TV Theatre: Nałkowska in Germany, Anouilh in Poland. Once again in Germany I re-wrote someone else's script (*A Long Conversation with a Bird*). The Author (Tankred Dorst) did not withdraw his name from the credits, even though I did everything otherwise than he intended.

CSK. *When will we see the next Zanussi/Wilson collaboration?*

KZ. I'm always ready. I've got so many ideas for Scott. I just need some ideas for financing!

---

[2] *Black Hawk Down.*

The Place and Prospect of a Polish Prelate as Pope:
Provisional Reflections on the Papacy of John Paul II
GEORGE HUNTSTON WILLIAMS

In his address to the diplomats accredited to the Holy See, Pope John Paul II on October 18, 1978 said that while he was aware of the "particular richness in the diversity of cultures, histories, and languages," he would be found from henceforth serving as a Christian and still more as Pope in a witness "to universal love" and that "the particular nature of the country" of his origin was "from now on of little importance."[1] Thus to discuss the Polish component in the new Papacy would appear to countervail the Pope's express intentions. Nevertheless, his very recognition of the plentitude of human cultures and the varieties of the modalities of Catholicism itself, pulsating, as he expressed it in his inaugural encyclical, "in full awareness of their own identity and, at the same time, of their own originality within the universal unity of the church," surely legitimates any attempt to understand him as a Pole, however cosmopolitan and ecumenically Catholic he may be.

I. POLISH PRELATES AND THE PAPACY IN THE PAST

It comes to the mind of any Pole that on at least two earlier occasions a Polish prelate is known to have been seriously considered for election to the See of St. Peter and on each occasion Christendom was at a momentous juncture in its history. After Gregory XI (1370-78) returned the Papacy from Avignon to Rome at the urging, among others, of Catherine of Siena (whom John Paul would invoke as the patroness of his pontificate before her sarcophagus in Santa Maria sopra Minerva), Latin Christendom had become monstrous with three rival claimants to the headship of the Church, the third claimant having resulted from the effort of the Council of Pisa to elect the Greek Alexander V in the hope that the Popes of Avignon and Rome would abdicate. Poland sided with the Pisan Pope along with France, England, the majority of the bishops

---

[1] Boston *Pilot,* Vol. CL, 20 October 1978.

of the Holy Roman Empire (but not by the rival royal contender Rupert and many German princes), and many of the states of the Italian peninsula. The second Pisan Pope John XXIII Cossa (1410-15)[2] convened the Council of Constance (1414-18), at the instigation of Emperor Sigismund (1410- 37) of Luxemburg. It was decided that the vote should be by nations, each having one vote (the university pattern prevailing over prelatical heads), and the Polish bishops were included in "the German nation," one of five only recognized, the Spanish being included in 1416, after their abandonment of the Avignonese Pope, Gregory XIII de Luna. Archbishop Nicholas Trąba of Gniezno had, on receiving the invitation to Constance from John XXIII, called a provincial synod at Uniejów on the Warta to discuss the problem of the Teutonic Knights and to choose representatives to the Fourteenth General Council. King Władysław Jagiełło had made Trąba his plenipotentiary and he had been accompanied to Constance by four bishops, two laymen, and a delegate of the Jagiellonian University, Rector Paweł Włodkowic, known as Paulus Vladimiri. When at Constance, after the flight of John XXIII, fearing the loss of votes by the plan to vote by "nations," Cardinal Peter D'Ailly headed the drawing up of the IV Articles of Constance, the charter of Gallicanism and notable for claiming that the assembled council derived its authority directly from God. After the cardinals had refused to promulgate the Articles, it fell to Bishop Andrzej Laskary of Poznań to announce them. During the ensuing deliberations on the basis of the Articles, Trąba was elected procurator of the "German" nation. At the time of the election of a Pope, when each nation was permitted to have a delegation of six persons with one vote, Trąba received a significant number, there being only six composite votes; but he, in the interest of unity, threw them to

---

[2] Neapolitan Baldassare Cossa was elected and crowned Pope in the Roman line and came to have the largest following among the three papal rivals. After his flight from Constance, he was brought back by force, imprisoned, and deposed in 1415 as simoniacal and as an Antipope. He was eventually released from prison and made Cardinal Bishop of Tusculum by Martin V in 1419. It is interesting that genial Pope John XXIII Roncalli (1958-63) should have chosen to take the very name of an earlier Antipope!

Cardinal Odo Colonna, who took the style of Martin V and raised Gniezno to the primatial dignity.[3]

It was not until the close of the Third Period of the Council of Trent (1545-63) that, so far as we know, a Pole came again anywhere near close to ascending the papal throne. Cardinal Stanisław Hosius (1504-79) of Warmia (Ermland), widely regarded throughout Europe, by reason of the many editions and translations of his spirited *Confessio Catholicae fidei Christiana* [Confession of the Catholic Christian Faith] as a major theological defender of the faith against Lutheranism (and Calvinism), was one of the legates for Period III (1562-63) and became legatine president during the last three sessions. He knew Lutherans well enough to be certain that concessions such as communion in two kinds for the laity, a vernacular liturgy, and even optional marriage for priests, some of these favored by the Polish Queen, the Emperor, and the duke of Bavaria, and the eucharistic option even by the Pope — would only weaken the Reformed Catholic Church and yet, Hosius well knew, would bring back scarcely a single Protestant. As a result of his theological prowess and scripturally and patristically undergirded defense of Reformed Catholicism, many cardinals rallied around Hosius as the appropriate successor to Pius IV (1559-65), but he almost immediately returned to the Polish Lithuanian Commonwealth to implement the reform through a national synod and through the introduction of the Jesuit Order.[4]

There have no doubt been several other conclaves, since the last non Italian Pope, Dutch Hadrian VI (1522-23), when prelates of various Italian states or the Kingdom Republic of Italy have come possibly closer to the throne of St. Peter than Archbishop Trąba or Cardinal Hosius, but these two Polish prelates are appropriately recalled now that the first Pole does sit on the throne. Before placing this Papacy in its general historical setting, we do well to

---

[3] Andrzej Laskary, "Poznańskie biskupstwo" [The Diocese of Poznań] "Schyzma" [Schism] "Trąba," *Podręczna Encyklopedya* [Portable Encyclopedia] 42 vols. (Warsaw, 1904-15); Tihomil Drezga, "Włodkowic's *Epistola ad Sbigneum Episcopum cracoviensem,* 1432 [W.'s letter to Zbigniew, Bishop of Kraków]." *The Polish Review.* XX, No. 4 (1975), pp. 43-64.

[4] G. H. Williams, "Cardinal Stanislas Hosius," *Shapers of Traditions in Germany. Switzerland. and Poland.* ed. by Jill Raitt (Yale, 1979).

make seven generalizations about the "country of origin" of Pope John Paul as they do bear on his pontificate.

II. POINTS IN THE POLISH BACKGROUND OF JOHN PAUL II

The first point relates to St. Stanisław, bishop of Kraków from 1072, who was put to death by order of King Bolesław II the Bold (1058-79) in the church of St. Michael in Kraków on April 11, 1079. After his canonization by Pope Innocent IV at Assisi in 1253, his cult spread beyond the Poles to the Lithuanians and the Ukrainians, and his feast day was fixed at May 8.

As Primate Stefan Cardinal Wyszyński and Metropolitan Karol Cardinal Wojtyła had long been making preparations for the celebration of the nine hundredth anniversary of the martyrdom of the Polish Thomas à Becket, it was natural that the Pope would have very much desired to return to his native land and former see for precisely that history-laden celebration of the patron saint of Poland. It is of interest, however, that the extremely well read Pontiff had long been aware of the ambiguity of the symbolic as well as the factually historic significance of his martyred predecessor in Kraków. At least two works appeared in the fifties about St. Stanisław, Danuta Borawska, Z dziejów jednej legendy [From the History of a Legend], Warsaw, 1950, and Tadeusz Wojciechowski, Szkice historyczne jedenastego wieku [Historical Essays from the XIth Century], Warsaw, 1951 (a reissue of a work originally published in Kraków, 1904).

Bishop Stanisław arose in rebellion with many magnates and Bolesław's brother, and likely successor, Władysław Herman, in protest against the King's protracted war against the Principality of Kiev; and, no doubt, Bishop Stanisław was particularly opposed to Bolesław's personally immoral life and the cruelty of his government. In any case, Stanisław was put to death as a traitor and as a pro-German. On the issue of investiture he had stood with many northern bishops against the international reform movement of Pope Gregory VII, Hildebrand (1073-85), whereas Bolesław had favored the reform against Emperor Henry IV and his numerous episcopal allies. It is quite likely that Pope John Paul, on his first return to his homeland, given his historical acumen, would have, rather in the spirit of St. Thomas à Becket of Canterbury, a "pro-Gregorian" of a later century (martyred 1170), defended the universal and the moral mission of the Church and of her bishops in whatever land but he would have quite likely taken occasion also to point up the ambiguities of power, both sacral and secular, and might well have found precisely at that altar the platform on which to erect his theory of the proper role of Christians and non-Christians in a pluralistic global society and within an ideologically Marxist state.

Although Pope John Paul II expressly referred to the approaching celebration of the ninth centenary of St. Stanisław in his inaugural homily, the only passage censored in the televised version in Poland (which the Pope later had beamed from Vatican Radio intact), I am inclined to think that the much publicized shifting of dates for the Pope's return to Poland, now fixed at June 2, has not been due wholly to the Polish government, which would have been under tremendous popular pressure if the Pope had insisted on returning on the feast of St. Stanisław, May 8.

One may surmise in the light of his policy in Poland as Cardinal, and especially of his stance in Latin America, that he had counted on gaining widespread popular support for placing peaceful social change in the interest of personal freedom from poverty and coercion under the aegis of the spiritual prerogative of bishops and priests, demonstrating that he could be socio-religiously influential without being politically provocative; for surely he knows that the Soviet Union, if it were to fear that increased internal freedom in Poland or elsewhere in the Socialist Bloc would lead to the breakup of the Warsaw Pact, could act recklessly. As the trip to Poland now stands, Pope John Paul has a calculated better chance of effecting the maximum church-state changes in his homeland, without arriving in the midst of the celebration that will be sufficiently emotional even without his presence.[5]

A second point in the Pope's historical background is the fact that Church and State and eventually Nation [Naród] were indeed very closely intertwined among his ancestral peoples. The

---

[5] *Editor's note*: The Pope's first visit to Poland took place between 2 — 9 June 1979.

cathedral, to the high altar of which the remains of St. Stanisław were translated by Bishop Lambert III in 1088, with the cathedral renamed, was from the beginning an integral part of Wawel, the royal complex of buildings atop and about the massive outcropping of limestone rock.

The proximity of cathedral and royal palace in Kraków is related to another distinction in the Polish constitution from the period of the First Commonwealth up to the Partitions and especially important after the extinction of the Lithuanian dynasty of the Jagiellons in 1572: The Primate of Poland was, during any interregnum, pending the election of a new King, the Interrex with the plenary authority of Church and State, presiding over the Diets, including the Election Diet (In only one other country of Christendom, East or West, namely, the Primate of the Apostolic Kingdom of Hungary residing at Esztergom, has the Primate or his counterpart had a comparably substantial role in the constitution.)[6] Although this right lapsed with the Partitions and was, of course, not to be revived in the Second and the Third Republic, respectively after the end of the First World War and the Second,[7] still the Archbishop of Gniezno and Warsaw and the Metropolitan of Kraków and their fellow bishops and priests have tended to be bearers of Polish national and political self-consciousness.

And to this day, something of the resonance and something of the stately demeanor of an Interrex can be detected in the voice and bearing of the present Primate Stefan Cardinal Wyszyński,[8] as

---

[6] Primate József Cardinal Mindszenty, after the establishment of the Communist government, behaved to his death as the bearer of Hungarian constitutional legitimacy by reason of his special interregnal status.

[7] *Editor's note:* Since the regaining of complete independence by Poland following the elections of 1989, a popular debate has surged around the terminology that Williams accepts here rather uncritically. Was the Polish People's Republic (PRL) the "Third Republic," or should that term be reserved for today's post-Communist state? Most people today accept the semi-autonomous PRL as a hiatus of sorts, and date the III RP from 1989.

[8] *Editor's note:* Stefan Cardinal Wyszyński (1901-1981) lived to see Karol Cardinal Wojtyła elected to the See of Peter; after his death, he was succeeded by József Cardinal Glemp (b. 1929), who had been Wyszyński's personal secretary from 1967-1979. The personal union of the Archbishop of Gniezno and Warsaw in the person of the Primate was abolished in 1992. With Cardinal

192

he, with his fellow bishops, prepared the Polish people systematically for the celebration of the millennium of Christianity in their land (966-1966). Subliminally felt by all Poles to be still a kind of Vicar of the Virgin Sovereign, declared in 1658 Queen of Poland by King Jan Kazimierz at a crucial juncture during the Swedish Deluge (1655-60), Wyszyński has stood up many times in his cardinal colors in the squares of Polish cities and places of pilgrimage as the veritable symbol of a Kingdom not wholly of this world.

Not only the Primate, however, and the prelates but also the Church in its priesthood and faithful laity have together been the bearers of Polish nationality, language, and culture up to the creation of the Second Republic. The Jews, driven out from western Europe, whom the Kings and nobility of the Royal Polish-Lithuanian Commonwealth welcomed from medieval times, during the period of many uprisings against the three Partitioning powers, often, especially under the Tsars, preferred to keep themselves free from the charges of sedition (suffering Russian pogroms as it was without provocation); thus the ethnic Poles became, contrary to their usual behavior during the Commonwealth, nationalistically disappointed when Jews living among them failed to join conspicuously in the several efforts to reconstitute the Polish Commonwealth in the nineteenth and twentieth centuries up to 1918-20. The quite recent episodes and personalities connected with the establishment and the personnel of the bureaucracy of the Third, the People's Republic under Soviet Communist auspices temporarily aggravated a latent feeling, despite the earlier common plight of ethnic Poles and Jews of Polish citizenship in the Nazi death camps. Yet for all these several reasons of ethnocentricity, the fact is that Polish Catholicism is today far more cosmopolitan in its outlook and concerns than many another national branch of Catholicism. Indeed, something of the sense of a messianic role of the Polish nation as suffering servant in the literature of Poland has been in modern times transferred to the Church and transmuted all the more easily into a truly universal Catholicity, all the more so for

---

Glemp's death or abdication, the title of Primate of Poland is to return to the Archbishop Metropolitan of Gniezno.

the reason that the intellectual leaders in Poland have come to see, how in contrast to the programmatically ethnic jurisdictions and liturgies of Orthodoxy, the Catholic Church to which Poles have been so long devoted, even when their national interests were often compromised by the very Papacy to which they remained steadfast, has everywhere become fully conscious of its global mission of fostering personal freedom and of upholding the rights of the poor — the proletariat which has been the alleged preeminent concern of the Communist parties. And finally, on this point, a distinction should probably be made between Catholics in Poland under such magnificent hierarchical leadership and the Poles of the extensive diaspora (Polonia beyond the boundaries); for those who built in Nowa Huta the parish church known as the Ark, dedicated to the Virgin and to the dead of all the extermination camps in their land, and all those tenacious builders like them, have met the new totalitarianism and found new modalities of freedom despite harassment and often second-class citizenship which the older among ethnic groups in the New World and Australia, looking back could scarcely imagine. Now that Poland is ethnically homogeneous [*naród jednolity, rdzenny* — Roman Dmowski] by reason of the actions of the Nazis and then the Soviets, the Catholic Church in Poland, thanks also to the Vatican Council, has come conspicuously to defend the universality of the Church and to revive the tolerant motif of the multiconfessional Commonwealth rather than to perpetuate the nationalist motif of the post-Partition generations.[9] The free Catholic University of Lublin, founded in 1918, has recently established a chair in Yiddish studies to foster an understanding of the Jewish component in the history of Polish culture and society.

A third point is related to the second. The Polish-Lithuanian Commonwealth of the sixteenth century was the largest state of Europe. The plenipotentiary of King Zygmunt Stary [Sigismund I the Old], acting on behalf of his relation, the Jagiellonian minor king of Bohemia, who was *ex officio* one of the seven electors of the Holy Roman Emperor, voted in Frankfurt on

---

[9] Feliks Gross, "Tolerance and Intolerance in Poland: The Two Political Traditions," *The Polish Review.* XX, No. I (1975), pp. 65-69.

the Main for Charles V and was present with his splendid Polish and Bohemian retinue at the royal coronation at Aachen in 1520 (the king to be crowned emperor later at Bologna by the Pope). The Commonwealth, two thirds of whose subjects were of the Byzantine rite, in the sixteenth and seventeenth century counted itself as fully part of the West. This was true even of the Ukrainians, for Kiev was a palatine capital in the Commonwealth, and many youthful Ukrainian nobles studied in Kraków and further west. The library of Erasmus of Rotterdam was purchased by the nephew of the Primate of Poland and transferred to Kraków by one of the great European publicists and social reformers, Andrzej Frycz Modrzewski. The Commonwealth became indeed a kind of Erasmian state with reference to toleration, and the yearning for peace and social justice. Indeed, the Commonwealth, already multinational, became also multiconfessional and instinctively reluctant to use coercion in the realm of the conscience. For a while a kind of Erasmian Gallicanism prevailed at court and in episcopal libraries and dining halls. Surely, Poland "was a state without stakes" (Janusz Tazbir). Stephen Bathory, before his election as King (1576-86) had said that God had reserved three things to himself: to create something out of nothing, to have foreknowledge of future events, and to be lord over consciences.[10]

The tolerance and magnanimity of the Polish aristocracy has over the intervening centuries been democratized. The *liberum veto* of the sovereign Senator or Deputy of the Sejm of the Old Commonwealth (constitutionally impractical) and the sense of individual worth and self-determination, the sense of inner sovereignty — to idealize a bit — of every *szlachcic* [nobleman] and his spouse all live on today in the heart of every Pole, regardless

---

[10] Bathory first said this at the Diet of Medgyes while Prince of Transylvania. Georgio Biandrata, M.D. was his court physician and orator at the Election Diet at Wielka Wola where the King-elect repeated the axiom. Georg Haner, *Historia ecclesiarum transylvanicarum* [History of the Transylvanian Churches] (Frankfurt am Main, 1694), p. 295. Previously in this section, the object of the satisfaction has been made clear: "He [Christ] it was and he alone, who satisfied the Father's eternal love, that fatherhood that from the beginning of the world found expression in creating the world, giving man all the riches of creation."

of class origin or perhaps even party affiliation. It was thus more than a personal trait of Bishop and then Archbishop Wojtyła to have defended in the basilica of St. Peter during Vatican II the liberty of conscience, joining in support of the American Jesuit political theorist, John Courtney Murray. Moreover, as in most cases, the prelate of Kraków was on this view of civil liberty, too, no doubt the spokesman of the entire Polish episcopate.

A fourth point about the Polish background of the Pope has to do with his eventual ecumenical moves towards the Orthodox Churches and the Protestants and other "ecclesial communities." In the sixteenth century the Roman Catholic Church recouped its losses to Protestant territorial churches in Europe by the Union of Brześć-Litewski of 1595, whereby a large portion of the dioceses, parishes, and monasteries of the Orthodox Church, stretching from roughly Chełm to several hundreds of miles beyond Kiev, became Byzantine-rite Uniate Catholic. Although the Union suffered setbacks after the Partitions, at least in Austrian Galicia as well as in parts of the Austro-Hungarian Empire, the Byzantine-rite Uniates were consolidated and constituted by far the larger portion of the Ukrainian immigrants to Canada and the United States. But apart from this New World diaspora of the Uniates, the achievement was completely shattered in the geographical recontouring of the People's Republic of Poland, which left most of the surviving Uniates in the former Polish territory from Wilno to Lwów as citizens of the Soviet republics of Lithuania, Byelorussia, and western Ukraine, subject by order of Joseph Stalin, to submission to the jurisdiction of the Patriarch of Moscow. With some exceptions, most Polish Catholics, including the Primate, have come to regard the Union of 1595 as the wrong way to have achieved Catholic unity amid diversity of rites. Thus precisely because the present Pontiff is a Pole with some Ukrainian blood in his veins and fluent in Ukrainian and Russian, it is predictable that his approach to the Orthodox Churches will be well informed by both the achievement and the failure of the Union of Brześć-Litewski.[11] One may expect

---

[11] *Editor's note*: The many overtures of John Paul II to the Russian Orthodox Church, especially following the dissolution of the USSR in the early 1990s, were uniformly rebuffed by the Orthodox patriarchy, who chose to see the establishment of Roman Catholic dioceses on Russian soil, intended to serve

John Paul II, in his earnest and urgent search for new and more viable modalities of ecumenical union, instructed by the past and convinced by observation in the Synod of Bishops of which he had been a member of all five meetings from 1967 to 1977 (from 1971, a member of the Secretariat) that Christianity is indigenized in many wonderfully different ways.

And this leads to a fifth point, which brings up again a theme in Polish history but with redoubled intensity. The multiconfessional Polish-Lithuanian Commonwealth had in it not only Catholics and Orthodox, but also Armenians, then invading Tartars, converted to Islam, and resident in quarters of many towns still named after them "Tatary." In the fifteenth century came the Czech Brethren, particularly to Great Poland with their chief center Leszno (Jan Ámos Komenský), and in the sixteenth century Lutherans, first in the Polish royal fief of Ducal Prussia in 1525, then the Mennonites in the Lower Vistula of Royal Prussia, then the Calvinists, out of whom emerged by 1565 the Unitarians centered in Raków. But then there were the Jews, organized in four synods or "kingdoms" under royal charter in Poland and a comparable number in Lithuania and that part of the Grand Duchy which became Crown Poland after the Union of Lublin in 1569. All this is to say that the Polish Pontiff, more than any one from another land with the possible exception of a cardinal coming out of the American pluralistic religious experience, will, as we already know from Cardinal Wojtyła's deeds and words in Kraków and as a member of the Synod of Bishops in Rome, have a special perspective to bring to bear on the interfaith level of ecumenism, with special reference to Jews and Muslims. We shall presently note some of the specifics, but as Switzerland and the Swiss character cannot be imagined without the Alps, nor Holland without its canals and its welcome to Jews driven out of the Iberian peninsula in 1492, who became integral parts of Dutch culture, so Poland, though in different ways, cannot be thought of without mindfulness of the once teeming

---

Russian Catholics, as proselytization of traditionally Orthodox Christians. The relations between Roman Catholics, Uniate Catholics, and Orthodox in the Ukraine have also been strained, especially in the area of the restitution of parishes and other property incorporated into the state-sponsored Orthodox Church during the Communist years.

millions of Jews of its past. Although the Polish Jews did not become so fully integrated in Polish cultural life as, say, the Jews in Holland or the United States, I would still conjecture that the distinctively Polish and solemnly loving and intimate sharing of the *opłatek* [unconsecrated communion wafer] in the Advent season in forgiveness and pledge of mutual support for the ensuing year derives by cultural osmosis from the annual Jewish Atonement (Yom Kippur) with its act of letting bygones be bygones, in order to start the New Year on a fresh basis. In any case, no cardinal of the Old World or the Third World could have been chosen who could have a more highly developed sensitivity to Judaism and surviving Jewry than the present Pontiff, the poetic and philological survivor of the Nazi underground, who emerged to write his habilitation doctorate on the ethical system of the phenomenologist Max Scheler, son of mixed Jewish-Protestant German family, who for a season became a Catholic.

There is a sixth point before we follow these motifs into the new pontificate, and that is a distinctive feature of Polish spirituality, notably the Catholic season of Advent. Elsewhere in the Catholic world, the four Sundays of Advent, while the lectionary remains roughly uniform throughout Catholicism, in Poland it retains features of its liturgical origin, not as the preparation for Christmas but as the penitential preparation, at the end of the liturgical calendar, for the Second, the judicial Advent of Christ. The lovely Polish carols are not sung openly until the midnight Christmas Mass, when Christ, instead of appearing as the Judge at the Last Judgment, turns out to be once again Christ the Babe of Bethlehem; and the solemn joy of those carols reflects the subliminal feelings that one has another year to become truly faithful to the Christ, growing in wisdom and stature, as did He. The coming of the Magi at Epiphany is never confused in popular celebration, so that the liturgical calendar still fully governs the modalities of Christian celebration interrupted by the quite different mood when "Sylvester" (the New Year's Eve festivity) temporarily takes over, the vestige of the pagan beginning of the year, only mildly Christianized!

There is perhaps a seventh point: the forests of Poland. The last bison of Europe were preserved by the Poles in a royal forest and swamp now divided between the Polish People's Republic and the Soviet Union, near Białystok.[12] The forests and the High Tatra Mountains, part of the Carpathian Chain, have also been the fastnesses which have sheltered the bivouac fires of the freedom fighters in Polish history into most recent times. Fox-fur hats and other furred garb give the big and small cities of Poland in winter even today a wilderness aspect that is absent from the cities of other Eastern countries, generally less sophisticated than Poland. An outside observer feels that the concern for wildness on the beautifully variegated Polish postage stamps no less than in the environmental studies in grade school curricula in Poland suggest a national trait that in sublimated ways will find new expressions in the undergrounder, the elegant skier, the folklorist, and the canoeist now helmsman of the Bark of Peter.

III. The Pontificate of John Paul II with Special Reference to His Inaugural Homily and His Inaugural Encyclical

With these Polish motifs in mind, we turn to John Paul II more directly. First as to his installation with the pallium, it is inconceivable that a non-Italian would have been emboldened to break with tradition and to dispense with the papal tiara. That was the achievement of Pope John Paul I, former Patriarch of Venice, who also appropriately dispensed with the two Franciscans and their frail guttering tapers and the warning: *Sic transit gloria mundi* [thus all earthly pomp passes away]; for Albano Luciano had already renounced the glory of a triumphalist Church in declining to be crowned. Had Karol Wojtyła been elected in the first conclave after the decease of Pope Paul VI, he would surely have been crowned with the tiara, as would, indeed, any other non-Italian, the first after 455 years. Moreover, there is reason to surmise that pastoral and humble though he is, the Cardinal of Kraków, though not yet the primate of Poland, as he might well in due course have become, would as an intellectual, as one knowledgeable in Polish history, been appreciatively conscious and retentive of the principal symbol

---

[12] *Editor's note:* The present border (2006) runs between Poland and Belorussia.

of sovereignty and temporality. He had once seen his own Primate effective in a Warsaw square, when the electronic equipment "strangely" broke down as he was about to speak to an immense throng, effective precisely because Wyszyński was wearing the royal purple (scarlet), reflective of the glory of the coming Kingdom (and also because of his powerful voice on its own). Cardinal Wojtyła would also have recalled the primatial interrex during the royal elections in the Commonwealth, and would have been mindful of the immense symbolic significance for world Catholicism of its being administered from a sovereign, however small, Vatican City State. Thus he well might have assumed the tiara in full recognition of the Apostolic mission of the Church as *Mater et Magistra* to, and among, the nations. He would have been aware of its complex history, of the original Phrygian cap that had evolved by the pontificate of Clement V (1305-14), the first of the Avignonese Popes, to symbolize the sovereignty of the Pope over the Church militant, the Church expectant, and the Church triumphant. But with the renunciation of the tiara by John Paul I, another meaning could be attached to the three crowns; and, as though caressing the tiara never again to be worn, John Paul II in his inaugural homily of 22 October 1978 related it reflectively to the *triplex munus Christi* [triple office of Christ]. He observed that with the assumption of a Petrine ministry in collegiality with fellow bishops and with support from the lay apostolate, the three offices of Christ could now be said in the fullness of time to be devolving up on all within the Church, the royal priesthood and the priestly kingdom (1 Peter 2:9).

In his inaugural encyclical *Redemptor hominis,* 15 March 1979, which corresponds to the inaugural encyclical of Paul VI, *Ecclesiam Suam,* which was enunciated while the Vatican Council II was still in progress, John Paul II with an even more comprehensive vision of the whole of the created order and of mankind, its history and salvation, than *Ecclesiam Suam,* which he quotes, for the first time in so authoritative a pronouncement deals with the Redemption of man through Christ, the Second Adam, and in Christ, the salvation of the whole world, "groaning in travail" and "futility," even in an age of such marked technological advances of which with legitimate praise but also warning John Paul II gives the marvelous details. Redemption, which is the central transaction in

Christian salvation and hence in theology, has notwithstanding never been dogmatically defined, remaining a cluster of not wholly convincing "theories" and metaphors: the Christus Victor Theory, the Theory of the deceptive Ransom paid to the Devil, and the Theory of Theosis or progressive Divinization, all these of the Patristic Age, the Satisfaction Theory of St. Anselm of Canterbury, the Exemplary Theory of Peter Abelard, the Acceptance Theory of the Scotists with the concept of *potestas absoluta* [absolute power] and *potestas ordinata* [ordained power] of God, the Penal Theory of the divine-human Mediator of Philip Melanchthon and John Calvin, and in some forms of Protestantism also the Governmental Theory of Hugo Grotius. But now for the first time John Paul II makes Redemption the central theme of a papal pronouncement, and significantly in his inaugural or programmatic encyclical.

In his cosmic, historic, and humanistic vision the Pope can still perceive in primordial sin and the collective sins of mankind, quoting from the *Exultet* of the Easter Vigil, that "happy fault . . . which gained us so great a Redeemer."[13] According to the central pronouncement of the encyclical, perhaps consciously against the background of the enormous suffering of his own Polish people during the Second World War and in the past and, also of the enormity of the Nazi genocidal assault upon the People of the Old Covenant, the Pope shifts the emphasis in the Atonement from expiatory suffering to redemptive love. He perceives as the central action of the Son of God, one in Person with the Man Jesus Christ, his becoming "our reconciliation with the Father," in that "he alone . . . *satisfied* the Father's *eternal love,* that fatherhood that from the beginning found expression in creating the world, giving man all the riches of creation and making him 'little less than God,' in that he [man] was created 'in the image and after the likeness of God.'"[14]

In almost all theories of Redemption or the Atonement hitherto articulated the Son or Mediator has either conquered Satan or satisfied *the outraged honor* of God (not His love), or suffered in substitution for the penalty due sinful man from Adam and Eve on, or given a moral example of utter obedience unto death to be

---

[13] *Redemptor Hominis,* translated as *The Redeemer of Man,* Boston: Daughters of St. Paul, 1977, §I, a.

[14] *Redemptor Hominis,* §§8, 9.

followed perhaps by readiness for martyrdom, or has given that agonizing token of obedience to the old Law on the cross to the Ruler and Lawgiver of the universe and mankind, as a warning that the Transcendent Ruler brooks no infraction of his laws. Here suddenly in a papal encyclical is an emphasis rather upon the "tremendous mystery of love in which creation is *renewed* — at its deepest root, the fullness of justice in a *human heart* — the heart of the first-born Son," "who therein *satisfied* that *fatherhood* of God and that love which man" is again and again failing to see or to live by, however constantly it is ever being offered.[15]

The fruit of this Redemption becomes available to each human being ("man" in the text) in a personal encounter with love[16] which the Church through her sacraments facilitates. In this connection, with his stress upon personal accountability, the Pope reasserts the value of private confession in penance in advance of the Mass without disparaging the more generalized and public repentance at Mass as in the worship of the classical Protestant churches.

Notable in the first encyclical is the prominence of Marian devotion and at the same time the care with which her role in the history of Redemption is clarified. Mariology in its fullest scope covers Mary as the New Eve and hence ecclesiology, Mary as the Co-redemptrix with her Son, hence soteriology, Mary as the obedient handmaiden of the heavenly Father, hence anthropology, and, with an eye toward the Eastern Church, the embodiment of holy wisdom, hence sophiology. In the encyclical the Virgin is preeminently the ideal freely acting and assenting person, who said "Fiat," and remained the responsible and accountable, suffering and loving person that she was.[17] The Mother of God, the Queen of Poland, becomes in the most authoritative of the asseverations to date of her devoted subject and venerator the Mother of the Church, as she was so proclaimed by Pope Paul at the close of the third session of Vatican II, and perhaps primarily the redemptive Exemplar; but John Paul, while speaking of Mary as unique in the history of Redemption, eschews mention of her Bodily Assumption,

---

[15] *Redemptor Hominis*, §§8, 9.
[16] *Redemptor Hominis*, §§10, 8.
[17] *Redemptor Hominis*, §22.

the only dogma defined *ex cathedra* on the basis of papal infallibility (Vatican I) in the apostolic constitution of Pius XII, *Munificentissimus Deus* (1 November 1950). Sensitive also to the Orthodox idea of the simpler Dormition and the weaker or non-existent Marian doctrine among Protestants, John Paul was no doubt ecumenically tactful, when he added the words "with full respect and love for the members of all the Christian communities," as he stood firm in the (Latin) tradition without specifying any further Mary's role beyond Exemplar and intercessor.

The Pope opens the encyclical on Redemption and the doctrine of Man not in the mood of eschatological anxiety but rather with joy and expectation, despite the enormous difficulties ahead which he does not fail to spell out.

While looking to the year 2000, at which jubilee it is reasonable to hope that John Paul II will himself still be on the throne of St. Peter at the age of 79, in his encyclical with that double millennium in mind, he is fully aware of the enormous threats to humanity and even the globe itself which could be lethally contaminated by a nuclear holocaust. Yet he speaks in restrained but faith-grounded hope that mankind will safely reach that jubilee; and from "the threshold" of the two Popes of Vatican II, along with his immediate 33-day predecessor who genially bethought himself of the programmatic double name, "guided by unlimited trust in and obedience to the Spirit that Christ promises," John Paul II speaks four times of that moment ahead as an Advent, not in the sense of Second Advent and a Last Judgment but rather as "a new Advent, a season of expectation,"[18] of "this new Advent of the church connected with the approaching end of the second millennium,"[19] of "the church of the new Advent, . . . the church that is continually preparing for the new coming of the Lord, . . . the church of the Eucharist and penance, "[20] and then again more comprehensively of "humanity's new Advent."[21] It is striking that for his first encyclical John Paul should have picked up the theme of Advent out of season — he had already done so a week earlier than the first Sunday of

---

[18] *Redemptor Hominis*, §1.
[19] *Redemptor Hominis*, §7.
[20] *Redemptor Hominis*, §20.
[21] *Redemptor Hominis*, §28.

Advent at a general audience, "Advent relives the Mystery of God's Coming to Man,"[22] and also that five of the 205 annotations specify his use in the encyclical of phrases from other seasons in the liturgical year.[23]

The first encyclical is, indeed, of considerable interest in respect to the sources cited. As many of the notes are very full, one can give only the statistical contour of John Paul's *Redemptor hominis*. The most numerous quotations or citations are scriptural. He cites his first papal namesake twice, and the second at least a dozen times. Of course, both John XXIII and Paul VI are implied in his citation of documents of Vatican II twenty eight times. As Cardinal, the active participant and spokesman of the whole Polish hierarchy during that Council, 1962-65, he once wrote a systematic (rather than genetic) study in Polish of the decrees and constitutions of the Council, *U podstaw odnowy* [English translation: Sources of Renewal: the Implementation of the Second Vatican Council] (Kraków, 1972) and knew it, therefore, as both participant and as analyst thereof, perhaps as well as any body of authoritative material. He quotes Vatican I four times, Pius XI once, Pius XII thrice, and Fathers and Schoolmen four times. His first encyclical, though balanced and highly structured, nevertheless does have a stress upon the immediate past and the future that reflects, in fact, a further effort from the vantage point of his own new authority to accelerate "the realization of Vatican II," not failing to cite himself in three footnotes with reference to his addresses in the Caribbean and Mexican visits.

The inaugural encyclical, indeed, bears throughout the distinctive language of the former Cardinal of Kraków. Alluding to his inaugural homily, when the Pontiff had, with respect to the *triplex munus Christi,* symbolized in the three-crowned tiara, said that "everyone in the people of God shares in this threefold ministry," in the inaugural encyclical he further defines the three offices, a major thematic structure within the pronouncement. John

---

[22] Daughters of St. Paul, *Talks of John Paul II* (Boston, 1979), pp. 348-63.

[23] *Editor's Note:* In his apostolic letter *Tertio millennio adveniente* (10 November 1994) John Paul II was to continue to link the jubilee year 2000 with the Incarnation and birth of Christ, as well as to underscore the "providential" nature of Vatican II as preparation for the Third Millennium.

Paul now makes very clear what he meant by the devolution of the kingly office of Christ, making it applicable to the *sacerdos* and the lay person alike: the sovereignty over oneself in one's calling through conscience and a sense of accountability. This definition represents an authentically traditional and yet a freshly relevant interpretation of the priesthood of all human vocations. He goes beyond Martin Luther in developing the idea of reform in order in this new age of technological advances, of tedium, of unemployment, and above all of alienation in a profound sense from the very work of our hands and minds, to maximize the importance of the preeminence of God's calling persons to various activities according to their aptitudes and their free choice of profession and also of inner directness, to employ a term from the social theory of David Riesman. He also repristinates at its best the idea of sovereign individuality of the Polish *szlachcic* of the Commonwealth period, whether virtually a yeoman with a few helpers or a prince and owner of many towns and villages. Moreover, the very title of the first encyclical is significant, emphasizing the redemption of each man, each individual, although ultimately all humanity. For that is there, too, in a striking formulation which intimates more than the scholastic realist or the patristic interpretation of the Logos made flesh or humanity, for the Pope says that the eternally begotten Son became a man in such a way, by the intention of the (Triune) Godhead, that all of humanity should be potentially touched and permanently affected for the good by the incarnation of the Logos as the Second and obedient Man (Adam).[24]

The Pontiff has in mind salvation and wholeness now as well as in the afterlife of every accountable human being wherever. In stressing the redemption of the person in the present as well as in the life to come, John Paul II is enhancing the preciousness of each sovereign human being of whatever race, class, or ideology in his this-worldly development and progressive liberation from all the various kinds of bondage of our age. He would enable each acting person to find whatever personal self-realization is possible and within the full range of natural and voluntary associations and

---

[24] *Redemptor Hominis,* §§13, 14.

groupings in which the disciplined person is strengthened, nurtured, sustained, and encouraged to share with others.

As for the other two offices of Christ, symbolized by the other two crowns of the tiara, the priestly and the prophetic, John Paul has said in the installation homily, in several subsequent addresses, and now in *Redemptor hominis* much to enrich our concept of the threefold office of Christ, though surely most perceptively with respect to the inner discipline in a freely accepted vocation betokened by the kingly crown. He makes clear in the encyclical that the prophetic office of Christ is "shared by the whole People of God," and he alludes to the responsibility for truth on the part of all "specialists in the various disciplines . . . , the natural sciences and letters, physicians, jurists, artists, and technicians, teachers at various levels." He does not directly connect the prophetic office of prelate or lay Christian with the forthtelling of Israel's prophets (as distinguished from retelling and foretelling), and in any case John Paul deplores "the excesses of [ecclesiastical] self-criticism."[25] Yet he is himself, like an ancient prophet, critical of all social and ideological systems, and retells in fresh language the history of the covenant of God with man, and enhearteningly foretells a brighter era for all mankind as the advent of the twenty-first century approaches.

As a vigorous spokesman of collegiality in the Council and exponent of it in the Episcopal Synods, 1967-77, he stresses in the encyclical the same theme and speaks with mounting conviction and specificity about his own role as successor of Peter in the ministry of service to which his fellow bishops have been likewise called, referring both to the Synod of Bishops in Rome and something somewhat new in phraseology and conceptualization, "The College of Bishops, which is growing more and more over all the earth remaining united with and under the guidance of the successor of St. Peter," an allusion to his own very high view of the Conference of Latin American Bishops, over which he presided for a few hours at Puebla. Stressing the ministry also of the Redeemer, the Pope never speaks in the encyclical of the vicariate of Christ and it is conceivable that with the renunciation of the tiara he may quietly

---

[25] *Redemptor Hominis,* §4.

decline in the future the imperial title which was ascribed to the Popes from the twelfth century on,[26] and use instead the title assumed by Gregory I the Great, and think of himself as Vicar of Peter, Bishop of Rome, Primate of Italy, Patriarch of the West, *primus inter pares, servus servorum Christi.* In any case, in the encyclical pope John Paul speaks of himself only as "successor of the apostle Peter."[27]

With his understanding of the plentitude of the Christ event, which affects all who come into the world whether they believe or not, John Paul in the encyclical defends with recurrent emphases and conviction that what is most precious about man, the truth about personhood, is the desire for responsible freedom, which he spells out in detail. He recognizes that neither "consumer civilization [capitalism]" nor state-controlled socialism inhibits the terrible menace of group and personal alienation wherein the technologies and the products of whatever the socio-economic system turn man and groups against themselves.[28]

It turns out to be easier for John Paul than for some of the less globally minded predecessors to see with Vatican II in "the firm belief of the followers of the non-Christian religions . . . an effect of the Spirit *of truth* operating outside the visible confines of the Mystical Body [of Christ]."[29] Yet John Paul in the encyclical does not go much beyond the schema of concentric circles of *Ecclesiam Suam* and the Vatican II decrees on non Christian religions with special attention to Jews and Muslims, except in his emphasis, in a missionary context, on "a feeling of deep esteem. . . for what man has himself worked out in the depths of his spirit," wherever and whenever.[30] It may be expected, however, that in connection with the peace between Israel and Egypt, John Paul II will find occasion to go even further than his immediate predecessor and namesake, who is known to have personally addressed a letter to "Mayor Teddy Kolek of Jerusalem, State of Israel," thereby according Israel

---

[26] *Editor's Note:* Pope John Paul II was never to cease to use the title "Vicar of Christ."

[27] *Redemptor Hominis,* §2.

[28] *Redemptor Hominis,* §16.

[29] *Redemptor Hominis,* §6.

[30] *Redemptor Hominis,* §11.

papal recognition until then not recognized by any such gesture.[31]

With respect to Church unity John Paul II sounds an urgent note. He says near the start: "To all who, for whatever motive, would wish to dissuade the [Roman Catholic] Church from seeking the universal unity of Christians the question must once again be put: Have we the right to do it? Can we fail to have trust. . . in our Lord's grace as revealed recently through what the Holy Spirit said and we heard during the Council?"[32]

This stress upon an ongoing revelation of the Holy Spirit promised as Guide and Comforter runs through the encyclical and is related, perhaps, to John Paul's first doctoral dissertation, on *The Problem of Faith in [the Mysticism of] St. John of the Cross*, some of whose propositions — as for example, that the night of faith deprived the rational part of the soul of the light of reason, blinding it to help it attain union with God — during the time of the beatification process were denounced as Illuministic. The modalities of revelation must have for some time concerned the Pope, who took St. Catherine, Dominican tertiary of Siena, patroness of Italy, and *doctor ecclesiae* (as of 1970) as patroness of his own pontificate, for she not only agitated for the return of the Papacy to Rome, but also had transcribed by her followers her *Dialoghi* with God. In other words she is an authoritatively recognized recipient of ongoing personal revelation.[33]

In the realm of international cooperation and the prevention of war, of the redistribution of wealth within a country and among nations, and of the denunciation of the use of nuclear weapons of any degree, the Pope is vigorous in all his pronouncements and notably in the encyclical, where he urges the strengthening of the United Nations.[34]

Finally, it may be said that in probably no papal document to date has there been given such prominence, as in John Paul's

---

[31] *Editor's Note:* This was achieved in the Fundamental Agreement signed in Jerusalem on December 30,1993.

[32] *Redemptor Hominis,* §6.

[33] *Editor's Note:* For more information on John Paul II, ecumenism, and the Catholic Church in reference to other religions and ecclesial communities, see the Introduction to the present volume.

[34] *Redemptor Hominis,* §§15, 16, 17.

encyclical, to ecology and conservation, wherein he warns about "the threat to man's natural environment." In all parts of the world new technologies and the exploitative mentality "alienate him [man] in his relation with nature and remove him from nature. Man often seems to see no other meaning in his natural environment than what serves for immediate use and consumption. Yet it was the Creator's will that man should communicate with nature as an intelligent and noble 'master' and 'guardian,' and not as a heedless 'exploiter' and 'destroyer.'"[35] "By submitting man to tensions created by himself, dilapidating at an accelerated pace material and energy resources, and compromising the geophysical environment, these [socio-political and technological] structures increasingly make the areas of [human] misery spread, accompanied by anguish, frustration and bitterness."[36]

EPILOGUE

All the great formulations of Vatican II reappear in this programmatic encyclical of one who was even then a much heeded voice in the basilica. He has brought all the anthropological and redemptive insights and proclamations of the Council and its two Popes together and has in powerful, at times nearly personal language, though holding close to Scripture, Tradition, and the most recent conciliar decrees and constitutions, fashioned a deep doctrine of man directed to scientifically sophisticated moderns in various disciplines related to our emerging conception of ourselves as individuals and as collectivities and has suggested a formulation of a doctrine of Redemption that has sublimated or rendered all the traditional salvific motifs into a compelling affirmation that the love of God and the love of which man was created capable of evincing — to the depths of suffering and to the heights of sovereign righteousness — was given the fullest "mediation" in Jesus Christ, "the center of the universe and of history,"[37] on the human side fashioned from the dust of the cosmos and the debris of human yearnings and catastrophes to become by his resurrection and

---

[35] *Redemptor Hominis*, §15.
[36] *Redemptor Hominis*, §16.
[37] *Redemptor Hominis*, §1.

ascension the hope to all that at Christ's Second Advent God will be all in all.

Karol Wojtyła came to the chair of St. Peter at a much more crucial juncture in the history of mankind than Polish prelates Trąba at the time of the Great Western Schism and Hosius at the close of the Council of Trent and the beginnings of the Counter-Reformation, for these memorable Poles would have been dealing only with schisms within western (largely Latin-rite) European Christendom, whereas John Paul II faces the schism of mankind into three "worlds" and the possibility of Last Things to be brought about by mankind itself. In his encyclical on the true dignity of man, created and recreated in the image of God, he in solemn joy and knowledgeable confidence, has directed not only the Church but all mankind with the fragile planet itself, beheld in our time as a blue-white globe as at once our terrestrial and our heavenly home, to a clear goal; and he has pointed the way to that personal encounter with the Spirit of Christ, which he calls an Advent, even as he looks forward to a more comprehensive Advent of that longed-for harmony among men and nations, with heaven and the seas, the dry land and all nature singing, duly guarded from exploitation, as all nature, long groaning in travail awaits the adoption of the sons of men.[38]

The national messianism of nineteenth-century Poland, long since sublimated, has now been transmuted into ecclesial and humanitarian goals, a confident global expression of hope for all mankind.

* * *

Perhaps at the end of this article, written before the Pope's triumphal return to Poland in June 1979, one should add that John Paul was in his homeland very much the Pole, "this Slavic Pope," as well as the universal Pontiff — clearly moved by the subliminal hopes of his own people for a long time, so well expressed in the titleless poem of 1848 of the Romantic Juliusz Słowacki (1809-49):

---

[38] *Redemptor Hominis,* §8.

We need the strength to lift
this world of God
Thus here comes a Slavic Pope,
a brother of the people *(Ludowy brat).*[39]

---

[39] Juliusz Słowacki, *Dzieła* (Works, 3rd ed.), ed, by Julian Krzyżanowski, Wrocław, 1959, l, pp. 250f. The *incipit* of the poem is "Pośród niesnasków Pan Bóg uderza":

> Among the discords the Lord God strikes
> at a bell immense
> For a Slavic Pontiff
> he opened the throne.

The "Slavic Pope," as John Paul II called himself in Poland with a sense of wonder himself, could not have been unmindful, poet and philologist that he is, that the poem of Słowacki, written during the Springtime of Nations, had a special meaning for Poles, Czechs, Slovaks, Slovenes, Croatians, and possibly even Ukrainians; for the Slavic Congress of Prague, February 2 to June 12, 1848, envisaged freedom of precisely these Catholic and partly Byzantine-rite Catholic Slavs and not the Great Russians under whom and under the Prussians and the Austrians these people lived, In the line translated at the end of the article, if the adjective had been *Narodowy,* it would have meant Polish brother, but *Ludowy* suggest the brother of all the common people or the working classes; in the mind of the present-day Poles and others who heard and understood the allusion to the poem and to Prague, the brother of the faithful working classes of the world united! The phrase used by the Pope of himself in Poland was a coded message to which every high school student and many more would have held in their heart's memory the key. *Editor's note:* This poem, with English prose translation, is included as the last position in this book.

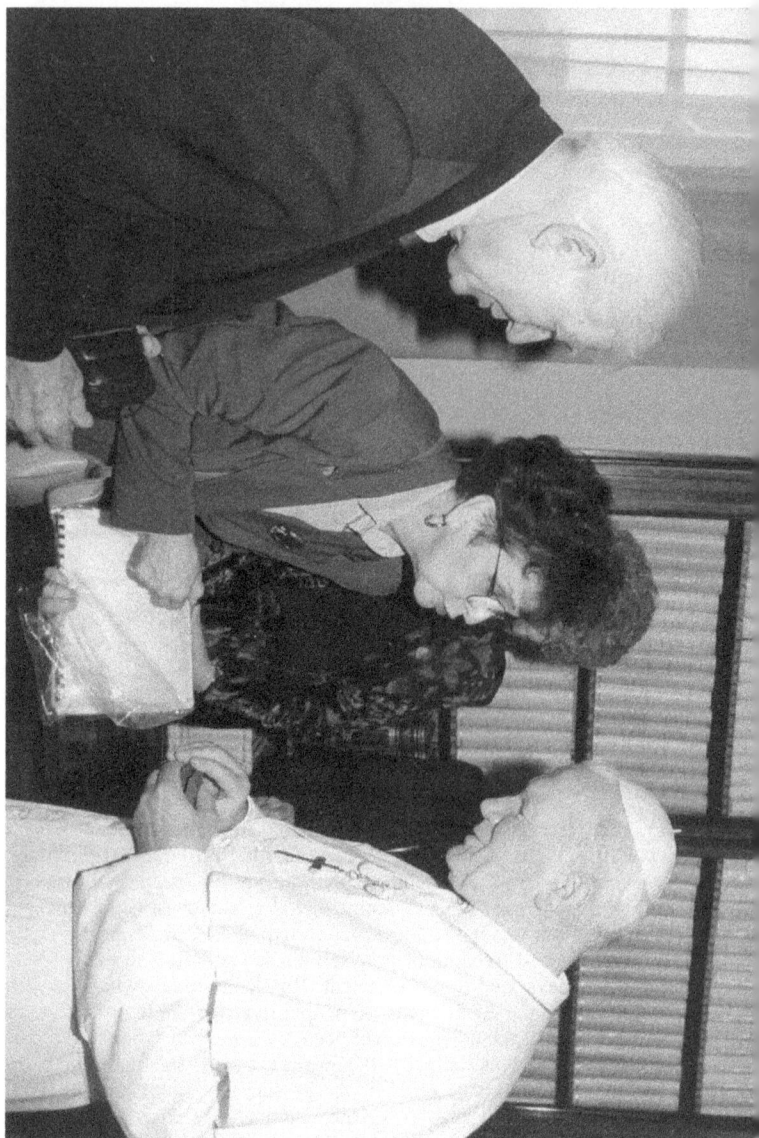

"

A Pope of Great Hopes

JOSEPH L. LICHTEN

Pope John Paul II is a man of great expectations not only for Catholics the world over, but for all men who cherish their human rights, their religious freedom and who are looking forward to a continuous dialogue of all faiths — to a dialogue of mutual respect and understanding which will have as its final goal the common good of all persons and the communities which they created.

When Noah shut the doors of the Ark and darkness closed in upon the world, legend has it that he hung high the true philosopher's stone to give light to every living creature he had preserved from destruction. The spirit of man forever reaches for the light. Through the ages, peace and freedom, truth and fulfillment of the human spirit have been sought in the aura of that light by mankind's inspired philosophers and leaders.

With the passage of time, man has come closer to the ideal and the promise, though there have been fearful setbacks, even in our own day. Yet men and women remain undaunted. They nurture the human spirit. They speak out for human decencies. They fight for human rights. They seek unremittingly that fulfillment for man which is the ultimate freedom.

These words, written on a different occasion and cited by the organization which I represent in Rome,[1] come to mind when we reflect upon the personality and life of the new Pope. His pontificate has only begun and it is too early even to attempt any meaningful synthesis of its significance. We can speak at this time about the Pontiff rather than about the Pontificate.

Volumes and a countless number of articles, stories and memoirs have already been written about him — some of them serious, factual, refreshing, others rather superficial and haphazardly manufactured in pursuit of an easy sensation. While glancing through all this rapidly assembled material, we can notice

---

[1] *Editor's note:* Dr. Lichten served as Director of the Anti-Defamation League of B'nai B'rith's Department of Intercultural Affairs, and was present at Vatican II.

that the authors encountered one major difficulty. Pope John Paul II is a many-sided personality, almost without precedent, and it was impossible for one writer to grasp equally well all his talents, interests and knowledge. We, the generations of this century, became accustomed to a certain type, one may risk saying a stereotype, of a pontiff — a man whose life was almost from childhood predestined for his future ecclesiastical leadership, educated mostly in theology, either an able official or with predominantly pastoral inclinations, behaving rather formally, in a ceremonial way; a man who even when he physically relinquished his ornamental papal throne was still sitting on it symbolically. In John Paul II we encountered a really versatile man — a worker, a scholar, a sportsman, a writer, a poet, a theologian, a philosopher, an actor, a stage director, a singer. And even this list is not exhaustive. His life was unusual; he has one of the most varied backgrounds of any Pope in the history of the Church. But it is also characteristic that within each of his interests and specializations he is different from widely accepted clichés. He is a theologian but also a philosopher of his own school; he is an ardent student of modern philosophical thought, but at the same time pays great attention to the heritage of St. Thomas Aquinas; he respects the traditional doctrines and ways, but is modern at the same time; he is a theoretician with a well developed sense of the need for practical decisions; he experienced the onus of human life before deciding as a priest to lighten the hearts of men and women. These are the reasons that it is almost impossible for any individual, including this writer, to grasp and portray in its entirety all the talents, all the achievements and all the aspirations of the new Church leader.

We shall therefore only select a few facts and observations, hoping that they will contribute in a modest way to an overall portrait of Pope John Paul II.

When we look retrospectively on the events between the death of Paul VI and the election of Karol Cardinal Wojtyła or even further back to John XXIII, we notice a chain of events which logically led to the election of John Paul II. John XXIII created the Vatican Council and opened the window to the world beyond the walls of the Vatican perhaps even wider than he originally intended. Pope Paul VI, who presided over the imposing variety of the

Council Fathers, of all races and cultures, indeed coming from the whole world, will be remembered as the Pontiff who internationalized the College of Cardinals and the Roman Curia. The cardinals and bishops from far countries stopped being only visitors in Rome; they became an integral working part of the Church. Pope Paul VI a few years ago selected one of them, coming from *da lantano* [from afar] to lead him and his entourage in a solemn annual retreat. It was Karol Wojtyła. And then came the tragic interval — the reign and death of Papa Luciani, as he was warmly called. Pope John Paul I gave the papacy a new physiognomy, a different style, and in some ways he was like Pope John XXIII; he was a pastor, only loosely bound with the Vatican's officialdom.

When we recall all these facts and events, we find it rather surprising that not more people predicted the election of John Paul II. It seemed almost natural. One element probably made an obvious conclusion difficult — that the nigh five-centuries-long tradition of Italian Pontiffs would be at this time so unhesitantly cast aside. Each of the electors was probably motivated by his own subjective evaluation of the personality of the new spiritual leader. Each of them wanted to see in the candidate a virtue or virtues closest to his predilections, and the possibility of choice was in this case indeed manifold.

The aspect which above all attracted my attention was Pope John Paul II's fascination with man as a human being. It will be sufficient to quote from his Christmas message *Urbi et Orbi.*

"A human being is an object to be counted, something considered under the aspect of quantity, one of many millions. Yet at the same time he is a single being, unique and unrepeatable."[2] He used the expression "unrepeatable" five times in the text. Man's acts, particularly his moral acts, are the summit of the reality surrounding him. The assessment of a human act, its essence, its value, should occupy *homo sapiens* all the time. Such an assessment would enable us to detect both negative and positive elements of our behavior. Consequently, every manipulation of human thought and

---

[2] *Editor's note:* From the Urbi et Orbi message, 1, Christmas, 1978. The original reads: *L'uomo, oggetto del calcolo, considerato sotto la categoria della quantità; uno fra miliardi. E nello stesso tempo, uno, unico e irripetibile.*

action, every infringement of human conscience, becomes an offense against man and a profanation of his dignity.

On the contrary, social, economic, political and cultural systems must be sensitive to the needs of man, to his complete good.[3] This "complete good" includes such essential prerequisites as human rights and individual freedom. "The great effort of our times, which aims at defining and consolidating 'human rights' in the life of present-day mankind, peoples and states, must be evaluated from this point of view."[4]

It is worthwhile to add that for Judaism and for Jews human rights always were among their highest concern, in theory and practice. Man has a right to freedom, to religious freedom. Freedom is at the same time offered to man and imposed upon him as a task. It is in the first place an attribute of the human person and in this sense it is a gift of the Creator and an endowment of human nature. For this reason it is also the lawful right of man; man has a right to freedom, to self-determination, to the choice of his life career, to acting according to his own convictions.[5]

Many writers are continuously asking themselves and others a perennial question — Will "Papa Wojtyła" be a "conservative" or a "progressive" Pope, or perhaps will he be conservative in Church matters and open and progressive in social problems? It seems to me that neither of these clichés applies to

---

[3] *Editor's note:* Lichten refers here to the General audience from November 8, 1978. See pt. 3: *Non può essere l'uomo per il sistema, ma il sistema deve essere per l'uomo. Perciò bisogna difendersi dall'irrigidimento del sistema. Penso ai sistemi sociali, economici, politici, culturali che debbono essere sensibili all'uomo, al suo bene integrale, debbono essere capaci di riformare se stessi, le loro proprie strutture secondo ciò che esige la piena verità sull'uomo.* [Man cannot be for the system, but the system should exist for man. For this reason, one must protect oneself from the rigidity of the system. I am thinking here of social systems, economical, political and cultural systems, which should be sensitive to man, to his integral good, which should be capable of reforming themselves and their own structures according to what the full truth of mankind requires of them.]

[4] *Da questo punto di vista occorre valutare il grande sforzo dei nostri tempi, che tende a definire e a consolidare "i diritti dell'uomo" nella vita dell'umanità odierna, dei popoli e degli Stati.* From the same text, pt. 3.

[5] Karol Wojtyła, "The Eucharist and Man's Hunger for Freedom," Homily for the Eucharistic Congress in Philadelphia, Aug. 3, 1976.

John Paul II. As a scholar of great philosophical and theological culture he is, in the words of a prominent Polish writer, "bound to the traditional doctrine of the Church . . . but also open to the historical development of theological thought and in fact a promoter of this development himself."[6] On the other hand, the Pope knows and understands the sufferings, miseries and anguish of man today, and not only sympathizes with him but is prepared to do everything in his power to alleviate his hardships. In this respect his goal is general and specific at the same time.

The Pope's goal "is the elaboration of a new moral conscience, one based on the concern of every human for every other person: the foundation of a new human community."[7] This humane approach to the problems of the world to a large extent accounts for the attachment of John Paul II to the idea and documents of the Second Vatican Council. Participating in Vatican II, the then Archbishop Karol Wojtyła had been confronted with the great spiritual problems of the world, which undoubtedly deeply influenced his outlook. This influence was later so noticeable that he was called by many in Kraków "a man shaped by the Council." One may venture to say that the Council paved the way to his election fifteen years later. The Pope is conscious, it seems, of his conciliar links and constantly refers to the conciliar documents. One of his books is totally devoted to the achievements of Vatican II. In the very first sentence of the foreword to the book the then-Cardinal Wojtyła acknowledges: "The bishop who participated in the Second Vatican Council feels the need of repaying the debt."[8]

Many aspects of this work are, to this writer, of special interest. One of them is devoted to the concept of dialogue and not only within but also outside the Church. Dialogue in a practical sense means, according to the author of the book, an exchange of ideas; it means questions and answers, or even a whole cycle of questions and answers. The idea of a dialogue with people "of different convictions" . . . carries along deep moral values, which

[6] Jerzy Turowicz in *Il Giornale,* Oct. 18, 1978.
[7] Anna Teresa Tymieniecka in *The New York Times,* Nov. 26, 1978.
[8] Karol Wojtyła: *U podstaw odnowy. Studium o realizacji Vaticanum II* [The Foundations of Renewal. A Study on the Realization of Vatican II] (Kraków: Polskie Towarzystwo Teologiczne, 1972).

condition the existence and the development of the human family in the world."[9] The concept of a dialogue logically leads to the concept of ecumenism. And on this subject we perceive in the views of the future Pope a refreshing approach, thus although in a proper sense it (the ecumenical approach) means an attitude to the separated Christians, in some measure it also expresses itself in an attitude to non Christian religions.[10] The above statement obviously applies also to Christian-Jewish relations. This writer has always been of the opinion that the Christian-Jewish situation is too unique and special to be totally eliminated from ecumenical considerations. A concept of ecumenism understood only as the unity of Christians is perhaps too rigid and restrictive. In the history of ecumenism, that question came perhaps closest to a dramatic confrontation at the Second Vatican Ecumenical Council. We recall that the now famous "Statement on the Jews" was originally proposed as a constitutive part, Chapter IV, of the schema on ecumenism. Those of us who were present at Rome during the sessions watched with anxiety as the Statement was juggled among its conciliar proponents and opponents, who were compelled to take into consideration a variety of theological and political factors. Its stormy peregrinations demonstrated, among other things, how much uncertainty even the bishops and *periti* [the experts] felt concerning the relationship of the Jews to Catholics — and to ecumenism — after centuries of historical and theological isolation.[11]

The Pope returned to this subject once more after his election and this is what he said: "But the ecumenical effort has an even wider significance. It indicates indirectly the ways that lead to rapprochement, coexistence, cooperation and union among men. And here, too, it is necessary to start from respect for man."[12]

---

[9] Tymieniecka, pp. 26,28.

[10] Wojtyła, *U podstaw odnowy*, p. 269.

[11] Joseph L. Lichten, *IDO-C-Information Documentation on the Conciliar Church.* Rome. No. 60-35, Aug. 25, 1968.

[12] John Paul II, Angelus Message, 21 January 1979, 2. *Ma lo sforzo ecumenico ha ancora più ampio significato. Indica indirettamente le vie che conducono all'avvicinamento, alla convivenza, alla cooperazione e all'unione degli uomini. E anche qui bisogna iniziare dal rispetto per l'uomo.*

The book also reflects upon the relationship of Christianity with religions "outside Christianity." The awareness of what links together the followers of various religions, including those outside Christianity, dictates a certain sense of unity and makes one well-disposed to overcoming mutual inhibitions.[13] The Pope, frequently quoting from the conciliar Declaration on the Relationship of the Church to non-Christian Religions, interprets positively and with attention the attitude of the Council to the "followers of the religion of the Old Testament."[14]

Pope John Paul II in his studies and as a priest was not only confronted with Judaism as a religion in all its traditional and historical aspects, but since his early childhood also knew Jews individually and was familiar with the Jewish community. He attended elementary and secondary schools with Jewish boys and made friends with some of them. One of his classmates recollected: "There was a lot of anti-Jewish sentiment at one point in the local high school, but young Karol refused to adopt his classmates' prejudices." Another classmate stressed that in the *gymnasium* which he attended with young Karol there existed much less anti-Semitism than in other schools. As a schoolboy he was a frequent visitor in Jewish homes, where he had the opportunity to familiarize himself with the Jewish way of life. Together with Jewish youths he pursued various sports and theatrical activities. A friendship with one Jewish schoolmate was renewed after the war and continues to this day.

The synagogue in Wadowice had an excellent cantor (leader of the religious services, trained to chant the prayers), Moshe Kussowicki, who later won world fame. Young Wojtyła often accompanied his Jewish friend to the synagogue on Friday evening or Saturday morning to admire the beautiful voice of the cantor. That liturgical chant stayed in the future Pope's memory, because as a Cardinal many years later he recalled the impression which Kussowicki's voice had made upon him. He again visited a synagogue on Friday night many years later in Kraków when he was already a Cardinal. The high prelate spoke to the remnants of

---

[13] Wojtyła, *U podstaw odnowy* , p. 270.
[14] Wojtyła, *U podstaw odnowy* , p. 270.

the once flourishing community and expressed interest and concern over their efforts to keep the synagogue open and functioning.

And then came the trying times of the Nazi occupation of Poland. Karol Wojtyła was then already living in Kraków. He began his studies at the underground university; among many subjects he also studied acting in an underground theater. A few years later, still during the war, he began his preparation for the priesthood in an underground seminary.

The dreary and tragic war years made a deep impact upon Karol Wojtyła. "May it [World War II] never be repeated in the history of Europe and of the world" — he reflected many years later already as Pope. And several times he stressed the fact that he is the product of underground studies. In order to avoid deportation for compulsory labor in Germany, the young student worked as a laborer first in a quarry near Zakrzówek and then in a chemical plant "Solvay," near Kraków. In both plants there was set up an underground radio station and military units were organized — a part of a national underground army — which engaged in acts of sabotage against the enemy. Karol Wojtyła was also active in an underground Christian organization. It is because of his activities that he was placed on a blacklist by the Nazis and a warrant for his arrest was issued.

While active in the underground, Karol Wojtyła also assisted hunted and persecuted Jews. Many sources report that he helped several Jewish families to escape from the ghettoes in and near Kraków, assisted them in finding shelter, and obtained false "Aryan" identification papers which saved them from deportation to concentration camps. Toward the end of the war he was hidden in the cellar of the mansion of Cardinal Adam Sapieha to avoid arrest by the Nazis. It must have been a strange feeling to return as a new occupant and the successor of Cardinal Sapieha to that palace where he once had hidden from the Nazis. The future Pope's interest in the welfare of the Jewish community, or rather in what remained of it, has not ceased with the end of the war. During the last thirty-five years many occasions arose when his intervention was needed and welcomed.

More than once in his homilies and sermons he touched on the problem of anti-Semitism. He did that again during a retreat for physicians.

As an archbishop and then as a cardinal he showed an interest in the preservation of the Jewish cemetery in Kraków and helped to organize permanent care of it by Catholic students. It is also reported, although there is conflicting information about the exact year of this event, that more than once the tombstones in that cemetery were defiled. Cardinal Wojtyła again mobilized Catholic students to clean and set in order the desecrated relics. In a sermon during the celebration of Corpus Christi he denounced the perpetrators of those acts.

When the infamous excesses of 1968 took place in Poland, when thousands of Jews were deprived of their jobs, ways and means of living and finally literally compelled to leave the country, Cardinal Wojtyła became very active. In a sermon in Kraków's cathedral he deplored the painful fact of the policy of persecution aimed at "Jews of Polish descent" and made an effort to convince the Polish episcopate that it should issue a formal declaration condemning these acts. As a faculty member of the Catholic University of Lublin (the only one of its kind in Poland and in all of Eastern Europe), he proposed that the Jews, who were denied admission to the State universities, be admitted to the Catholic University — a fact without precedent.

At the same time the Polish Catholic weekly *Tygodnik Powszechny* [Universal Weekly] opened its columns to the Jewish writers, poets and newspapermen who were denied the right to publish their works in the State-controlled press and publishing houses. One may add that this weekly always devoted and still devotes as much space as possible to the Holocaust and Christian-Jewish relations all over the world, reporting with great objectivity and understanding of the issues. Cardinal Wojtyła always played *the* guiding role in the policies of this very important Catholic publication.

The first Pope from Poland stepped into the fisherman's shoes with a rich, many-sided and admirable background. By taking the names of his three predecessors, he undoubtedly intended to continue in many respects their labors. The greatest achievement, of historic dimension, in that period was the Second Vatican Council. It was also one of the most interesting and unforgettable periods in this writer's life. It was a crucial moment for the future of Christian-Jewish relations. It would therefore be appropriate to conclude with a quotation from *Nostra Aetate,* one of the documents of Vatican II to which the Pope refers so often.

Since the spiritual patrimony common to Christians and Jews is thus so great, this sacred Council wishes to foster and recommend that mutual understanding and respect which is the fruit above all of Biblical and theological studies, and of brotherly dialogues.

Rome, February 1, 1979

"Pośród niesnasków Pan Bóg uderza"
JULIUSZ SŁOWACKI

Pośród niesnasków Pan Bóg uderza
　　W ogromny dzwon.
Dla Słowiańskiego oto Papieża
　　Otwarty tron.
Ten przed mieczami tak nie uciecze
　　Jako ten Włoch,
On śmiało, jak Bóg, pójdzie na miecze,
　　Świat mu — to proch!

Twarz jego, słońcem rozpromieniona,
　　Lampą dla sług,
Za nim rosnące pójdą plemiona
　　W światło — gdzie Bóg.
Na jego pacierz i rozkazanie
　　Nie tylko lud —
Jeśli rozkaże, to słońce stanie,
　　Bo moc — to cud.

　　*

On się już zbliża — rozdawca nowy
　　Globowych sił;
Cofnie się w żyłach pod jego słowy
　　Krew naszych żył;
W sercach się zacznie światłości Bożej
　　Strumienny ruch,
Co myśl pomyśli przezeń, to stworzy,
　　Bo moc — to duch.

A trzebaż mocy, byśmy ten Pański
　　Dźwignęli świat:
Więc oto idzie Papież Słowiański
　　Ludowy brat; —
Oto już leje balsamy świata
　　Do naszych łon.

"'Midst squabbling dissension strikes the Lord God"
JULIUSZ SŁOWACKI

'Midst squabbling dissension strikes the Lord God —
  His bell intones:
And behold: the Holy Father, a Slav
  Ascends his throne.
Before the hostile sword he will not flee
  Like that Pius;
Bold, like God, he'll face the sword, for he'll see
  The world as dust.

The sun's splendor will illuminate his face
  Just like a lamp,
And it will lead all men, of every race,
  Where God encamps.
And when he'll pray, at his very command
  Not only people,
But Nature will heed him — the sun will stand:
  Might is miracle.

*

He's on his way already, to ordain
  A new global course;
At his word, the very blood of our veins
  Will re-seek its source;
And through our hearts God's luminosity
  In torrents will roll,
And what thought, thus enlightened, thinks, will Be:
  Might is of the soul.

And might is what we need, to raise this globe,
  This divine clay.
And thus it is that he, the Slavic Pope,
  Is on his way.
The peoples' brother, with balsam our wounds
  He will repair;

225

Hufiec aniołów kwiatem umiata
    Dla niego tron.
On rozda miłość, jak dziś mocarze
    Rozdają broń,
Sakramentalną moc on pokaże,
    Świat wziąwszy w dłoń.

        *

Gołąb mu słowa usty wyleci,
    Poniesie wieść,
Nowinę słodką, że Duch już świeci
    I ma swą cześć.
Niebo się nad nim piękne otworzy
    Z obojgu stron,
Bo on na tronie stanął i tworzy
    I świat — i tron.

On przez narody uczyni bratnie
    Wydawszy głos,
Że duchy pójdą w cele ostatnie
    Przez ofiar stos.
Moc mu pomoże sakramentalna
    Narodów stu,
Że praca duchów będzie widzialna
    Przed trumną tu.

        *

Wszelką z ran świata wyrzuci zgniłość
    Robactwo, gad,
Zdrowie przyniesie, rozpali miłość
    I zbawi świat;
Wnętrzy kościołów on powymiata,
    Oczyści sień,
Boga pokaże w twórczości świata,
    Jasno jak dzień.

Already choirs of seraphim with blooms
    His throne prepare.
He will distribute love, as this world's kings
    Toss bullet and bomb;
For sacramental is the might he brings,
    The world in his palm.

*

From his lips the dove of the Word shall fly,
    And what it says
Is God's sweet news: the Holy Ghost is nigh
    And has His praise.
Above him will the heavens open, huge
    From zone to zone,
For he ascends his throne and thus renews
    Both world — and throne.

He will make brothers of all nations, this
    Will move men's souls
To heed his voice in unselfish witness
    And work towards goals —
One hundred nations of them — celestial,
    Bent to the plough,
The fruits of spirit labor visible
    Both here and now.

*

The world's sores he shall heal, vermin remove
    In the decay curled;
Health shall he restore by igniting love —
    He will save the world.
He will sweep out the nave of every church,
    Each apse and bay,
And show us God in the things of this earth,
    As clear as day.

CONTRIBUTORS

Kazimierz Braun is a director, writer, playwright, and scholar. He studied at the University of Poznań and at the National School of Drama in Warsaw. He was artistic director and general manager of professional theaters in Poland, including the Contemporary Theater in Wrocław. He has directed in Poland, the United States, Canada, Germany, Ireland, and several other countries. He has taught at both Wrocław University and Poznań University, as well as at several American universities. He has published more than 30 books, including scholarly works, novels, and plays. He has obtained several artistic and scholarly awards for theater, literature, and scholarship, including the awards of the Guggenheim Foundation and the Fulbright Foundation. Currently, he is professor of Theater at the State University of New York at Buffalo. He also holds the title of professor in Poland.

Thaddeus V. Gromada received his PhD in East Central European History from Fordham University under the mentorship of the eminent Polish historian, Prof. Oskar Halecki, who was also the first Director of PIASA. Until his retirement in 1992 he was on the faculty of New Jersey City University where he attained the rank of full Professor of European History and Coordinator of Multi-Ethnic and Immigration Studies. He now holds the rank of Professor Emeritus at NJCU. He became Executive Director of the Polish Institute of Arts and Sciences of America in 1991. Earlier he served as PIASA's Secretary General. He is editor of and contributor to several books dealing with Polish foreign policy, Polish-Czech-Slovak relations, and Polish Immigrant Ethnic studies. He has authored many articles that have appeared in various scholarly journals in both the U.S. and Poland. He edited and prepared for publication Oskar Halecki's posthumous monograph *Jadwiga of Anjou and the Rise of East Central Europe* which he presented to Pope John Paul II in 1993. Together with his sister Janina Kedron, he founded and co-edites a bilingual folkloristic quarterly, *Tatrzański Orzeł [The Tatra Eagle]*.

Richard J. Hunter, Jr. is Professor of Legal Studies and Faculty Fellow of the Institute for International Business at the W. Paul Stillman School of Business, Seton Hall University. Dr. Hunter is a longtime member of the Polish Institute of Arts and Sciences of America, which he served for many years as Treasurer. He has written extensively on Eastern and Central European business, politics, law, and economics. Professor Hunter is the author or co-author of more than 30 research articles on aspects of political and economic transformation in Poland. Along with Leo V. Ryan, C.S.V., Professor Hunter co-authored *From Autarchy to Market: Polish Economics and Politics, 1945-1995* (Praeger) and more recently *Poland: A Transitional Analysis* (with Leo V. Ryan and Robert E. Shapiro), published by PIASA Books. He is also a frequent presenter at numerous international conferences and symposia and a contributor to the United Nations Institute for Training and Research (UNITAR) Annual Conferences on "Foreign Direct Investment For Development Financing" in New York City and Hiroshima, Japan.

Janusz A. Ihnatowicz is an ordained Roman Catholic priest, Doctor of Sacred Theology, and Professor Emeritus of Theology at the University of Saint Thomas in Houston, Texas. He is one of the poets associated with the *Merkuriusz Polski* [Polish Mercury] and *Kontynenty* [Continents]. He has authored five volumes of poetry as well as numerous articles on patristics.

Charles S. Kraszewski was born in 1962 and holds a PhD in Comparative Literature from Penn State University. The recipient of two Fulbright grants, he both studied and taught at Jagiellonian University in Kraków, Poland. Currently, he teaches in the English Department of King's College in Wilkes-Barre, PA. Series editor of PIASA Books and associate editor of *The Polish Review,* his main scholarly interests are Polish and Czech literature.

Joseph L. Lichten was born in Poland and received his Doctor of Law degree from the University of Warsaw. He served as director of the International Affairs Department for the Anti-Defamation League of B'nai B'rith, which organization he represented in Rome

229

during the Second Vatican Council in the early 1960s. A tireless proponent of respectful Jewish-Catholic relations, he died in Rome, in December, 1987.

Héctor Lozada is Associate Professor of Marketing and Faculty Fellow of the Institute for International Business at the W. Paul Stillman School of Business, Seton Hall University and is Director of the Institute for International Business. Professor Lozada is the author or co-author of over 20 research articles on marketing, environmentalism, and international business. He is a frequent participant at various conferences and symposia in the United States and abroad and is also a contributor to the United Nations Institute for Training and Research (UNITAR) Annual Conferences on "Foreign Direct Investment For Development Financing" in New York City and Hiroshima, Japan.

Harold B. Segel is professor emeritus of Slavic Literatures and of Comparative Literature at Columbia University. A native of Boston, he graduated from Harvard University with a PhD. in Slavic Languages and literatures in 1955. At Columbia, he has held manifold appointments, including director, Institute on East Central Europe, 1978-88. He has been a member of the Board of Trustees, The Kościuszko Foundation, 1992-98, and a member of the Board of Directors, Polish Institute of Arts and Sciences of America since1999. Professor Segel was twice decorated by the Polish government for contributions on behalf of Polish culture. His extensive publications fall into several areas: Polish literature; Russian literature; East European studies, German and Austrian literatures; and comparative literature. Among his major publications are: *Polish Romantic Drama*, *Stranger in Our Midst: Images of the Jew in Polish Literature*, *Political Thought in Renaissance Poland: An Anthology in English* (PIASA Books, 2003), *The Literature of Eighteenth-Century Russia: A History and Anthology*, *The Vienna Coffeehouse Wits, 1890-1938*, *Body Ascendant: Modernism and the Physical Imperative*, and *The Columbia Guide to the Literatures of Eastern Europe Since 1945*. Professor Segel and his family currently live in Tucson, Arizona.

Juliusz Słowacki (1809-1849) needs no introduction for anyone even remotely interested in Polish literature. Along with Adam Mickiewicz, Zygmunt Krasiński and Cyprian Kamil Norwid he is generally recognized as one of the leading poets of the Romantic period in Polish literature. The creator of numerous important dramas of a Shakespearean cast, he was also creative in the lyric genre, narrative poetry, poetic prose, and self-ironic poetic narratives of a witty, Byronic tint. During the 1830 November Uprising, he served the revolutionary government as a diplomatic courier in England, after which, like many of his generation, he lived in exile in Paris. Both Słowacki and Mickiewicz were critical of the stance assumed by the Holy See in regard to the Polish insurrections of the nineteenth century. The "Italian Pope" so bitterly referred to by Słowacki in the opening lines of "Pośród niesnasków" is Pius X (Giovanni Count Mastai Ferretti, b. 1792; *reg.* 1846-1878), who was constrained to flee Rome on November 24 , 1848 after Italian revolutionary forces laid siege to the Quirinal, seeking, unsuccessfully, his blessing for a rising of the Papal States against Austria. His poem "Pośród niesnasków" was rendered into English for this volume by Charles S. Kraszewski.

Bolesław Taborski was born in 1927 in Toruń, Poland. He is a poet, essayist, translator, and writer on theatre. He fought and was wounded in the Warsaw Uprising of 1944; since 1946 he has lived in England, where he co-founded the émigré journals *Merkuriusz Polski* [The Polish Mercury] and *Kontynenty* [Continents]. He is the author of many books of poetry and criticism, including *Karola Wojtyły dramaturgia wnętrza* [The Interior Dramaturgy of Karol Wojtyła, 1989] and *The Collected Plays and Writings on Theatre of Karol Wojtyła/Pope John Paul II* (1987).

Piotr Wandycz was born in Kraków in 1923. He holds a PhD from the London School of Economics and Political Science. During World War II he served in the Polish Forces in the West, and has been in the United States since 1951. Currently Bradford Durfee Professor of History at Yale University, emeritus, he is author and co-author of 18 books and over 400 articles and book reviews in Polish, East Central European and European Diplomatic History published in several languages. Prof. Wandycz is Doctor honoris causa of Wrocław University, Jagiellonian University, Lublin Catholic University (KUL) and the Sorbonne. He is a member of both PAU and PAN, an honorary member of the Polskie Towarzystwo Historyczne [Polish Historical Association], and President of the Polish Institute of Arts and Sciences of America.

George Huntston Williams (1914-2000) was Hollis Professor of Divinity Emeritus at Harvard Divinity School. A Congregationalist minister, Mr. Williams was ordained in the Church of the Christian Union in Rockford, IL in 1940. He was Winn Professor of Ecclesiastical History at Harvard from 1956-1963, and Hollis Professor of Divinity from 1963 until his retirement from the university in 1980. Guggenheim fellow and IREX scholar, among Mr. Williams' publications are titles such as *The Radical Reformation, The Mind of John Paul II* and *The History of the Polish Reformation: Stanisław Lubieniecki and Nine Related Documents.* On April 27, 1979 at a Mass for Christian Unity concelebrated by Humberto Cardinal Madeiros, Rector John P. Boles of St. Paul's Church in Cambridge, Massachusetts, and other priests, Rev. Williams was honored by a special papal award and a decorated Knight of St. Gregory the Great.

Krzysztof Zanussi was born in 1939. One of the most important film directors in Europe, Zanussi serves as Consultant to the Pontifical Council for Culture and has served as president of the Fédération Européenne des Réalisateurs Audiovisuels and Eurovision. Since 1966, he has realized some forty full-length films, most of them from his own screenplays. His most recent film is *Persona non grata* (2005). He has worked in Great Britain, Germany, Italy, France, Sweden, Denmark and South America as well as his native Poland. Truly a Renaissance man, he began his university studies in Physics and continued in Philosophy at the Jagiellonian University in Kraków before enrolling in the Director's program at the Film School of Łódź. Since 1992, he has taught at the University of Silesia in Katowice, and since 1979 has been Head and Artistic Director of TOR Film Studios in Warsaw.

Józef M. Życiński was born in 1948. He is Professor of Philosophy at the Catholic University of Lublin, Poland, Archbishop of Lublin, Grand Chancellor of the Catholic University of Lublin, Member of the European Academy of Science and Art in Salzburg, the Pontifical Council for Culture, and the Russian Academy of Natural Sciences. He is author of 40 books in philosophy of science, relativistic cosmology, history of the relationship between natural sciences and Christian faith. Some of his titles are: *The Structure of the Metascientific Revolution*; *Three Cultures: Science, the Humanities and Christian Thought*; *Theism and Analytic Philosophy*; *Die Zeichen der Hoffnung entdecken* [To Discover the Signs of Hope]; *God of Postmodernists*; *God and Evolution. Basic Questions of Evolutionary Theism.*